Alan G. Futerman • Walter E. Block

The Austro-Libertarian Point of View

Essays on Austrian Economics and Libertarianism

Springer

Alan G. Futerman
Department of Economics
University of the Latin American
Educational Center
Rosario, Santa Fe, Argentina

Walter E. Block
Harold E. Wirth Eminent Scholar Endowed
Chair and Professor of Economics, College
of Business
Loyola University New Orleans
New Orleans, LA, USA

ISBN 978-981-16-4690-4 ISBN 978-981-16-4691-1 (eBook)
https://doi.org/10.1007/978-981-16-4691-1

This Springer imprint is published by the registered company Springer Nature Singapore Pte Ltd.
The registered company address is: 152 Beach Road, #21-01/04 Gateway East, Singapore 189721, Singapore

This book is dedicated to Ludwig Von Mises and Murray N. Rothbard

Foreword

Suppose you are the sort of economist whom in their fine book Alan Futerman and Walter Block and all the wide world these days would call "neoclassical." That is, suppose you are an orthodox economist of the British and especially the post-War American sort, now spread around the world. If so, you need to read and consider this book of "Austrian" economics, because you have spent decades *not* reading and considering what the Austrians are saying, and have made a scientific mistake.

Yet the truth is that the wide world's definition of "neoclassical" here is misleading. (Futerman and Block use the word in the misleading if commonplace sense some fifty times.) "Neoclassical" properly understood, as Futerman and Block do deeply understand, refers to the Marginal Revolution in economic thinking during the 1870s. In a spectacular case of simultaneous discovery in science, on the order of Newton-Leibnitz or Darwin-Wallace, the new thinking was discovered independently by William Stanley Jevons (1835–1882) for English speakers, by Leon Walras (1834–1910) for French speakers, and by Carl Menger (1840–1921) for German speakers. And Menger was, after all, the founder of the Austrian School.

The Revolution overturned the rigid, average-cost, already-given "structure" characteristic of the Classical economics of David Ricardo—and nowadays characteristic of neo-Marxists such as Thomas Piketty or Marianna Mazzucato. The "minor Ricardian" Karl Marx died in 1883, a decade after the Revolution. But like his followers since then he refused to learn from the neoclassicals such as Menger. I do wish the neo-Marxists nowadays, some of whom are my dear friends, would learn the core of Economics 101, that is, neoclassical and especially Austrian economics. But, following The Master, with rare exceptions (Burczak 2006), they don't.

The revolutionaries of the 1870s put at the center of their analysis not the given social structures of the Classicals but "choice at the margin," which is why such economics is also called "marginalism." Harriet chooses whether or not to buy a little more (a "marginal" amount of) coffee, or to supply a little more labor. She keeps on choosing until the increment of happiness she gets from the marginal unit has declined (according to the core law of diminishing marginal utility, the fourth cup of coffee gives less pleasure than the first) to meet the rising marginal opportunity cost of acquiring it. Then she stops. Harriet will have maximized her pleasure net of the pleasure from whatever else she could have done. Hurrah!

As Futerman and Block put it, following their master Ludwig von Mises' axiom of action, "the contention [is] that every acting man [and woman, dears] is eager to substitute a more satisfactory state of affairs for a less desired one." Harriet's choice, interacting with Tom's and Dick's, though it is no part of their intentions, imparts a spontaneous structure to the economy—not rigid and given and predictable, but emergent. Hurrah again: self-interest yields riches for us all.

The Austrians *are* such neoclassicals. You, the orthodox economist whom Futerman and Block steadily criticize in the book, are better therefore called "Samuelsonian." The amiable Paul Anthony Samuelson (1915–2009) created the orthodoxy in economics, the sort I myself was trained in and practiced for decades, before gradually seeing the Austrian heterodox light. The orthodox economists, it must be said, were fortunate that Samuelson (who in case you need to know was for a long time my mother's mixed doubles tennis partner in league tennis in Boston) was our very own Blindingly Intelligent MIT Leader. Linguistics, which shares interesting parallels with economics, such as the spontaneous order emergent from individual human actions, also had such a leader at MIT. Too bad for the linguists: he was the decidedly non-amiable Noam Chomsky (b. 1928; I'll bet he didn't play tennis), who has ruined the field.

Samuelson was open at least to logic, if not so much to evidence, and so he treated with respect if not agreement that Marxian one among the three streams of economic thinking. But, following our leader, we Samuelsonians tried to ignore the third stream flowing from the specifically Austrian highlands of neoclassical economics, in Menger, Mises, Hayek, Lachmann, Kirzner, Rothbard, Lavoie, Boettke, Rizzo, Klein, Tucker, Boudreaux, and in Futerman and Block.

The Samuelsonian economist, being mainly in charge of modern economics worldwide, is prideful. Pride is a grave sin in science, because it closes the ears to logic and evidence. As the novelist and philosopher Iris Murdoch wrote in 1967, its opposite, humility, "is not a peculiar habit of self-effacement, rather like having an inaudible voice. It is selfless respect for reality and one of the most difficult and central of all virtues" (Murdoch 1967 [1970], p. 95; cf. McCloskey 2006). To be a good economic scientist, as to be a good novelist or philosopher, one must listen intently. But the proud, non-humble Samuelsonian is already an expert, and so she won't listen. An expert, said the American president Harry Truman, doesn't want to listen to anything new, because then she wouldn't be an expert. Nor does she want to relinquish the rewards in academic bishoprics and political power that the orthodox acquire.

I confess that I acted just like that for decades, until awakened from my dogmatic slumbers by Don Lavoie, Donald Boudreaux, and Walter Block. Now Futerman and Block here lucidly explain Austrian economics, and then apply it to various matters of policy, from the minimum wage to hyperinflation. No excuses, you Samuelsonian. Get to reading.

I admit that I do not agree with every single sentence in the book, though agreeing mostly on matters of policy. Frankly, I think Austrians create pointless opposition to their scientific and policy ideas by insisting fiercely on what seem to me unnecessary claims about epistemology. For example, the Austrian economist who is now emeritus at the University of Nevada, Hans Hermann Hoppe, regularly attacks his natural allies because they do not agree with his apriorism. So here, minus the authoritarian tendencies of Hoppe, Futerman and Block explain that Mises was a Kantian in believing in the synthetic a priori. We followers rather of the empirical Scots of the eighteenth century, Hume and Smith, do not.

On the other hand, I have come to agree with Futerman and Block in favor of "methodological dualism," which argues that a slavish imitation of what they believe is the character of physical science—the impulse leading Samuelsonians so far astray—does not suffice for social science. Mises, though, erroneously claimed that social science was different because it was not experimental. Such a definition would exclude evolutionary biology or most of geology from the physical sciences. The actual difference is that humans speak, even if only to themselves, and make projects of human action together or apart. The Austrian economist Fritz Machlup asked early in the 1940s what physics would look like if atoms could … speak to each other, or themselves make plans with their liberty of the will. His question remains a powerful Austrian challenge to the Samuelsonian and Marxist projects.

I would suggest the next step for Austrian economics—something that the other hero of the book, Murray Rothbard, scornfully opposed, but that is at least implicit in Hayek and Lachmann and Kirzner and their students—should be taking human speech seriously, in what has been called "humanomics" (Smith and Wilson 2019; McCloskey 2021).

Futerman and Block say that their book is not a manual, which I suppose it is not. But it is a collection of highly pertinent essays, from which you can understand what is mistaken in the orthodoxy of economics, law, and politics. The central term of art in Austrian economics is that phrase "human action." It is the exercise of human will, not the blind bumping of one molecule against another or one organism against another, as in the physical sciences. Samuelsonian economics at the individual, marginal level and Marxist economics at the aggregate, class level are concerned exclusively with *re*-action in the style of physical science. Their actors have no liberty of the will, to put it in theological terms (McCloskey 2021). They don't speak and reflect and plan. They *re*-spond to mechanically given conditions of utility or the relations of production.

Futerman and Block distinguish Austrian economics as a scientific enterprise based on liberty of the will from "libertarianism" as an advocacy based on policies implied by such liberty. "Although Austrian economics is positive and libertarianism is normative," they write, "this book shows how both are related; how each can support the other." Indeed, they do.

§

Let me explain in my own humanomical way how Austrian emphasis on human action overturns Samuelson. Mises spoke on action: "Man is in a position to act because he has the ability to discover causal relations which determine change and becoming in the universe. Acting requires and presupposes the category of causality" (Mises (1949 [1998], p. 22). My point, with which I think Futerman and Block would agree, is that Samuelsonians and Marxists are terminally confused about causal relations.

The great philosopher, historian and archaeologist R. G. Collinwood explained long ago, in a passage that could just as well have come from Mises or Hayek, that "the historian … is investigating not mere events (where by a mere event I mean one which has only an outside and no inside) but actions, and an action is the unity of the outside and the inside of an event" (Collingwood 1950 [1993[, pp. 214–215; my italics).

Collingwood, you see, is using "action" as the Austrians do. A mere "event" is his term for merely physical happenings, observable in positivist/Samuelsonian style from the outside. He gives the example of Caesar crossing the Rubicon. The physical action of the crossing of the river was an "event" in a behavioral sense. But its purpose was the purposeful violation of Roman law, and its meaning depended on the ability to discover causal relations, in this case an intentional act towards the fall of Roman Republic —an action rather than an outwardly observed *re*action to stimulus. The man in orthodox Samuelsonian economics, a sociopathic fellow known as Mr. Max U, is external in this way. The analyst is forbidden in behaviorist dogma to know *why* Caesar did it—or at best would reduce his action to a cost/benefit calculation in view of the constraints he faced. It is a *re*action, not the action of a liberated will.

Collingwood continues, giving another example: "When an historian asks 'Why did Brutus stab Caesar?' he means 'What did Brutus think, which made him decide to stab Caesar?' The cause of the event, for him, means the thought in the mind of the person by whose agency the event came about: and this is not something other than the event, it is the *inside* of the event itself." The Max-U model slides past the *inside* of the event, turning it so to speak inside out the better to reduce thought to "observable," "behavioral" reactions to "objective" constraints. (My scare quotes here put a check mark beside the philosophically naïve dogmas in Samuelsonian economics, and in Marxism, too; I do not entirely exempt Austrian economists from the charge of a similar scientistic naiveté.)

Samuelsonian economics therefore confuses necessary with sufficient conditions, and confuses helpful side conditions with inspiring casual conditions. For example, the idea overused in Samuelsonian economics of the "production function" (which I myself overused for decades, after learning it in graduate school) says that a book of alternative recipes for products is necessary. Certainly, it is, whether literally written down or not. Put together such and such a tonnage of coke (from coal), iron ore, and limestone into a blast furnace with such and such specifications run by a certain number of laborers with such and such skills, according to page 106 of the book of recipes, and you get a ton of pig iron. Use instead the recipe from page 26, which entails much more labor, and is charged instead with charcoal (from wood, instead of coal), and you get the ton of pig iron, but with differing opportunity cost of the inputs used. Good to know.

But to stop at the recipe book as the "cause" of the pig iron is to confuse the book with the human action sufficient and inspiring that yielded the very book, such as an engineering self-education and craft traditions, and a liberal society encouraging having a go at exercising them. And most basically it ignores the human creativity that suffices for education and craft and betterment, when the society permits.

True, French cuisine still depends to some degree on *Le Guide Cuisinaire* (1903; also called *L'art culinaire*) by Auguste Escoffier, as for example in its five "mother sauces": béchamel, espagnole, velouté, hollandaise, and tomate. Escoffier's *Guide* is a necessary input, or at least a helpful one, into *Mastering the Art of French Cooking*, and into Julie's 365 days of dinners cooking from it. But the sufficient and inspiring causes of French cuisine are not such items in the present supply chain. They are the social and intellectual arrangements in French kitchens and restaurants that made for the books in the first place, from Guillaume Tirel in the fourteenth century and Catherine de Medici in the sixteenth century down to untold thousands of wives, and then husbands, too, inventing crème caramel and bouillabaisse, with the millions of French eaters insisting on getting a good meal, "Slow Food," and willing to chat about it endlessly. The "causes" in a sense relevant to serious scientific description, and to proposals for policies to encourage haute cuisine, were not recipes but the *ideas* for the recipes, the human creativity along with the conditions such as *liberté*, and then practice, practice. (How do you get to Guy Savoy, Monnaie de Paris, 11?) The causes were not production functions—not the routine, bookable recipes helpfully teaching how to combine ingredients and to practice, practice by chopping potatoes. The sufficient cause under some broadly available necessary conditions, such as the existence of labor and sunlight and Paris, was human creativity.

The production function construed as causal confuses necessary with sufficient conditions; it is to confuse modestly helpful pedagogy (on the "outside" in Collingwood's terminology, as for example the Samuelsonian economist's ill-named "growth theory") with powerfully inspiring conditions on the "inside" for human action in creation. It leads away from a proper understanding of economic growth, among lesser topics in economics.

Establishing property rights under a rule of law, to instance the behaviorist, neo-institutionalist's favorite cause, is necessary and helpful, of course, for the life of man, quoth Thomas Hobbes, is solitary, poor, nasty, brutish, and short. You can therefore explain why nations *fail*, and can discern the origins of poverty, by noting the nasty incentives that have led most nations for millennia far enough away from the rule of law and of alienable property rights and the rest to hobble the economy (Acemoglu and Robinson 2006, 2012).

But you can only explain why nations *succeed,* and then discern in a proper economic science the origins of our startling modern prosperity, by noting with Francis Hutcheson of Belfast and Glasgow the sufficient cooperativeness, and noting with his student Adam Smith of Glasgow and Edinburgh the inspiring liberties, jointly sufficient, that led a few nations such as Holland and Britain early and the USA and Sweden and Japan later towards enterprise and betterment. Even if *Le Guide Cuisinaire* had been a deeply flawed book, you could still explain some outcomes in bad cooking. But, in any case, excellent cooking, and excellent economic science, comes from human creativity liberated—such as exhibited by the admirable

Escoffier and the admirable Samuelson. We should seek to know the sufficient conditions for such creativity. That's economic science, and it is in particular in Austrian economics when it seeks, as it should, to explain the Great Enrichment, 1800 to the present.

Elevating a necessary condition for the production function such as property rights to the cause of modern growth would be like elevating the existence of the tomato in Europe after the Columbian Exchange to the cause of *sauce tomate.* It was necessary, obviously, but not sufficient, equally obviously. The British and the Dutch and the Germans had the necessary tomatoes, too, but did not have the sufficiencies that made for their glorious Italian and then French use. Tomatoes, labor, and capital in France made for French cuisine; in Germany, German. (I rest my case.)

Once you have such understanding, you stop believing in simple formulas for improving lives by coercing people, what Futerman and Block call "the fallacy of a priori statism." My friends on the left, and quite a few on the right, too, believe that the government is a swell bunch of folks with amazing abilities to instruct us all in how to live. They can solve easily the "knowledge problem" that Hayek articulated in 1945—an essay still neglected by most Samuelsonians and all but one or two Marxists. That is, these swell folks can know from Washington or Brussels or for that matter from Moscow or Beijing just what you need today in the way of haute cuisine.

One of my two college roommates, David, was a brilliant electrical engineer. David on the banjo, with Derek and I on guitars, would leave off studying late of an evening to belt out labor songs. I was a socialist then—to this day I know more labor and socialist songs than my leftwing friends. The songs fit well with the economics that Derek and I were being taught at Harvard College in the early 1960s—Keynes and social engineering to help the poor, by running their lives. Derek and I then believed Keynes's lofty assurance in 1936 that an economist is "in a position to calculate the marginal efficiency of capital-goods on long views and on the basis of the general social advantage" (Keynes1936, Chapter 12, Section VIII). To an old classical liberal nowadays such brisk statism seems, as the British would put it, daft, loony, bollocks, bonkers, stark raving mad—and very much not helpful to the poor. But it was highly flattering to young American economists in the 1960s just learning such magical ideas as the Keynesian multiplier and the creation of supplies of goods and services out of demanding them.

Therefore, Derek and I, the official students of economics in our room, scorned David's reading, during breaks from solving second order differential equations, of Ludwig von Mises's *Human Action.* I can still see David tilting back in his chair, puffing on an unfiltered Gauloise cigarette and sipping occasionally on a cup of espresso, with the old Yale Press edition of Mises propped on his lap.

Had I picked up the book and read with humility, instead of sneering at it from a proud statism of long views able so easily to discern the general social advantage, I would have saved a lot of time—I mean, three or four decades late in which I slowly, slowly left statism for a true liberalism, and the Austrian (and neoclassical) economics and the libertarian policies of Futerman and Block.

Works Cited

Acemoglu, Daron, and James A. Robinson. 2012. *Why Nations Fail: The Origins of Power, Prosperity, and Poverty*. New York: Crown Business.

Acemoglu, Daron, and James A. Robinson. 2006. *Economic Origins of Dictatorship and Democracy*. Cambridge: Cambridge University Press.

Burczak, Theodore. 2006. *Socialism After Hayek.* Advances in Heterodox Economics. Ann Arbor: University of Michigan Press.

Collingwood, Robin George. 1946 (1993). *The Idea of History*, Oxford: Clarendon Press, 1946; revised edition, with an introduction by Jan Van der Dussen, Oxford: Oxford University Press,

Hayek, Friedrich. 1945. The Use of Knowledge in Society. *American Economic Review, 35* (Sept): 519–530.

Keynes, John Maynard. 1936. *The General Theory of Employment, Interest and Money*. London: Macmillan.

McCloskey, Deirdre Nansen. 2006. Humility and Truth. *Anglican Theological Review* 88: 181–196.

McCloskey, Deirdre Nansen. 2021. *Bettering Humanomics: A New and Old Approach to Economic Science.* Chicago: University of Chicago Press.

Mises, Ludwig von. 1949 [1998]. *Human Action: Scholar's Edition*. Auburn, AL: Ludwig von Mises Institute.

Murdoch, Iris/ 1967 (1070). The Sovereignty of Good over Other Concepts. Leslie Stephen Lecture, 1967, reprinted in Murdoch, *The Sovereignty of Good* (London: Routledge, 1970, reprint of 1985).

Smith, Vernon and Bart J. Wilson. 2019. *Humanomics*. Cambridge: Cambridge University Press.

Deirdre Nansen McCloskey

UIC Distinguished Professor of Economics
and of History Emerita, Professor of English
Emerita, Professor of Communication Emerita
University of Illinois at Chicago
Chicago, IL, USA

Acknowledgments

Several people helped us throughout the journey of writing the series of essays that comprise this work. We mention in this regard our co-authors William Barnett II and Kevin Aguilar.

We especially want to thank the wonderful Deirdre McCloskey, who wrote an extraordinary (and very generous) foreword to our book.

To Lucie Bartonek, Aarthi Padmanaban, R. Rathika and Mariëlle Klijn from Springer, who were always very kind and attentive in their help and suggestions.

To Professor Robert T. Miller, for making us think further on objections to the Anarcho-Capitalist ideal.

Of course, to our families and friends.

And last, but not least, to Ludwig Von Mises and Murray Rothbard, who fundamentally developed the economic and philosophical approach that we follow and defend in this work.

Introduction

Austrian Economics and Libertarianism

This book ranges widely over a number of topics, not all of them that usually fit inside the covers of any one book.

What is the thread that runs through them all, apart from the fact that we two coauthors of this book have written all of them? Well, there are several threads. For one thing, we are both animated and inspired by the libertarian philosophy of our beloved mentor, Murray N. Rothbard. We do not agree with him 100% of the time, but even when we diverge to the greatest degree possible, we are inspired by his example. That is the normative thread. The other is Austrian Economics, i.e., the economic perspective we use in order to analyze the subjects treated in this book, ranging from epistemology and methodology of economics to international economics. That is the positive thread.

Hence, this book covers several areas of economic theory and political philosophy from the viewpoint of Austrian Economics and libertarianism. As such, we deal with Epistemology and Methodology, Microeconomics, Macroeconomics, Labor Economics, International Economics, Political Philosophy, Law, and Public Policy, all from our Austro-Libertarian perspective.

Thus, this book offers the reader an integrated view of libertarianism and Austrian economics in the light of recent debates in economic science and political philosophy. Moreover, this volume builds from the foundations of our approach (epistemology and methodology), applying to the individual on the microeconomic level, which in turn allows us to deal with subjects in macroeconomics. We also analyze issues in law, politics, and public policy. Thus, this book gives readers a unified view of our entire approach, in a logical progression, allowing them to judge it in full.

We do not here offer a manual, but rather a collection of cases analyzed in the light of our perspective, hence illustrating what a typical textbook on economics or political philosophy explains only on the theoretical level. By reading these essays, the reader is introduced to applications of Austro-libertarianism, which will concretize what is often explained only in theory.

Following Israel Kirzner's book entitled *The Economic Point of View: An Essay in the History of Economic Thought* (with an Introduction by Laurence S. Moss. Kansas City: Sheed Andrews McMeel, 1976), this book is named *The Austro-Libertarian Point of View: Essays on Austrian Economics and Libertarianism.* The idea is to show how our point of view explains economic phenomena, and how it applies to issues in law and politics. Although Austrian economics is positive and libertarianism is normative, this book shows how both are related; how each can support the other.

Despite being structured in a logical progression, the reader can choose to read any individual chapter according to their interests as these are all self-contained works.

Chapter 1 deals with the epistemology and methodology of economics. It builds on Ludwig Von Mises' action axiom, and develops its implications. The central idea is to give the reader an exposition of praxeology, in the Misesian tradition. This insight by the Viennese economist allows us to derive the fundamental features and implications of human action, including value, scale of value, scarcity, abundance, profit, loss, uncertainty, causality, and others. We also deal with objections and try to present different approaches to its foundation. As it can be seen, this is not only relevant for human behavior as such, but also to its economic applications. It is crucially important to extol the benefits of economic laws which are necessarily true, and not mere tautologies.

Chapter 2 is focused on analyzing neoclassical microeconomics, especially with regard to consumer choice, and how and in what respect the Austrian perspective diverges from it. We analyze the concepts of utility maximization and indifference, and argue how they are not fully capable of explaining consumer choice, as is often presented by neoclassical economists.

Chapter 3 consists of an application of the Austrian approach to government intervention in general and minimum wages in particular, on the basis of a paper which we co-authored with Kevin Aguilar. We object not only to the level of any particular minimum wage, but also to its very existence. Some people (Bernie Sanders!) might dismiss this as callous, and indifferent to low skilled workers. We demonstrate that the very opposite is true.

Once we have surveyed some of the main subjects in microeconomics, we are ready to deal with issues in macroeconomics.

In Chap. 4, we present the Austrian Business Cycle Theory and, on the basis of a paper co-authored with Dr. William Barnett II, analyze the feasibility of extending it to economies with large government sectors (big in both scale and scope) and how this affects the original ABCT.

Later, in Chap. 5, we deal with subjects regarding international economics: first, by analyzing Nassim Nicholas Taleb's critique of David Ricardo's Law of Comparative Advantage, and defending its validity, and second, by rejecting the Prebisch-Singer theory of the deterioration in the terms of trade on an Austrian basis, thereby, in both cases, defending international free trade, both for developed and underdeveloped economies.

The burden of Chap. 6 is devoted to libertarianism and political philosophy. Specifically, we present the ideal of a private property society, or Anarcho-Capitalism. First, we oppose the idea of the state as an ideally legitimate or efficient entity. We define the fallacy of *a priori* statism to refute claims that only the government can solve issues of so-called market failure. Secondly, we take to task the views of those who critique (private property) anarchism, on the basis of our reply to Professor Robert T. Miller's objections to our approach. We thereby defend laissez faire capitalism based on its most radical interpretation.

Chapter 7 offers a libertarian interpretation of the US Constitution. Hence, we apply libertarianism to law, and analyzing US history by so doing. This chapter in particular is also helpful in order to understand the slow and complex institutional path by which a society becomes more and more interventionist.

Chapter 8 treats subjects in public policy according to libertarian law. The first essay analyzes the subject of drugs legalization. The second, is a very brief exposition of how a libertarian society would deal with a pandemic such as COVID-19.

We share some final thoughts with the reader in Chap. 9.

In sum, this book offers our analysis of different areas of thought and reality on the basis of an Austro-Libertarian perspective. We hope the reader enjoys reading them as much as we enjoyed writing them.

And now, let us begin.

Contents

Chapter 1
Epistemology and Methodology

Praxeology, Intentional Action and the Methodology of Austrian Economics

"Economics is not about goods and services; it is about human choice and action."

Ludwig Von Mises (1949, 491).

Abstract The concept of Intentional Action is at the core of Praxeology, as developed by the Austrian economist Ludwig von Mises. Under this unique approach, defined as the science of human action and designed to study the field of the social sciences, Mises created an axiomatic-deductive system starting from the "action axiom": the contention that every acting man is eager to substitute a more satisfactory state of affairs for a less desired one. From this axiom, the Austrian scholar is able to derive the fundamental features and implications of human action; such as value, scale of value, scarcity, abundance, profit, loss, uncertainty and causality, among others. This chapter intends to present the praxeological perspective on intentional action and its epistemological implications; it also attempts to answer objections to this thesis.

Keywords Mises · Action · Praxeology · Logic · Austrian economics

---

This chapter is based on our paper Futerman, Alan G. and Block, Walter E. 2017. "A Praxeological Approach to Intentional Action". *Studia Humana*, Vol. 6:4, October, pp. 10-33. Available at http://studiahumana.com/pliki/wydania/10443-Volume6_Issue4-02_paper.pdf (last visited April 11, 2021).

A. G. Futerman, W. E. Block, *The Austro-Libertarian Point of View*,
https://doi.org/10.1007/978-981-16-4691-1_1

1.1 Introduction[1]

Praxeology[2], defined as the "Science of Human Action" and thoroughly developed by the Austrian School economist Ludwig von Mises[3] in his *magnum opus* "Human Action" (1949 [1998]), is based on a unique approach towards the fundamental nature of intentional action. Mises, best known for his contributions to the debate on Economic Calculation under the Socialist system (1922 [1962]), is widely regarded today, along with Friedrich A. von Hayek, as the most important representative of the Austrian School of Economics in the twentieth century.[4] The foundation of his entire defense of the free market system,[5] in the tradition of classical liberalism, is based on the concept of action defined as purposeful behavior, i.e. intentional action.

This approach is of a special kind, since among the students of human behavior, Mises is one of the rare ones whose work consists in the development of an axiomatic-deductive system, which could pretend to explain the fundamental nature of human action as the basis for understanding the field of economics.[6,7] Thus, "Economics, as a branch of the more general theory of human action, deals with all human action, i.e., with man's purposive aiming at the attainment of ends chosen, whatever these ends may be" (Mises 1949 [1998]:880). As we shall argue throughout this chapter, praxeology is able to explain the basic nature of human action, and to do so under a unique epistemological foundation.

In order to make a case for praxeology's usefulness in understanding the nature of intentional action, first we will present its methodology and theory as an axiomatic-deductive system. Then we will analyze its postulates and their epistemological status, which will allow us to respond to possible objections and finally to present our conclusions.

---

[1] The authors wish to thank Rafael Beltramino for helpful comments on an earlier draft of this essay.

[2] For another approach on praxeology, see Kotarbinski (1965).

[3] Lemberg, Austria, 09/29/1881 – New York, United States, 10/10/1973.

[4] The present authors would include in this regard Murray N. Rothbard, even though he is lesser known that those two. The latter's perspective can be seen in Rothbard (1951, 1960, 1962, 1971, 1973, 1997a, b, c, d).

[5] A "defense of free enterprise" is normative. The action axiom is an aspect of positive economics. Never the twain shall meet? See below.

[6] Others include Block (1973, 1980, 1999), Batemarco (1985), Fox (1992), Hoppe (1989, 1991, 1992, 1995), Hulsmann (1999), von Mises (1957, 1998), Polleit (2008, 2011), Rizzo (1978), Rothbard (1951, 1960, 1962, 1971, 1973, 1997a, b, c, d), Selgin (1988). Further, virtually all of these are in effect standing on the intellectual shoulders of Mises.

[7] By focusing on human action as such, Mises tried to identify what Sarjanovic (2008, 20) defines as a "pre-scientific metaphysics". As such, it primarily deals with the nature of human action (and behavior), and only secondarily with economic theorems (*catallactics*).

1.2 The Methodology of Praxeology

We shall begin explaining Mises's specific ideas with respect to human action by showing his views on methodology. This is essential to the entire approach and the reason will be clear by the end of this section.

Mises can be defined as a methodological dualist, since he regarded the method of the natural sciences as necessarily different from that of the social sciences, due to the idea that the former study regularities in nature, while the latter study concrete cases where human action is involved. This kind of phenomena, under a social context, constitutes complex phenomena, and therefore requires a different methodology for its analysis. As such, Mises explained:

> "Action is a category that the natural sciences do not take into account. [...] There are constant relations between entities that enable the scientist to establish the process called measurement. But there is nothing that would suggest aiming at ends sought; there is no ascertainable purpose" von Mises (1962: 6–7).

Methodological dualism is based on the fact that Mises identifies an ontological dualism between physical concretes and human actions, where the latter cannot be reduced to the former (Scarano, 2004: 2). Thus, this implies that both phenomena must be treated differently while at the same time preserving a scientific approach to their study.

In the words of Mises:

> "The natural sciences too deal with past events. [...] But the experience to which the natural sciences owe all their success is the experience of the experiment in which the individual elements of change *can be observed in isolation*. [...] The experience with which the sciences of human action have to deal is always an experience of complex phenomena. No laboratory experiments can be performed with regard to human action. *We are never in a position to observe the change in one element only, all other conditions of the event remaining unchanged*. [...] The information conveyed by historical experience cannot be used as building material for the construction of theories and the prediction of future events. Every historical experience is open to various interpretations, and is in fact interpreted in different ways. The postulates of positivism and kindred schools of metaphysics are therefore illusory. It is impossible to reform the sciences of human action according to the pattern of physics and the other natural sciences. There is no means to establish an a posteriori theory of human conduct and social events. History can neither prove nor disprove any general statement in the manner in which the natural sciences accept or reject a hypothesis on the ground of laboratory experiments. *Neither experimental verification nor experimental falsification of a general proposition is possible in its field*" (emphasis ours); von Mises (1949 [1998]: 30–31).

As Mises explains, there is no such thing as *ceteris paribus* in the field of human action[8], although we may use such a concept in order to *illustrate* a specific idea (or

---

[8] Although it could be said that there is no such thing as *ceteris paribus* in any science, it is certainly possible to distinguish among different conditions for the application of the concept: 1. When the exact formal conditions which allow the application of a proposition hold; 2. When the variables not included in the theory are irrelevant or constant; 3. When such variables are neither relevant nor constant but have turned out to be so in a laboratory; and 4. The variables not included in the theory

conceive it).[9] Thus, since no necessary regularities could be identified in this field,[10] any use in the social sciences of concepts or methodological tools originated in the natural sciences would be an illegitimate extrapolation[11]. Therefore, he naturally rejected the positivist approach as presented by the Vienna Circle (in the same way he fought the German Historical School).

The absence of regularities in human action, in turn, brings us a problem since we cannot proceed by generalizing from specific instances. Rather, we must utilize the hypothetic-deductive model of causal realism. Therefore, we cannot count on past events in order to create any specific model of human behavior, which we could use to predict future behavior, since "statistics is a method for the presentation of historical facts concerning prices and other relevant data of human action. It is not economics and cannot produce economic theorems and theories. The statistics of prices is economic history" (von Mises 1949 [1998]: 348). In effect, without theory we are not even able to understand past behavior[12]. Thus, "there is no such thing as quantitative economics" (von Mises 1949 [1998]: 348). Mises also explained:

> "The historian can never derive theorems about *cause and effect* from the analysis of the material available. [...] This shows why it is wrong to contend that 'it is from observation

---

are neither constant nor irrelevant nor established in a laboratory, but we accept the current hypothesis arguendo until we can make a new one which includes them. See Gordon (1993). We can infer that Mises refers here to the fact that formal sciences apply for 1, the natural sciences for 2 and 3, but economics pertains to 4. For a different approach, see as an example Roth (1988).

[9] A similar situation pertains with regard to equilibrium, or the evenly rotating economy. States von Mises (1922: 163) in this regard: "To assume stationary economic conditions is a theoretical expedient and not an attempt to describe reality. We cannot dispense with this line of thought if we wish to understand the laws of economic change. In order to study movement we must first imagine a condition where it does not exist. The stationary condition is that point of equilibrium to which we conceive all forms of economic activity to be tending and which would actually be attained if new factors did not, in the meantime, create a new point of equilibrium. In the imaginary state of equilibrium all the units of the factors of production are employed in the most economic way, and there is no reason to contemplate any changes in their number or their disposition.

> "Even if it is impossible to imagine a living—that is to say a *changing*—socialist economic order, because economic activity without economic calculation seems inconceivable, it is quite easy to postulate a socialist economic order under stationary conditions. We need only avoid asking how this stationary condition is achieved. If we do this there is no difficulty in examining the statics of a socialist community. All socialist theories and Utopias have always had only the stationary condition in mind." (emphasis in the original).

[10] There are no constants in economics as there are in the natural sciences, such as gravity, or the periodic table of the elements in chemistry. There are, however, particular features of human action *as such*, identified by praxeology, that can help us make sense of human behavior, but these praxeological laws and theorems are of a formal kind. Hence, regularities do exist in the social sciences, but only in a formal sense, not in a material sense. Hence, events are unique. See below for further clarification on this regard.

[11] See Mises on Case Probability and Class Probability (1949 [1998]: 107–113). This fundamental distinction can allow us to understand why certain industries, such as insurance, are both of the utmost importance in a society and at the same time *can* and *do* work with certain regularities, i.e. those subject to class probability.

[12] This insight by Mises was later adopted by philosopher of science Karl R. Popper (1957 [2002]).

that even deductive economics obtains its ultimate premises.' What we can 'observe' is always only complex phenomena. What economic history, observation, or experience can tell us is facts like these: Over a definite period of the past the miner John in the coal mines of the *X* company in the village of *Y* earned *p* dollars for a working day of *n* hours. There is no way that would lead from the assemblage of such and similar data to any theory concerning the factors determining the height of wage rates" (emphasis ours); von Mises (1962: 74).

What then, is the alternative to empirical scientific models in order to study human action? In Mises's view, to understand this field we need an axiomatic-deductive model. The central axiom of such a model should be a *self-evident* truth[13] (thus expressing its axiomatic nature[14]) by which theorems ought to be derived. These are later applied to the field of economics (*catallactics*[15]) in order to understand social phenomena. Such an axiom is defined as the "action axiom"[16]. Thus, praxeology is based on the foundation of such an axiom. The fact that we could not know the ultimate end of every action[17] does not imply that we could not engage in studying its structure.

The basis for the axiom as being self-evident is that we cannot deny it without engaging in a contradiction[18]. This, in turn, provides the reason for its foundation as an irrefutable truth. In effect, its axiomatic nature implies that there is neither a possible nor a thinkable world where the axiom does not apply[19]. Thus, it is non-falsifiable[20].

---

[13] Although the conception of axioms as self-evident has been abandoned at the beginning of the XXth century, this in turn works in favor of Mises, since it does not oblige him to justify the action axiom as the only and most fundamental basis for any knowledge, or knowledge as such. Despite of the fact that Mises indeed wants to prove that it is an axiom.

[14] "Axiomatic Nature" is to be regarded in the sense of the self-evidency. However, as we have previously said in the previous fn., if axioms need not be self-evident, but chosen for a system, then there is no such a thing as axiomatic nature. Even so, we use the phrase as to follow Mises's idea on this regard; which does not alter the reasoning. The action axiom is apodictic, since any attempt to deny it is *also* a human action.

[15] "[…] to distinguish precisely, within the broader field of general praxeology, a narrower orbit of specifically economic problems […] All that can be contended is this: Economics is mainly concerned with the analysis of the determination of money prices of goods and services exchanged on the market. In order to accomplish this task it must start from a comprehensive theory of human action […] it must not restrict its investigations to those modes of action which in mundane speech are called 'economic' actions, but must deal also with actions which are in a loose manner of speech called 'noneconomic'" (von Mises 1949 [1998]: 233–235).

[16] Although not everything that *seems* evident is irrefutable nor everything that is irrefutable *is* evident, we will address possible objections throughout this chapter in order to defend this view with respect to the action axiom.

[17] The causes of the ends aimed by every action is studied by the field of psychology.

[18] Following Aristotle´s performative contradiction.

[19] Despite of the fact that if we are to adopt the analytic/synthetic distinction we may discard the empirical validity of the action axiom as a mere *analytic* truth (or a tautology), and thus analyze this approach from a strict positivist view, we will deal with this objection by pointing out its contradictions further in the text.

[20] Since we are approaching this subject matter from the point of view of methodological dualism, a falsifiability criteria such as Popper's need not apply to define this approach as scientific or not.

Since we have explained the specific methodological approach taken by Mises, let us now examine what is the nature and scope of praxeology, based on the action axiom.

1.3 The Logic of Intentional Action

Mises defines human action as "[…] purposeful behavior. Or we may say: Action is will put into operation and transformed into an agency, is aiming at ends and goals, is the ego's meaningful response to stimuli and to the conditions of its environment, is a person's conscious adjustment to the state of the universe that determines his life. Such paraphrases may clarify the definition given and prevent possible misinterpretations. But the definition itself is adequate and does not need complement or commentary" (von Mises 1949 [1998]: 11). As such, the action axiom consists in the fact that every "Acting man is eager to substitute a more satisfactory state of affairs for a less satisfactory" (von Mises 1949 [1998]: 13). Thus, the acting agent chooses those means that he *subjectively* identifies as the best in order to achieve his ends.

Although Mises rejects mathematical economics[21], it can be useful to illustrate the action axiom and its theorems with the help of mathematical functions[22]. In effect, if we say that every action (A) is a function of specific ends (E), then:

$$A = f(E) \tag{1.1}$$

[21] See von Mises (1938 [2000]). For a critique see Moorhouse (1993). Other Austrians, too, reject mathematical economics. Austrian economists who object to the hyper-mathematicalization of the dismal science include: Anderson (2002), Barnett (2003, 2004), Barnett and Block (2006a, b, 2010), Brätland (2000), Bylund (2011), Callahan (2001), Hazlitt (1959), Herbener (1996), Hutt (1979), Jablecki (2007), Kirzner (1990), Leoni and Frola (1977), Menger (1973), von Mises (1977, 1998), Murphy (2008), Murphy et al. (2010), Reekie (1984a, 1984b), Rizzo (1978), Ropke (1956), Rothbard (1960, 1962, 1988, 1997b, 2011), Shostak (2002), Spadaro (1956), Wutscher (unpublished). There are even some economists not usually associated with the Austrian School who also oppose this hyper-mathematicalization of economics: Boulding (1971), Champion (2008), Dolan (1976), Ingrao and Israel (1987), Ischboldin (1960), Mirowski (1988).

[22] It is possible to formalize the theory with the help of symbolic logic, but functions are useful as well and we pursue that path at present. Why? Garrison (1994, 2001) inverted the triangle of Hayek (1931) and Rothbard (1962 [2009]), placing time on the horizontal, not the vertical axis. Why did he do so? This was done in order to make the triangle, a pillar of Austrian business cycle theory, more amenable to mainstream economists, who are accustomed to that practice and might reject the triangle out of hand for this one characteristic. It is only in like manner that we employ mathematical format; for the same precise reason: to render Austrian economics more palatable to the profession, which is mainly neoclassical, and more than likely to reject praxeology for that reason alone (The popularity of Coase 1960, is an exception to this general rule.). As for the present authors, we join Barnett and Block (2006a, b) in rejecting the triangle holus bolus, and, also, with the economists mentioned, *supra*, in the present footnote, who reject mathematical notation.

This is so because if the acting agent has no ends he wishes to attain, then he will not engage in any action whatsoever. It must be also said that, in this respect, action always aims at a change in existing conditions, whether with respect to the acting man itself (*autistic* exchange), or to other/s (*interpersonal* exchange) (von Mises 1949 [1998]: 195–196). In this regard, the focus of any specific action is irrelevant with respect to its fundamental character: it always purports to remove or alleviate some uneasiness.

In effect, human action is based on the presupposition that the subjective value that the individual gives to the end (vE) he wishes to attain is higher than the subjective value he gives to his effort or means (vM) to achieve it.

$$\text{If } vE > vM \rightarrow \exists A \tag{1.2a}$$

$$\text{If } vE \leq vM \rightarrow \nexists A \tag{1.2b}$$

Mises explains:

> "The most general prerequisite of action is a state of dissatisfaction, on the one hand, and, on the other, the possibility of removing or alleviating it by taking action. (Perfect satisfaction and its concomitant, the absence of any stimulus to change and action, belong properly to the concept of a perfect being. This, however, is beyond the power of the human mind to conceive. *A perfect being would not act.*)" (emphasis ours); von Mises (1933 [2003]: 25).

At any specific point in time, man wishes to attain several different ends, and therefore he will try to achieve those which he identifies as priorities according to his scale of preferences. How do we know it? Because if we follow [1.1] and [1.2a], then it is obvious that the individual will act in order to achieve the end that he regards as most important, leaving the rest for a later time (according to his means). This is so because human action takes place in time (T), and depends on means (M); and since man cannot attain all the ends (E) he wishes simultaneously,[23] he must necessarily choose. Such choice will be made according to some standard, thus ordering the ends with respect to the individual's judgment and values:

$$E_1, E_2, E_3, \supset, E_n \tag{1.3a}$$

$$vE_1 > vE_2 > vE_3 > \ldots > vEn \tag{1.3b}$$

$$vE_n = f\left(E_n\right) \tag{1.3c}$$

As we can see in [1.3c] the value that the individual gives to any specific end will depend on the position of such end in his scale of preferences. Now we may turn our attention to means themselves. As every human action makes use of some means for the attainment of its ends, these means (M) are also valued by the acting agent. We

[23] If he could do so, we would have achieved post scarcity. Then, there would be no need for human action, nor economics, which is its study.

call this valuation *utility* (U), and it will be proportionate to the value that the individual gives to the end that could be attained with such unit of means.[24]

$$M_1, M_2, M_3, \supset, M_n \tag{1.4a}$$

$$U_1, U_2, U_3, \supset, U_n \tag{1.4b}$$

$$M = F(E) \tag{1.4c}$$

$$M_n = F(E_n) \tag{1.4d}$$

$$U_n = F(vE_n) \tag{1.4e}$$

Since the individual chooses the means he subjectively regards as the best in order to achieve its ends ([1.4c] and [1.4d]), according to his value scale ([1.4a] and [1.4b]), we can see that the utility of every (unit of) means is determined by the value that the individual gives to the end that could be achieved with it [1.4e]. Thus, the utility of every unit of means is ultimately a function of the specific end that could be achieved with it and its value for the acting man:

$$M_n = F(E_n) \rightarrow U_n = F(vE_n) \tag{1.4f}$$

This in turn implies that, in many cases certain units of means may be used for different ends, while at the same time being interchangeable and equally relevant, i.e. any of them could be used for the attainment of any end, regardless of their ranking in the individual's scale of preferences. Therefore, the utility of every unit will be determined by the value of the last possible end (or lower ranked) that could be achieved with them (since this last end is the *first* one the individual would be willing to sacrifice if he had one less unit of means). Since the last end is called the *marginal* end (because it is on the margin[25]), and the last unit of means is called the marginal unit, the utility of this last unit is called marginal utility:

$$M_1 = M_2 = \ldots = M_n \rightarrow U_n = f(vE_n) \tag{1.5a}$$

This is the foundation for the law of marginal utility. Since every end is arranged under a scale of preferences [1.3a] and the value of each end depends on how it is ranked in such a scale [1.3b], then utility will necessarily decrease as the individual

[24] Are we now treading in the direction of illegitimate cardinal utility? Austrianism is only compatible with ordinal utilty. Let us reassure the reader that we are not. That is why we say that the individual orders his ends in a ranking, and he values his means in *proportion* to how he values the ends he intends to achieve with them; i.e. in relation to them. But we do not say that the value of the means is *equal* to the value of the ends. We intend to say that, for example, the individual values E1 more than E2 (vE1> vE2); and the unit of means with which he intends to achieve E1 will be valued according to how he values E1 (vE1). Note that the values do not equalize; or that we can somehow measure them. Formalization is offered only for illustrative purposes.

[25] Menger [1871 (2007)], by using the word "marginal" meant "additional".

adds additional units to his stock and evaluates them [1.4f]. Such is the fundamental reason behind *diminishing* marginal utility[26]. Thus, as the individual increases its supply of units of means, U will consequently decrease [27,28]:

$$\frac{\partial Un}{\partial Mn} < 0 \tag{1.5b}$$

$$U_1(M_1) > U_2(M_2) > U_3(M_3) > \ldots > U_n(M_n) \tag{1.5c}$$

Given the fact that each individual always has a specific amount of units of means to achieve its ends, if the amount of the former (Mq) is lower than that of the latter (Eq), therefore the individual will face scarcity. Thus, scarcity is a subjective evaluation of means with respect to ends, and not a real feature of any given good (means).

$$0 < \mathrm{M}q < \infty \tag{1.6a}$$

$$\mathrm{E}q > \mathrm{M}q \tag{1.6b}$$

$$\mathrm{vS}_{x+1} > \mathrm{vS}_{x} \tag{1.6c}$$

Given [1.6a] and [1.6b], the acting agent faces scarcity. If he had enough units of means in order to achieve every end (and even more), then the marginal utility of each unit would fall to zero, and at this point he would not engage in any purposeful behavior (to achieve more ends), i.e. he would no longer act[29]. This is because [1.2b] would apply, where the effort to attain a specific end is valued more than the end itself. Moreover, the individual will prefer a larger stock of means rather than a smaller one [1.6c], since more ends can be achieved with the former.

Until this point, we have only analyzed action *ex ante*. Let us now turn our attention to the implications of action *ex post*. The individual faces multiple possible

---

[26] Let us note that the praxeological deduction of diminishing marginal utility is based on the fact that the first unit of means is used for the attainment of the highest ranked end, the second unit for the second ranked end, etc. regardless of the *psychological* satisfaction (reported utility) that the individual gets at each time. On the other hand, Gossen's (1854) Law (which is often used by neoclassical economists in order to illustrate this theory) is based on the idea that successive consumption of units of the same commodity will provide less utility each time. However, this depends on the commodity and the individual. For instance, the second unit may provide more satisfaction than the first one, and the third more than the second, etc. It is only eventually that we reach a point of diminishing returns. As such, it cannot be necessarily true, as are the categories of praxeology. In effect, this in turn implies that for praxeology marginal utility theory is not based on psychologism, and as we will see in section V.i., this is relevant for the entire praxeological approach towards human action.

[27] With respect to disutility, or discomfort, something similar takes place, e.g. The first scratch in the car bothers the owner more than the second, and so forth.

[28] Since there is no continuity in the field of human action (because man only regards discrete quantities as relevant for action), to derivate a function makes no *economic* sense. However, this formalization is intended to illustrate the postulates of praxeology, not to replace their conceptual truth, which is mainly shown in discursive reasoning.

[29] Thus, economic goods are those which are scarce.

different ends he could achieve with the means at his disposal. So, he will tend to choose which goals to attain according to his value scale[30] at any specific point in time ([1.3a] and [1.3b]). Thus, the concept of cost (C) is implicit in every human action. As Mises explained:

> "But acting man chooses, determines, and tries to reach an end. Of two things both of which he cannot have together he selects one and gives up the other. Action therefore always involves both taking and renunciation" (von Mises 1949 [1998]: 12).

The best-discarded alternative use of a unit of means would be the alternative cost of each action (or, as economic theory presents it, the "opportunity cost").

$$vE_1 > vE_2 \rightarrow A = f(E1) \text{ and } C = vE_2 \tag{1.7a}$$

$$vE_1' > vE_2 \rightarrow P \tag{1.7b}$$

$$vE_1' < vE_2 \rightarrow L \tag{1.7c}$$

As analyzed *ex post*, if the value the individual obtained by the action (vE1') is greater than that attained by the best other available option, then he has in fact profited (P) from such action. In case the opposite happens, he has experienced a loss (L).

We can infer from this that there is no such thing as indifference in the field of human action, ([1.2a] and [1.2b]), since a truly indifferent agent does not act; cannot act.[31] However, it may very well be the case that after the individual acts he may *say* he was indifferent with respect to acting in order to achieve E_1 or E_2. However, since this analysis is *ex post*, we do not have any other alternative but to assume that there was, *ex ante*, *something* in E_1 that he found more valuable than E_2[32]. Preference

---

[30] Let us be clear on this "value scale" business. It is not as if, on the one hand, we have the person, and on the other, his "value scale" that, perhaps, he is clutching in his hand, and consults, from time to time, before he acts. Rather, this value scale is *implicit* in his behavior. He chooses an apple instead of a banana, when offered both. On his value scale, the former ranks higher than the latter. We discover this, through his choice. However, he had no separate, perhaps printed, value scale, that he consulted. It is entirely possible, very likely even, that he was not thinking about fruit just before the moment he was offered this choice. It is highly plausible the even he did not know, beforehand, which he would partake in; that even he only discovered this ranking as he reached out his hand and grabbed up the apple.

[31] Thus, it would be impossible for anyone to demonstrate that he was indifferent between any two or more options. He could *say* he was indifferent, but how could he *reveal* (in the Rothbardian 1977) sense, that he was? He could not.

[32] Otherwise, why did he make that choice? Neoclassical indifference analysis is based on the idea that there is such a thing as indifference in human action (as presented in indifference curves and maximization analysis; see Chapter II). Nozick (1977: 369) argues that marginal utility theory requires indifference in order to explain why the agent may choose any of the units he possesses to achieve an end; thus, he avers, the Austrian rejection of the concept of indifference is self-refuting. But if the agent were truly indifferent between the aforementioned apple and banana, why, ever, would he pick one and not the other? For the Austrian critique of the concept of "indifference" in economics, see Barnett (2003), Block (1980, 1999, 2003, 2007, 2009a, 2009b), Block and Barnett (2010), Hoppe (2005, 2009), Hulsmann (1999), Machaj (2007). For a neoclassical rejection of this

always reveals in action, and, despite the psychological implications that the concept of "indifference" may have, it has no *economic* consequences whatsoever.

In the case of interpersonal exchange, the price (p) is the amount of money paid for an item, or the other good, in the case of barter. If there is no voluntary exchange, always based on [1.2a] and [1.2b], then there is no price (which can be expressed in monetary terms or as a simple ratio of exchange between two commodities).

Another implication of the action axiom is time (T), since every action takes place in time and requires time in order to manifest itself and give place to an outcome. This in turn implies that the very same fact that the individual acts due to [1.2a] and [1.2b], means that it must be the case that he valued more the attainment of the end chosen in t than in t+1 ([1.8a.]).

Now consider:

$$vE_1t > vE_1t+1 \tag{1.8a}$$

$$vE_1t < vE_1t+1 \rightarrow \nexists A \tag{1.8b}$$

In effect, time preference (the ratio between the subjective value of the present with respect to the subjective value of the future) is an essential implication of human action.

$$TP = \frac{vE1t}{vE1t+1} \tag{1.8c}$$

Thus, in order to sacrifice the achievement of the end at present for its accomplishment in the future, the individual will demand to receive in the future a higher value than that which he could have attained at present. In terms of present and future consumption, time preference (TP) explains the existence of interest and savings. The latter exists because it permits one to expand future consumption, which compensates for the sacrifice of postponing present consumption[33]. Therefore, the individual will demand future consumption according to his time preference in

---

Austrian view, and thus a defense of the mainstream doctrine of "indifference" see Caplan (undated, 1999, 2001, 2003, 2008), Nozick (1977), O'Neill (2010). See also on this Zanotti [1990 (2004): 22]: "Nozick has objected that from the fact that one person chooses *a* does not imply that it does not want nor prefer *b*. It is true. But our contention that every action implies choosing between *a* and *b* does not mean deducing that the person does not prefer *b*, rather that since not every necessity could be satisfied at the same time, then the acting agent must create a value scale and set his priorities, according to which he will option. Perhaps, respect to this observation by Nozick we may say that every action implies to choose between *a* and *non a*" (translated by the first of the present authors from the original in Spanish, with permission of the original author).

[33] Menger (2007 [1871]) classified economic goods in lower and higher order. Thus, lower order goods (or first order) are consumption goods, and those of higher order (or second, third, …, *n* orders) are those which are used in the production process of lower order goods, classified as such according to how far they are from the consumption stage. Savings implies economic agents sacrificing present consumption in order to create higher order goods, which in turn can increase future consumption.

order to sacrifice present consumption, i.e. the value of present consumption for the individual is defined by the present value of future consumption discounted by his rate of time preference.

An objection to the foregoing involved the famous ice-in-winter versus ice-in-summer example.[34] It is now winter. A man, surely, will prefer the latter to the former. This seems like a refutation of the Austrian view that people always desire a good sooner rather than later. The refutation of this objection as that these two are not the same good, economically, even though they are, but only chemically.

Another implication of the action axiom is the concept of causality. This is so because unless the acting agent *assumes* that by doing p (a specific action using specific means), he will not achieve q, then he would not engage in any action. In the view of von Mises (1949 [1998]: 22):

> "Man is in a position to act because he has the ability to discover causal relations which determine change and becoming in the universe. Acting requires and presupposes the category of causality. Only a man who sees the world in the light of causality is fitted to act. In this sense, we may say that causality is a category of action. The category *means and ends* presupposes the category *cause and effect*. In a world without causality and regularity of phenomena there would be no field for human reasoning and human action. Such a world would be a chaos in which man would be at a loss to find any orientation and guidance. Man is not even capable of *imagining* the conditions of such a chaotic universe. Where man does not see any causal relation, he cannot act. This statement is not reversible. Even when he knows the causal relation involved, man cannot act if he is not in a position to influence the cause." (emphasis ours)

Thus, man will act only if he wishes to attain q, *believes* he had identified a causal relation of the type $p \rightarrow q$, and is able to engage in p. This, of course does not imply that causality should have a metaphysical character (Scarano 2004: 3), but that it has to be *considered* by the acting agent as such, if he wants to engage in any action[35].

Should be clear by now what is the nature and corollaries (for praxeology) of intentional action, i.e. human action[36]:

> "As thinking and acting men, we grasp the concept of action. In grasping this concept we simultaneously grasp the closely correlated concepts of value, wealth, exchange, price, and cost. They are all necessarily implied in the concept of action, and together with them the concepts of valuing, scale of value and importance, scarcity and abundance, advantage and disadvantage, success, profit, and loss [...] There can be no doubt whatever concerning the *aprioristic* character of these disciplines." (emphasis ours); von Mises (1933 [2003]: 24–25).

---

[34] which takes place before the advent of refrigeration

[35] Thus, the metaphysical status of the category of causality is outside the scope of praxeology. This is so because it is irrelevant for the acting agent: Whatever its metaphysical status, it must take it into account for the very nature of intentional action as such.

[36] For a full analysis of praxeology see von Mises [1949 (1998)] and Zanotti [1990 (2004)].

1.4 The Epistemological Implications of Praxeology

Let us now analyze the epistemological implications of this unique approach toward intentional action. It must be clear by now that Mises ascribes to human action the condition of *rationality*. This requires further explanation, since this definition may at first sight appears as trying to justify every action as the *proper* one according to its specific context. But this is not the case, since Mises defines action as rational since it is always based in the selection of certain means for the attainment of specific ends, according to the *subjective* judgment of the individual who chooses to act. This in turn implies that, although the individual may be wrong, it does not follow that he did not regard the means chosen, at the *time* of choosing, as the best available to him. Mises defines as rational only the *structure* of human action, based on a means and ends approach, but not as an evaluative judgment. In other words, he does not regard rational action as necessarily the best choice that the individual could have made in a specific context (as judged by the best mind with the best knowledge in that context). But the fact that since he chose in a certain way, then it must necessarily follow that his judgment was made on the basis of his knowledge and based on his subjective considerations (value scale and preferences) as the standard.[37,38]

---

[37]As presented in the previous section [1.4c]. "Choosing means is a technical problem, as it were, the term 'technique' being taken in its broadest sense. Choosing ultimate ends is a personal, subjective, individual affair. Choosing means is a matter of reason choosing ultimate ends a matter of the soul and the will" (von Mises 1957 [2007]: 14–5).

[38]The idea of identifying economic principles in human action as such and analyzing different areas of human behavior by using economic tools or concepts is not such a controversial approach within economic science. In effect, for instance, Gary Becker pursued a similar path (only on a different basis). In his words:

> "My research uses the economic approach to analyze social issues that range beyond those usually considered by economists…
>
> "Unlike Marxian analysis, the economic approach I refer to does not assume that individuals are motivated solely by selfishness or material gain. It is a *method* of analysis, not an assumption about particular motivations. Along with others, I have tried to pry economists away from narrow assumptions about self-interest. Behavior is driven by a much richer set of values and preferences.
>
> "The analysis assumes that individuals maximize welfare *as they conceive it,* whether they be selfish, altruistic, loyal, spiteful, or masochistic. Their behavior is forward-looking, and it is also assumed to be consistent over time. In particular, they try as best they can to anticipate the uncertain consequences of their actions. Forward-looking behavior, however, may still be rooted in the past, for the past can exert a long shadow on attitudes and values.
>
> "Actions are constrained by income, time, imperfect memory and calculating capacities, and other limited resources, and also by the opportunities available in the economy and elsewhere. These opportunities are largely determined by the private and collective actions of other individuals and organizations.
>
> "Different constraints are decisive for different situations, but the most fundamental constraint is limited time. Economic and medical progress have greatly increased length of life, but not the physical flow of time itself, which always restricts everyone to 24 h per day…" Becker (1993, 385–386).

This also explains another feature of human action: uncertainty with respect to the future. Since man can experience both profit and loss, while he would always prefer to experience the former rather than the latter, it follows that he does not have *perfect* knowledge[39]. Otherwise, men would always profit from every action they undertake, thus implying that there would neither be a concept of loss *nor* of profit (since this would be the standard)[40]. Man cannot always be right, and automatically so.

We may also ask why the category of action, as presented in praxeology, is an axiom. Its axiomatic nature comes from the fact that there is no possible way of escaping its truth. Even in the act of trying to deny the validity of the action axiom, one would have to choose certain means (arguments) in order to attain an end (refute the action axiom). In addition, one would have to assume that the act of trying to refute the axiom makes one pass from a less satisfactory state to a more satisfactory one. Thus, any individual who tries to refute the action axiom affirms it in the very act of trying to deny it[41].

As can be seen by now, Mises was deeply influenced by Kant (von Mises 1933 [2003]; 1962). By talking about the category of action as *inherent* in the *structure* of the human mind, Mises regards it as a Kantian category[42]. In effect, the action axiom is presented as a *synthetic a priori* proposition. Its truth is independent from any experience (thus making it *a priori*), while it is also present in every human action in the real empirical world (thus making it *synthetic*).

This does not imply that the concept of action cannot be learned. The *a priori* refers here to the identification of an essential attribute in human nature, and therefore an intrinsic characteristic of man; not necessarily the concept of *a priori* as prior to experience (as developed by John Stuart Mill). What Mises tells us is that the axiom is independent of experience, not that no experience is required in order

[39] One of the characteristics of "Perfect Competition". See Kirzner (1963a).

[40] It is true that, supposing someone's actions always turned out for the best, nothing would prevent him from having the concept of cost or being aware of alternatives to his actions. It could be (reasonably) claimed that the presupposition of our argument is that in order to have the concept of loss one must be able to experience a loss, and this may not be necessary. Yet, in this scenario, the concept of loss would be, at least, *irrelevant*. This is a speculation in psychology, not praxeology: it is addressed to how people come to appreciate different concepts such as, in this case, alternative or opportunity costs.

[41] See Rizzo (1978: 50).

[42] Some disciples of Mises, such as the American economist Murray Rothbard, use an Aristotelian foundation for the action axiom. "All human beings *act* by virtue of their existence and their nature as human beings. We could not conceive of human beings who do not act purposefully, who have no ends in view that they desire and attempt to attain. Things that did not act, that did not behave purposefully, would no longer be classified as human." (emphasis in the original); Rothbard (1962 [2009]: 2); this author also cites Aristotle's *Ethica Nicomachea*, ch. vii, as the basis for his contention on the nature of action. See also Rothbard (1997b, d).

to gain conscious awareness of its existence. In effect, by identifying the action axiom one is in fact engaging in an action.

In the words of von Mises [1949 (1998): 64], "All that is needed for the deduction of all praxeological theorems is knowledge of the essence of human action. It is a knowledge that is our own because we are men; [...] no experience, however rich, could disclose them to a being who did not know a priori what human action is. The only way to a cognition of these theorems is logical analysis of our inherent knowledge of the category of action. We must bethink ourselves and reflect upon the structure of human action. Like logic and mathematics, praxeological knowledge is in us; it does not come from without".

In other words, the identification of the concept of action is *a posteriori* (in the sense of Mill), but the category of action itself is *a priori* since it responds to a fundamental attribute of human nature, independent of whether such an attribute has been conceptualized or not[43]. Thus, the action axiom is not to be understood as a tautology of the same kind as those in logic and mathematics, applicable to any universe possible or thinkable; rather, it is especially applicable to the concrete universe of experience of human beings and at the same time *necessary*.

Mises explains:

> "The a priori knowledge of praxeology is entirely different— categorially different—from the a priori knowledge of mathematics or, more precisely, from mathematical a priori knowledge as interpreted by logical positivism. The starting point of all praxeological thinking is not *arbitrarily* chosen axioms, but a self-evident proposition, fully, clearly and necessarily present in every human mind. [...] The characteristic feature of man is precisely that he consciously acts. [...] To act means: to strive after ends, that is, to choose a goal and to resort to means in order to attain the goal sought.
>
> "The essence of logical positivism is to deny the cognitive value of a priori knowledge by pointing out that all a priori propositions are merely analytic. They do not provide new information, but are merely verbal or tautological, asserting what has already been implied in the definitions and premises. Only experience can lead to synthetic propositions. There is an obvious objection against this doctrine, viz., that *this proposition that there are no synthetic a priori propositions is in itself a*—as the present writer thinks, false—*synthetic a priori proposition, for it can manifestly not be established by experience*" (emphasis ours); von Mises (1962: 4–5).

However, different objections have been raised against the praxeological perspective. Let us now review some of them, as well as offer possible replies.

[43] This fact may answer the contention that the *a priori* nature of mathematics and logic is demonstrable, while praxeology is not (Scarano, 2004: 11). "...axiomatic concepts are only *implicit* in experience. To identify them explicitly, to conceptualize them, requires a sophisticated development" (emphasis in the original) Binswanger (2014: 168).

1.5 Objections to the Praxeological Approach and Possible Answers

1.5.1 Psychologism and Polylogism

Although the arguments of Mises seem compelling, possible objections may arise. Despite of the fact that human action is rational action; how can we know, in any specific case whether the individual's behavior corresponds to an action or a "reflex"? Mises himself recognizes that "Human action is conscious behavior on the part of a human being. Conceptually it can be sharply and clearly distinguished from unconscious activity, even though *in some cases it is perhaps not easy to determine whether given behavior is to be assigned to one or the other category*" (emphasis ours); (von Mises 1933 [2003]: 24). If we do not have any criteria in order to identify human action as such, then praxeology, although true *a priori*, would be useless in practice (and the action axiom would no longer be a *synthetic a priori* proposition).

Mises replies that "[…] all experience concerning human action is conditioned by the praxeological categories and becomes possible only through their application. If we had not in our mind the schemes provided by praxeological reasoning, we should never be in a position to discern and to grasp any action. We would perceive motions, but *neither buying nor selling, nor prices, wage rates, interest rates, and so on*. It is only through the utilization of the praxeological scheme that we become able to have an experience concerning an act of buying and selling, but then independently of the fact of whether or not our senses concomitantly perceive any motions of men and of nonhuman elements of the external world. Unaided by praxeological knowledge we would never learn anything about media of exchange. If we approach coins without such preexisting knowledge, we would see in them only round plates of metal, nothing more. Experience concerning money requires familiarity with the praxeological category medium of exchange." (emphasis ours); (von Mises 1949 [1998]: 40).

In the same light, Mises said that, "No talk about irrationality […] can invalidate the statement that man makes use of his reason for the realization of wishes and desires. From the unshakable foundation of the category of human action praxeology and economics proceed step by step by means of discursive reasoning. Precisely defining assumptions and conditions, they construct a system of concepts and draw all the inferences implied by logically unassailable ratiocination. With regard to the results thus obtained only two attitudes are possible; either one can unmask logical errors in the chain of the deductions which produced these results, or one must acknowledge their correctness and validity" [1949 (1998): 67].

Similarly, Roderick T. Long explained:

> "Now we can begin to see why it is a mistake to assimilate what the praxeologist does to what a Cartesian rationalist does when he spins out the laws of physical motion a priori. The conclusions of praxeology are not in themselves empirical statements. They do not predict what people will do. For example, they do not predict how people will behave with regard

to metal disks and piles of wood. What they do predict is how people will behave *so long as they are buying and selling*. If that gives praxeology empirical content, then geometry has empirical content in just the same way. Geometry cannot predict how many edges your next slice of pizza will have; but it can predict how many edges it will have *so long as it is triangular*" (emphasis in the original) Long (2004: 356).

Although we could say that this answer to the problem makes sense, it is only a partial solution. We need a stronger foundation for praxeology, and as we will show next, we may find it in the work of the Austrian philosopher Ludwig Wittgenstein (as presented by Long 2004).

In order to further analyze the validity of the praxeological approach we need to respond to several objections against this view. The first one is what von Mises (1949 [1998]: 75–89) defined as "polylogism", the view that there is no such a thing as a universal logic. For praxeology, the problem with this view can be easily seen: if there is no universal logic, then there is no way to derive any empirical application (including economic theory) from the action axiom, which is based on the idea of identifying every human action as rational action. Here, the Austrian author is in the tradition of Frege[44] (Long 2004: 346–349), who in turn opposed the idea of "psychologism", the view that the laws of logic are nothing more than a *generalization* of how men think. This is an important distinction, since we can define two different views of polylogism (Long 2004: 347): normative and descriptive.

Frege explained that "the laws of logic are normative for thought because they are descriptive of reality; but they are not descriptive of thought" (Long 2004: 347). This implies a *reflectionist* view of logic, i.e. the idea that reality in itself is logical[45] and therefore our thinking, in order to reflect reality, ought to follow the laws of logic. The corollary of this approach is that logical thought is optional for man, meaning that although the proper way to think, if one wants to conform to reality, is by guiding thought according to the laws of logic, man can also think illogically. Now, for normative polylogism, which holds that "every group has its own logic, but they're all correct; each group's logic is valid for that group" (Long 2004: 347), the Fregean view described before is a proper response, since although men *can* think illogically, it does not follow that there *are* multiple logics.

But what about descriptive polylogism? This view maintains that "different principles of logic describe the thinking of different groups, but it does not follow that all these different logics are equally valid; one might well be right and all the others wrong" (Long 2004: 347). The problem here is more difficult, since although it could be said that there is no such thing as multiple logics, there is no standard by which to judge which one is correct. This is so because the Fregean approach could be easily dismissed by pointing out that what the Fregean *thinks* that are the laws of logic, is only what his group *regards* as the laws of Logic, which can be different from what other group may *think*. This in turn implies that there is no way of knowing which Logic is the correct one, and therefore normative polylogism appears

[44] Perhaps by the influence of Edmund Husserl.

[45] While we respect Frege, the present authors do not accept his view that reality is "logical." We maintain that it just *is*. See on this Wittgenstein, below.

again. In other words, in order to refute normative polylogism, one may very well fall into descriptive polylogism, thus finally returning to normative polylogism.

Although Frege discards this possibility by not paying attention to descriptive polylogism (implying that the only problem is normative polylogism), Mises does in fact recognize that there is a difficulty with descriptive polylogism that should be solved[46]. In order to do that he adopts an *impositionist* approach to logic, which holds that the Logic of reality is in fact an imposition made by the subject *to* reality due to the structure of the human mind. As we can see, this is a standard Kantian approach. Thus, by adopting this position, Mises is discarding any possibility of illogical thought, due to the nature and functioning of the reasoning mind itself. However, at the same time there is no way for Mises to discard the chance that other beings have other mental structures, and thus, impose different categories on reality.

In the words of Long (2004: 366), "[…] by granting that such categories apply to the world only because we impose them on it, it leaves open the possibility that creatures of another sort might impose different categories […] the reflectionist position, echoing Frege's view that logical principles are laws of reality rather than laws of though […] too seems vulnerable to polylogism. If the principles of psychology are normative for rather than constitutive of thought, then thought can depart from them; and once illogical thought is permitted, so is irrational action, and the fabric of praxeology is rent asunder" [47]. Therefore, this problem brings us back to normative and descriptive polylogism.

According to Long (2004: 355), the solution to this problem is to be found in the work of Ludwig Wittgenstein. Why? Because based on his work we may reject the approach of both Mises and Frege to the problem of polylogism. Instead, he presents a case for what we may define as a *unified* view on the subject of thought and reality. Thus,

> "[…] impositionism is rejected because it pictures logic as a constraint imposed by us on the world, while reflectionism is rejected because it pictures logic as a constraint imposed by the world on us. To think of logic as constraining something is to imagine, or try to imagine, how things would be without the constraint. Since neither talk of an illogical world nor talk of illogical thought can be made sense of, the whole question cannot be meaningfully asked and so may be dismissed in good conscience: 'in order to be able to draw a limit to thought, we should have to find both sides of the limit thinkable ….We cannot think what we cannot think; so what we cannot think we cannot *say* either' (Wittgenstein 1961:3, 49)" (Long, 366).

The unified view emanates from the fact that "It is a sign of confusion to say either that the logicality of the world has its source in the structure of thought or that the logicality of thought has its source in the structure of the world—as though the logicality of thought and the logicality of the world were two different facts that need to be hooked together, rather than being two sides of the same fact […]" (Long, 2004: 366).

---

[46] We follow Long's (2004) presentation; Mises does not present his case specifically in this way.

[47] And, as we have seen, Mises also points out that unconscious behavior may be difficult to distinguish from conscious behavior.

How do we make sense of the fact that praxeological concepts may not apply in practice all the time?

> "[...] although it is true that empirical considerations come into play in determining whether a praxeological concept is applicable in a particular case, such empirical considerations cannot confine themselves to the sorts of purely quantitative magnitudes and repeatable experiments with which the physical sciences (supposedly) deal, but must instead involve the intuitive, interpretive method that Mises and Hayek, borrowing from the hermeneutical tradition, call *verstehen*"[48] (Long 2004: 358).

Thus, "In solving Frege's problem, Wittgenstein has solved Mises' problem as well. There can be a priori economic laws, because the terms that occur in those laws will be applicable only to phenomena that in fact obey those laws. [...] Mises agrees with Wittgenstein that economic categories legitimately apply only to those items that play the corresponding role in people's actions. He too invokes the specific example of coins, which count as money only if they are actually used to facilitate indirect exchange. That use is *constitutive* of money" (Long 2004: 355). Therefore, as Long (2004: 359), explains by using a Kantian formula[49]: praxeology without thymology[50] is empty; thymology without praxeology is blind.

History, as such, is to be studied according to the previous approach since the historian identifies common phenomena according to praxeological concepts and deals with unique events by the use of *verstehen* (Scarano 2004: 8). Thus, it can deal with specific men, ideas, events, and other historical data by using *ideal types*. How does it create these? "The aspect from which history arranges and assorts the infinite multiplicity of events is their meaning. The only principle which it applies for the systemization of its objects-men, ideas, institutions, social entities, and artifacts-is meaning affinity. According to meaning affinity it arranges the elements into ideal types" (von Mises 1949 [1998]: 59).

As Wittgenstein explained, illogical thinking cannot count as thinking; and very much in the same way, irrational action cannot count as action. "To borrow a phrase from Hayek, the mind does not so much *make* rules as *consist* of rules (Hayek 1973:18); and a mind that 'consists of rules' cannot intelligibly be interpreted either as *making* rules (as though it might have left them unmade), or as having rules *imposed* on it (as though it might have been free of them)" (Long 2004:367).

Similarly, Mario Rizzo (2015: 377) explained that, "Wittgenstein's view is that we must go beyond the descriptive-normative dichotomy to the position that the

---

48 In Mises's analysis, *Verstehen* could be identified with Bergson's concept of *Intuition* (Scarano 2004: 6). However, the approach here is not the same. The concept of intuition often responds to subjectivism and thus to relativism, turning it into an invalid source for objective knowledge. The idea here is that experience is interpreted by *a priori* praxeological concepts, not that there is some kind of revelation that allows the individual to identify reality as it is without a specific means of cognition (in this case, the use of man's mind aided by praxeological concepts).

49 "Thoughts without content are void; intuitions without conceptions, blind" Kant (1787).

50 "'Thymology' is derived from the Greek *θυμός*, which Homer and other authors refer to as the seat of the emotions and as the mental faculty of the living body by means of which thinking, willing, and feeling are conducted." von Mises (1957 [2007]: 265–266).

laws of logic are *constitutive* of thought. Without logic there is no thought and without thought there is no objective substratum of communication" (emphasis ours).

Thus, praxeological categories are not only an essential feature of the human *mind*, but also are a fundamental part of our understanding of human action in *reality*. The example of Mises on money is a case in point: without the category of a medium of exchange, we would only see "round plates of metal". This example may be compared to that presented by John Wisdom when he discussed whether we can correctly deduce emotions by perceiving the external behavior of individuals in the case of a person's face and then deducing he is angry in the same way "we know a kettle's boiling – from the steam we guess at bubbles and the rest, and from the bubbles and the rest it's a deduction that it's boiling" (Wisdom 1968: 209). Here, Wisdom's point is that inferring someone's anger from his behavior was not like inferring that a kettle is boiling by looking at the steam, because we have no direct access to someone's else's mind. We can in effect see "inside" the kettle but not into someone else's mind. Although we may be making an illegitimate extrapolation by deducing a specific inner state from an external reaction, what underlies both examples is that in order to understand both phenomena one needs the correct *concepts*. Hence, it is not that we deduce the person is angry from his face, but we see anger in his face directly. In this respect, one also needs to have the concept of action in order to identify it in reality. Otherwise, one would never see *actions*, but only specific bodily movements. Getting back to Mises' example, aided by praxeological concepts, it is not that we see people with round plates of metal and we deduce that they are trading, but we *see* them trading directly.

We are able to find in the work of Wittgenstein a solid foundation for praxeology and another justification for Mises's contentions, and thus we can leave behind the problematic analytic/synthetic distinction[51]. Therefore, "Wittgenstein's arguments for the conclusion that whatever counts as *thought* must embody *logical* principles can likewise be deployed to show that whatever counts as *action* must embody *economic* principles" (Long 2004: 367).

1.5.2 *Praxeology and Logic*

Since Mises compares praxeological concepts with those of logic, in the sense that these are both *a priori*, this may lead to some confusion about their different natures in cognition. Praxeology consists of basic concepts, based on the action axiom, which are identifications of fundamental features of human nature. From this axiom, we derive the rest of the praxeological theorems.

However, it has been contended that no proposition could be derived from a concept, but only from another proposition (Scarano 2006: 4). Nevertheless, the

[51] See Quine (1951). Thus, we do not have to respond to the reasons for the rejection of *synthetic a priori* propositions as presented, for instance, in Scarano (2006: 5).

problem here is that the concept of action is not understood in praxeology primarily as a specific, articulated, proposition, but rather as an identification of a fact of reality: man acts. In addition, this fact may be stated in different ways, and later aid us in order to derive further implications of the axiom. Hence, it is not the proposition that defines "action" which gives rise to the concept or the theory that enables us to identify action in reality. Rather, it is the concept of action which in turn allows us to articulate it in a certain proposition. E.g., in order to define the concept "action", one must already have the concept; and the same applies for identifying action in reality, otherwise one would not be able neither to define it propositionally nor identify it in reality (for different ways of stating the action axiom see above von Mises 1949 [1998]: 11).

Scarano (2006: 4) contends that if praxeology is formal, then every proposition with the same structure of the action axiom should be regarded as a praxeological truth for sharing the same structure. I.e. if the action axiom ("every action is purposeful behavior") has the logical form "All S is P", then every other proposition with such form (e.g. "All swans are black") should be regarded as apodictically true. Further, Scarano explains that for Kantians every *synthetic a priori* proposition is not true due to its form, but because of its content:

> "Secondly, if praxeology is formal, then any sentence with the same form would be true. The statement 'every conscious action presupposes ends', has the logical form 'if P then Q' and, therefore the following should be praxeological truths, 'All men are happy', 'All whales have lungs'. None of these statements are considered as praxeological truths… Praxeological truths, or synthetic *a priori* truths as a Kantian would say, are not true for their form, but for their content!" (Scarano 2006: 4).[52]

However, Mises explains that the fact that man acts, i.e. he chooses means in order to attain certain ends, is true of any situation where such an event takes place, regardless of the means or ends chosen.

> "Praxeology is indifferent to the ultimate goals of action. Its findings are valid for all kinds of action irrespective of the ends aimed at. It is a science of means, not of ends. It applies the term happiness in a purely formal sense. In the praxeological terminology the proposition: man's unique aim is to attain happiness, is tautological. It does not imply any statement about the state of affairs from which man expects happiness" (von Mises 1949 [1998]: 15).

To act is to choose means to attain ends. As such, the form which Mises has in mind here is not the *logical* form of a proposition, but the specific *sequence of events* that are conceptualized under "action", i.e. choosing certain means in order to attain certain ends. The action axiom is not a logical proposition without content, but a specific concept, which abstracts from the given means and ends that any individual may choose, and only considers the structure of the event as such. Thus, the content of the axiom is its identification of a specific sequence of events that identify

[52] Translated by the first of the present authors from the original in Spanish, with permission of the original author.

any situation where such sequence or phenomena take place, regardless of the specifics involved in the situation[53].

Let us give an example from the field of mathematics in order to better illustrate the idea. A function is a set of ordered pairs where for each value of the independent variable corresponds a unique value of the dependent variable, but not necessarily *vice versa*. For instance, if we have the function $y = a_0 + a_1x + a_2x^2$, where $a_2 < 0$, there may be the same value of y for different values of x, but not the other way. As such, this function has the logical form of the *modus ponens*:

If P, then Q

$$\frac{P}{\therefore Q}$$

For any value of x there is a certain value of y

$$\frac{x}{\therefore y}$$

Let us assume that for this parabolic function, the value of y = 7 may correspond both to x = 2 and x = 4. As such, if we then conclude from the fact that y = 7 that x = 2 we are committing the fallacy of affirming the consequent, since it may also be that x = 4. This is so because the logical reasoning implicit in the function is (*modus ponens*):

If x = 2 then y = 7

$$\frac{x = 2}{\therefore y = 7}$$

But if we say:

If x = 2 then y = 7

$$\frac{y = 7}{\therefore x = 2}$$

This is false, since the conclusion may also be x = 4.

The point of this example is to show that the underlying logic behind this mathematical reasoning is the *modus ponens*, but there are many possible applications of the same logical structure to propositions of different nature. Because praxeology studies the logic of action, this does not imply that logic is to be understood here as

[53] This may be presented as the reason why Mises seems to avoid distinguishing between primitive and defined terms, as well as axioms and theorems in the strict sense. He also does not specifically state theorems nor constructs nor proves a definite system where praxeological truth belongs to both the axioms and the theorems (such is a part of the critique by Scarano, 2004: 9). The key here is that although the concept of action may be defined only ostensively, it is nevertheless axiomatic.

symbolic logic. From the fact that two reasoning have the same structure one cannot conclude that they have the same nature.

This example implies that although one may very well identify the logical *structure* of a certain reasoning, this does not imply that the reasoning itself is of a logical nature (in this case, its nature is mathematical). With the concept of human action something similar happens: we identify the underlying logic of the axiomatic proposition of action as purposeful behavior. Thus, Scarano's critique that praxeology is not sensible since it is not formalized and refers only to concepts such as those of logic is wrong; although the action axiom has logical implications, it is not by itself of a logical nature. In other words, although praxeology studies the structure of action, as logic studies the structure of reasoning and propositions, we must not conclude that praxeology is of the same nature as logic; only that both deal with the *a priori*.[54]

Praxeology has a conceptual nature, and if we are to identify the logical structure of the action axiom, then it is not "All S is P" but "S if and only if P" (biconditional[55]). This is so because there is action if and only if there is purposeful behavior, i.e. only the choice of certain means to attain certain ends can be regarded as action. Thus, Wittgenstein's approach as presented *supra* applies in this regard. How so? Because the concepts of praxeology can only be applied to those situations where they identify reality. As such the concept of action applies if and only if someone acts. Hence, the identity of the premises in the reasoning is the *content* of praxeology, but applicable to any phenomena which has the *form* of action, *any* action. It is not the same to say that "if there is behavior, then there is action", as to say, "If there is purposeful behavior, then there is action", despite of the fact that both propositions are of the form "If P, then Q".

---

[54] It might be argued that many of the theorems of praxeology are not apodictic since they are not necessarily true in every possible state of the world. For instance, there could be backward bending supply curves (as recognized by Rothbard (1962 [2009]), the equalization of profits as a tendency could not be attained if all entrepreneurs are stupid, the law of one price could not take place if pricing is done by senile people, and minimum wage laws could theoretically increase employment in the monopsony model (Block and Caplan 2015). Even if this were true, it would not mean that the concepts of praxeology are useless. They would still be a *model* for thought and, especially, action. This implies that it is not necessary for Mises' principle of human action to be necessarily regarded as axiomatic to be useful. However, none of these contentions are valid criticisms of Austrian economics. First there is nothing in all of praxeology that excludes the possibility of a backward bending supply curve of labor for an individual. After all, no one wants to work 24 h per day, even if it were humanly possible. If this is possible for one person, it is also possible for more. Second, profit equalization as a tendency would still operate no matter how unwise the entrepreneurs; losses would still more heavily impact those who failed to "buy low and sell high" to the greatest degree. Third the law of one price would still tend to obtain, since profits could thereby be made, even by the most ignorant people on the planet. On these last two points, see the Becker-Kirzner debate: Becker (1962, 1963), Kirzner (1962, 1963b). As to the fourth point, on "monopsony," this is a mainstream concept recognized as invalid from the praxeological point of view (Block and Barnett 2009).

[55] $A \leftrightarrow B$

1.5.3 Intuition and Introspection

Another critique of praxeology is that it not only depends on intuition[56] but also on introspection, and as such, it may be discarded as a form of subjectivism[57]. However, this is not the case, since the Austrian approach does not rely on introspection in general, but only as a means of identifying the truth of the action axiom. How so? Since introspection is by itself an action, any introspective inquiry uses and thereby confirms the validity of the action axiom; regardless of the content of one's introspection (thus it is valid for inter-subjectivity).

As for the rejection of "concepts of consciousness" (on which introspection depends), Binswanger (2014: 54) explains:

> "The denial that we are self-aware is self-refuting: the denial maintains, in one form or another, that concepts of consciousness are invalid, that they do not represent an awareness of anything real. Since this claim presupposes knowledge of the distinction between contents of consciousness and external facts, it is just another form of denying the axiom of consciousness and commits the same stolen concept fallacy: the concept 'invalid' presupposes, implicitly or explicitly, the concept 'consciousness.' 'Invalid' refers to the status of an idea, a status that is differentiated from that of a valid awareness of fact. But making that distinction presupposes that we have recognized what it is to be aware of facts, which implies an act of self-awareness. The denial of introspective self-awareness presupposes what is being denied."

We are here attacking the idea that introspection is invalid as a source of knowledge, because if so, so is the case that praxeology is invalid as a methodology. Binswanger's approach is useful to explain why concepts of consciousness (which are the ones we reach by introspection, and give it validity) are valid (and reliable).

Further, it can be claimed that[58] if we accept that there can be such a thing as a "reflex" or behavior that is not purposeful, we cannot be sure that we are identifying action (as purposeful behavior) in any specific situation. However, this would be nothing more than a *reductio ad absurdum*, since it is a fact of daily life of any individual that his usual approach towards interacting with others is to assume that these follow the concept of action as presented here, i.e. they choose certain means to attain their ends[59].

The idea that human beings are motivated in general by "reflexes" or "unconscious movements" cannot be seriously contended nor applied as a usual policy. This is so because if a "reflex" would be the standard of human behavior, then with what are we to contrast it in order to arrive to the concept of action? How could we make sense of any process of thought if we must assume that we are motivated just by "reflexes" and not by conscious awareness? Thus, there would be no way to

---

[56] We discussed this problem in section V.i.

[57] Or, as a form of psychologism.

[58] As we have said in section V.i.

[59] The concept of reflex is only used to identify such behavior that cannot be said to be an action, i.e. purposeful behavior. But it is not nor cannot be used *primarily* as an approach to human behavior in general.

explain not only the daily events in which human beings are involved, but also, we would have to accept that civilization as we know it is the result of mere chance. Thus, an implication of the action axiom is that in every interaction with other individuals one has the expectation that these others will behave rationally (but, of course, not necessarily in a sensible way[60]); otherwise, no theory could be constructed so as to explain human behavior in society[61] (with its great complexity). An individual who acts has expectations that those with whom he exchanges w will act rationally. This is the regularity that permits us to construct economic theory (or any theory of social cooperation in general).

The standard for any theory of human behavior as such should be rational action, because if we would take, for instance, sleepwalking as a standard then there is no reason to distinguish between conscious and unconscious behavior in the first place. To state that an industrial civilization may be the outcome of mere "reflexes" or unconscious reactions is nothing more than a *reductio ad absurdum*. It cannot certainly be used as an argument against praxeology.

Moreover, rejecting the action axiom would imply that economic events (as a category of events in general) do not need to follow a means-ends structure not only in order to be understood, but also to exist at all. As Hayek (1973) explained (following Adam Ferguson), many fundamental human institutions may not be and are not the result of human design, but human action.[62]

Following Mises's approach we can say that they are nevertheless the *outcome* of human reason in pursuing individual ends. They are an *emergent*[63] outcome[64].

---

[60] Nevertheless, this pertains to evaluations, not mere descriptions of action as such. That is, their actions will be purposive, and rational in the *ex ante* sense. But they are of course not always so *ex post*. That is people make mistakes, but do not intend to do so.

[61] It could be contended that there are certain events where the individual expects the other parties to behave irrationally, such as in war. But here also the action axiom is valid, since even when human beings act to destroy each other, they choose what they regard the best means in order to achieve that end. Rational here refers only to 'instrumental' rationality.

[62] Examples include the spontaneous order creation of language and money. No one intended that they be created, but they came about as a result of human action.

[63] Austrian economics, especially of the Hayek (1945, 1968 [2002]; 1973, 1974 [2008]) variant, explain that the economy is a complex system where institutions appear as an emergent property, not due to design but because of *spontaneous orders*. This in turn explains why central planning fails: it does not take into account that emergent properties of certain systems, such as social organization, cannot be emulated by a central authority. There is, fundamentally, a knowledge problem that the price system (in part) tends to solve under a free market.

[64] In fact, the term *catallactics* already involves the idea of society as a spontaneous order, and the economic order as a process. In the words of Hayek (1988 [1992], 112): "Whately suggested 'catallactics' as a name for the theoretical science explaining the market order, and his suggestion has been revived from time to time, most recently by Ludwig von Mises. The adjective `catallactic' is readily derived from Whately's coinage, and has already been used fairly widely. These terms are particularly attractive because the classical Greek word from which they stem, *katalattein* or *katalassein*, meant not only 'to exchange' but also 'to receive into the community' and 'to turn from enemy into friend', further evidence of the profound insight of the ancient Greeks in such matters (Liddell and Scott 1940, *s.v. katallasso*). This led me to suggest that we form the term

The fact that reason is fallible[65] does not imply that it will necessarily be wrong. As such, whenever a certain behavior is interpreted as action while it was actually a reflex, we must conclude that there was an error of judgment, but not infer from this error that there is no such a thing as action, nor that a human being is unable, *in principle*, to identify it.

1.6 Conclusion

As we tried to show throughout this chapter, the work of Ludwig von Mises in developing the field of Praxeology is highly useful in order to shed light on the concept of intentional action. Moreover, aided by the developments of other authors, such as Friedrich Hayek and Ludwig Wittgenstein (as presented by Long 2004), a solid foundation for praxeology is provided and thus a deeper understanding of the concept of action is achieved.

Intentional action is, under this approach, rational action, and therefore purposeful behavior. Although there are problems in the exposition and formulation of praxeology as presented by Mises[66], it is nevertheless useful not only in identifying the nature of the category of action, but also its implications, thus expanding our knowledge on the concept of intentional action as such. Despite the fact that there have been enormous advances in the study of action in general and in the field of economics in particular[67], Mises's approach is able to give as a unique basis on the subject, that will guide us throughout this work.

Bibliography

Anderson, William. 2002. *Mathematics and Economic Analysis*. April 2. Available at https://mises.org/library/mathematics-and-economic-analysis. Last visited April 22, 2021.

Barnett, William I.I. 2004. Dimensions and Economics: Some Problems. *Quarterly Journal of Austrian Economics* 7 (1, Spring): 95–104.

Barnett, William I.I., and Walter E. Block. 2006a. Rothbard on V Shaped Average and Total Cost Curves. *Quarterly Journal of Austrian Economics* 9 (3, Fall): 61–66.

———. 2006b. On Hayekian Triangles. *Procesos De Mercado: Revista Europea De Economia Politica* III (2, Fall): 39–141.

catallaxy to describe the object of the science we generally call economics, which then, following Whately, itself ought to be called catallactics."

[65] This fact, (as we have seen in section III) is also recognized by praxeology, which in turn is the basis for the *uncertainty* of the future as well as for the existence of *both* profit and loss (section IV).

[66] We presented several objections to this methodology and their possible answers throughout this work.

[67] For an analysis of *Human Action* in the light of Experimental Economics, see Smith (1999).

Barnett, William, and Walter E. Block. 2010. Mises Never Used Demand Curves; Was He Wrong? Ignorant? No: The Antimathematicality of Demand Curves. *Dialogue* 1 (March): 23–31.

Barnett, William, II. 2003. The Modern Theory of Consumer Behavior: Ordinal or Cardinal? *The Quarterly Journal of Austrian Economics* 6 (1): 41–65.

Batemarco, Robert. 1985. Positive Economics and Praxeology: The Clash of Prediction and Explanation. *Atlantic Economic Journal, July* 13 (2): 31–27.

Becker, Gary S. 1962. Irrational Behavior and Economic Theory. *Journal of Political Economy* 70 (1, February): 1–13. Available at https://www.journals.uchicago.edu/doi/pdf/10.1086/258584. Last visited May 29, 2021.

———. 1963. Rational Action and Economic Theory: A Reply to I. Kirzner. *Journal of Political Economy* 71 (1, February): 82–83. Available at https://www.journals.uchicago.edu/doi/10.1086/258737. Last visited May 29, 2021.

Becker, Gary. 1993. Nobel Lecture: The Economic Way of Looking at Behavior. *Journal of Political Economy* 101 (3): 385–409.

Binswanger, Harry. 2014. *How We Know*. New York: TOF Publications.

Block, Walter E. 1973. A Comment on 'The Extraordinary Claim of Praxeology,' by Professor Gutierrez. *Theory and Decision* 3 (4, June): 377–387.

———. 1980. On Robert Nozick's 'On Austrian Methodology'. *Inquiry* 23 (4, Fall): 397–444. Spanish translation, *Libertas*, Vol. 14, No. 26, May 1997, pp. 71–131.

———. 1999. Austrian Theorizing, Recalling the Foundations: Reply to Caplan. *Quarterly Journal of Austrian Economics* 2 (4, winter): 21–39.

———. 2003. Realism: Austrian vs. Neoclassical Economics, Reply to Caplan. *Quarterly Journal of Austrian Economics* 6 (3, Fall): 63–76.

———. 2007. Reply to Caplan on Austrian Economic Methodology. *Corporate Ownership & Control* 4 (2, November): 312–317.

———. 2009a. Rejoinder to Hoppe on indifference. *Quarterly Journal of Austrian Economics* 12 (1): 52–59.

———. 2009b. Rejoinder to Machaj on Indifference. *New Perspectives on Political Economy* 5 (1): 65–71.

Block, Walter E., and William Barnett. 2009. Monopsony Theory. *American Review of Political Economy* 7 (1/2, June/December): 67–109.

Block, Walter E. and Caplan, Bryan. 2015. Walter Block vs. Bryan Caplan on Austrian vs. Neoclassical Economics. *YouTube*, August 25. Available at https://www.youtube.com/watch?v=wHIm2NRvcAQ. Last visited January 1, 2021.

Block, Walter E., and with William Barnett II. 2010. Rejoinder to Hoppe on Indifference, Once Again. *Reason Papers* 32: 141–154.

Boulding, Kenneth E. 1971. After Samuelson, Who Needs Adam Smith? *History of Political Economy* 3 (2, Fall): 225–237.

Brätland, John. 2000. Human Action and Socially Optimal Conservation: A Misesian Inquiry into the Hotelling Principle. *The Quarterly Journal of Austrian Economics* 3 (1): 3–26.

Bylund, Per. 2011. The 'Mystery' of the Endowment Effect. *Mises Daily*, December 28. Available at http://mises.org/daily/5839/The-Mystery-of-the-Endowment-Effect. Last visited April 22, 2021.

Callahan, Gene. 2001. Logical Economics vs. Mathematical Economics. *Mises Daily*, February 17. Available at https://mises.org/library/logical-economics-vs-mathematical-economics. Last visited April 22, 2021.

Caplan, Bryan. 1999. The Austrian Search for Realistic Foundations. *Southern Economic Journal* 65 (4, April): 823–838.

———. 2001. Probability, Common Sense, and Realism: A Reply to Huelsmann and Block. *Quarterly Journal of Austrian Economics* 2 (4, summer): 69–86.

———. 2003. Probability and the Synthetic *A Priori:* A Reply to Block. *Quarterly Journal of Austrian Economics* 6 (3, Fall): 77–83.

———. 2008. The Trojan Horse Example. *EconLog*, June 16; Available at http://econlog.econlib.org/archives/2008/06/the_trojan_hors.html. Last visited April 22, 2021.

———. Undated. *Why I Am Not an Austrian Economist*; Available at http://www.gmu.edu/depts/economics/bcaplan/whyaust.htm. Last visited April 22, 2021.

Champion, Rafe. 2008. *The Rise of Mathematical Economics*. Available at http://www.the-rathouse.com/2008/Ingrao-Israel.html. Last visited April 22, 2021.

Coase, Ronald H. 1960. The Problem of Social Cost. *Journal of Law and Economics* 3: 1–44.

Dolan, Edwin. 1976. Austrian Economics as Extraordinary Science. In *The Foundations of Modern Austrian Economics*, 3–18. Sheed & Ward, Inc.

Fox, Glenn. 1992. The Pricing of Environmental Goods: A Praxeological Critique of Contingent Valuation. *Cultural Dynamics* V (3): 245–259.

Garrison, Roger W. 1994. Hayekian Triangles and Beyond. In *Hayek, Coordination and Evolution: His Legacy in Philosophy, Politics, Economics, and the History of Ideas*, ed. Jack Birner and Rudy van Zijp, 109–125. London: Routledge.

———. 2001. *Time and Money: The Macroeconomics of Capital Structure*. London: Routledge.

Gordon, Scott. 1993. *History and Philosophy of Social Science*. Londres: Routledge.

Gossen, H.H. 1854 (1983). Entwickelung der Gesetze des menschlichen Verkehrs, und der daraus fließenden Regeln für menschliches Handeln. Braunschweig: Friedrich Vieweg und Sohn. English translation R. C. Blitz, *The Laws of Human Relations and the Rules of Human Action Derived Therefrom*. Cambridge, MA: MIT Press.

Hayek, Friedrich A. 1931. *Prices and Production*. London: Routledge.

———. 1945. The Use of Knowledge in Society. *The American Economic Review* 35 (4): 519–530.

———. 1968 (2002). *Competition as a Discovery Procedure*. Institut für Weltwirtschaft, Kiel University, No 56 Kieler Vorträge series. Trans. Marcellus S. Snow "Der Wettbewerb als Entdeckungsverfahren". *The Quarterly Journal of Austrian Economics* Vol. 5, 3 (Summer). pp. 9–23.

———. 1973. *Law, Legislation, and Liberty: A New Statement of the Liberal Principles of Justice and Political Economy, Vol. I, Rules and Order*. Chicago: University of Chicago Press.

———. 1974 (2008). *The Pretense of Knowledge*. Friedrich A. Hayek's Nobel Prize Lecture, Nobel Prize in Economics. Stockholm, Sweden. In "A Free Market Monetary System and The Pretense of Knowledge". Ludwig Von Mises Institute. Auburn.

———. 1988. (1992). The Fatal Conceit: The Errors of Socialism. In *The Collected Works of F.A Hayek*, ed. W.W. Bartley III. London: Routledge.

Hazlitt, Henry. 1959. *The Failure of the 'New Economics'*, 98–106. New Rochelle: Arlington House. See especially.

Herbener, Jeffrey M. 1996. Calculation and the Question of Mathematics. *Review of Austrian Economics* 9 (1): 151–162.

Hoppe, Hans Hermann. 1989. In Defense of Extreme Rationalism: Thoughts on Donald McCloskey's *The Rhetoric of Economics*. *Review of Austrian Economics* 3: 179–214.

———. 1991. Austrian Rationalism in the Age of the Decline of Positivism. *Journal des Economistes et des Etudes Humaines* 2 (2).; reprinted as Hoppe, Hans-Hermann. 1994. "Austrian Rationalism in the Age of the Decline of Positivism," in *Austrian Economics: Perspectives on the Past and Prospects for the Future*, Vol. 17, Richard M. Ebeling, ed., Hillsdale, MI: Hillsdale College Press, pp. 59–96.

———. 1992. On Praxeology and the Praxeological Foundation of Epistemology and Ethics. In *The Meaning of Ludwig von Mises*, ed. J. Herbener. Boston: Dordrecht.

———. 1995. *Economic Science and the Austrian Method*. Auburn: The Ludwig von Mises Institute.

———. 2005. A Note on Preference and Indifference in Economic Analysis. *The Quarterly Journal of Austrian Economics* 8 (4, Winter): 87–91.

———. 2009. Further Notes on Preference and Indifference: Rejoinder to Block. *The Quarterly Journal of Austrian Economics* 12 (1): 60–64.

Hülsmann, Jörg Guido. 1999. Economic Science and Neoclassicism. *Quarterly Journal of Austrian Economics* 2 (4): 1–20.

Hutt, W.H. 1979. *The Keynesian Episode: A Reassessment*, 99–103. Indianapolis: Liberty Press. See.

Ingrao, Bruna and Giorgio Israel. 1987 (1990). *The Invisible Hand: Economic Equilibrium in the History of Science*. Translated by Ian McGilvray, the MIT Press, Cambridge/London.

Ischboldin, Boris. 1960. A Critique of Econometrics. *Review of Social Economy* 18 (2, September): 110–127.

Jablecki, Juliusz. 2007. How Many Traders Can You Fit into a Model?. *Mises Daily*, August 23. Available at https://mises.org/library/how-many-traders-can-you-fit-model. Last visited April 22, 2021.

Kant, Immanuel. 1787 (2013). *The Critique of Pure Reason*. Available at http://www.gutenberg.org/files/4280/4280-h/4280-h.htm. Last visited April 22, 2021.

Kirzner, Israel M. 1962. Rational Action and Economic Theory. *Journal of Political Economy* 70 (4, August): 380–385. Available at https://www.journals.uchicago.edu/doi/pdf/10.1086/258665. Last visited May 29, 2021.

———. 1963a. *Market Theory and the Price System*. New York: D. Van Nostrand Co.

———. 1963b. Rational Action and Economic Theory: Rejoinder. *Journal of Political Economy* 71 (1, February): 84–85. Available at https://www.journals.uchicago.edu/doi/10.1086/258738. Last visited May 29, 2021.

———. 1990. The 'Austrian' Perspective on the Crisis. In *Austrian Economics*, vol. 1, 191–202. Edward Elgar.

Kotarbinski, Tadeusz. 1965. *Praxiology – An Introduction to the Sciences of Efficient Action*. Trans. Olgierd Wojtasiewicz. Pergamon Press: Poland.

Leoni, Bruno, and Eugenio Frola. 1977. On mathematical thinking in economics. *The Journal of Libertarian Studies* 1 (2, Spring): 101–110.

Liddell, H. G. and R. Scott. 1940. *A Greek-English Lexicon*. 9th ed. London: Clarendon Press.

Long, R.T. 2004. Anti-Psychologism in Economics: Wittgenstein and Mises. *The Review of Austrian Economics* 17 (4): 345–369.

Machaj, Mateusz. 2007. A Praxeological Case for Homogeneity and Indifference. *New Perspectives on Political Economy*. 3 (2): 231–238.

Menger, C. 1871. (2007). *Principles of Economics*. Auburn: The Ludwig Von Mises Institute.

Menger, Karl. 1973. Austrian Marginalism and Mathematical Economics. In *Carl Menger and the Austrian School of Economics*, ed. J.R. Hicks and Wilhelm Weber. Oxford: Clarenden Press.

Mirowski, Philip. 1988. *Against Mechanism: Protecting Economics from Science*. Rowman & Littlefield.

Moorhouse, John C. 1993. A Critical Review of Mises on Mathematical Economics. *History of Economics Review* 20 (1): 61–74.

Murphy, Robert P. 2008. Austrian Realists. *Mises Daily*, July 17. Available at https://mises.org/library/austrian-realists. Last visited April 22, 2021.

Murphy, Robert P., Robert Wutscher, and Walter E. Block. 2010. Mathematics in Economics: An Austrian Methodological Critique. *Philosophical Investigations* 33 (1, January): 44–66.

Nozick, Robert. 1977. On Austrian Methodology. *Synthese* 36: 353–392.

O'Neill, Ben. 2010. Choice and Indifference: A Critique of the Strict Preference Approach. *Quarterly Journal of Austrian Economics* 13 (1, Spring): 71–98.

Polleit, Thorsten. 2008. Mises's Apriorism Against Relativism in Economics. *Mises Daily*, April 25. Available at https://mises.org/library/misess-apriorism-against-relativism-economics. Last visited April 22, 2021.

———. 2011. True Knowledge from A Priori Theory. *Mises Daily* June 8. Available at http://mises.org/daily/5349/True-Knowledge-from-A-Priori-Theory. Last visited April 22, 2021.

Popper, K. 1957. (2002). *The Poverty of Historicism*. London: Routledge.

Quine, W.V. 1951. Two Dogmas of Empiricism. *The Philosophical Review* 60 (1): 20–43.

Reekie, W. Duncan. 1984a. The Austrian Response at a Micro Level. In *Markets, Entrepreneurs, and Liberty*, 27–55. Wheatsheaf Books.

———. 1984b. The Austrian Macro Retort. In *Markets, Entrepreneurs, and Liberty*, 56–84. Wheatsheaf Books.

Rizzo, M.J. 1978. Praxeology and Econometrics: A Critique of Positivist Economics. In *New Directions in Austrian Economics*, ed. Louis M. Spadaro. Kansas City: Sheed Andrews and McMeel, Inc.

———. 2015. The Problem of Rationality: Austrian Economics Between Classical Behaviorism and Behavioral Economics. In *The Oxford Handbook of Austrian Economics*, ed. Peter J. Boettke and Christopher J. Coyne, 364–392. New York: Oxford University Press.

Ropke, Wilhelm. 1956. The Place of Economics Among the Sciences. In *On Freedom and Free Enterprise*, ed. Mary Sennholz, 111–127. Princeton: D. Van Nostrand Co.

Roth, Alvin E. 1988. Laboratory Experimentation in Economics: A Methodological Overview. *The Economic Journal*. 98 (December): 974–1031.

Rothbard, Murray N. 1951. Praxeology: Reply to Mr. Schuller. *American Economic Review* 41 (5, December): 943–946.

———. 1960 (1997). The Mantle of Science. In *The Logic of Action One*, 3–23. Cheltenham: Edward Elgar. Originally published in *Scientism and Values,* Helmut Schoek and James W Wiggins, eds.

———. 1962 (2009). *Man, Economy and State*. Scholar's Edition, Second Edition. Ludwig Von Mises Institute. Auburn.

———. 1971. Lange, Mises and Praxeology: The Retreat from Marxism. In *Toward Liberty*, vol. II, 307–321. Menlo Park: Institute for Humane Studies. Reprinted in *The Logic of Action One: Method, Money, and the Austrian School*. Glos, UK: Edward Elgar Publishing Ltd., 1997, pp. 384–396.

———. 1973. Praxeology and the Method of Economics. In *Phenomenology and the Social Sciences*, ed. M. Natanson, vol. 2, 311–342. Evanston: Northwestern University Press; and *Austrian Economics: A Reader* Vol. 18, Richard M. Ebeling, ed., Hillsdale, MI.: Hillsdale College Press, 1991, pp. 55–91.

———. 1977. *Toward a Reconstruction of Utility and Welfare Economics*. San Francisco: Center for Libertarian Studies, Occasional Paper #3.

———. 1988. Chaos Theory: Destroying Mathematical Economics from Within? *The Free Market* VI (3), pages 1, 2 and 8.

———. 1997a. Praxeology as the Method of the Social Sciences. In *The Logic of Action One*, ed. Murray N. Rothbard, 28–57. Edward Elgar Publishing Limited.

———. 1997b. Praxeology: The Methodology of Austrian Economics. In *The Logic of Action One*, ed. Murray N. Rothbard, 58–77. Edward Elgar Publishing Limited.

———. 1997c. Praxeology, Value Judgments, and Public Policy. In *The Logic of Action One*, ed. Murray N. Rothbard, 78–99. Edward Elgar Publishing Limited.

———. 1997d. In Defense of 'Extreme Apriorism'. *Southern Economic Journal* January 1957: 314–320; reprinted in *The Logic of Action One*. Murray N. Rothbard, ed., Edward Elgar Publishing Limited, pp. 100–108.

———. 2011. Daniel Bernoulli and the Founding of Mathematical Economics. *Mises Daily*, February 10. Available at https://mises.org/library/daniel-bernoulli-and-founding-mathematical-economics. Last visited April 22, 2021.

Sarjanovic, Ivo A. 2008. Popper y los Austríacos: Atando Cabos. *Revista de Instituciones, Ideas y Mercados* 48 (May): 17–32.

Scarano, E. R. 2004.El Apriorismo de Ludwig Von Mises. *Revista Libertas*, N° 40. Mayo. Available at http://www.eseade.edu.ar/files/Libertas/1_2_Scarano.pdf. Last visited April 22, 2021.

———. 2006. "Las Dificultades de la Metodología Miseana". Congreso Internacional "La Escuela Austríaca en el Siglo XXI". Rosario, Argentina. Available at http://austrianeconomicsconference.org/ponencias/2006/Scarano01.pdf. Last visited April 22, 2021.

Selgin, George A. 1988. Praxeology and Understanding: An Analysis of the Controversy in Austrian Economics. *Review of Austrian Economics* 2: 19–58; and *Praxeology and Understanding*, Auburn, AL: Ludwig von Mises Institute, 1990.

Shostak, Frank. 2002. What is Wrong with Econometrics?. *Mises Daily*, April 17. Available at https://mises.org/library/what-wrong-econometrics. Last visited April 22, 2021.

Smith, Vernon. 1999. Reflections on *Human Action* After 50 Years. *Cato Journal* 19 (2, Fall): 195–209. Cato Institute.

Spadaro, Louis M. 1956. Averages and Aggregates in Economics. In *On Freedom and Free Enterprise*, ed. Mary Sennholz, 140–160. Princeton: D. Van Nostrand Co.

von Mises, Ludwig. 1922. (1962). *Socialism: An Economic and Sociological Analysis*. New Haven: Yale University Press.

———. 1933. (2003). *Epistemological Problems of Economics*. Auburn: Ludwig Von Mises Institute.

———. 1938. (2000). The Equations of Mathematical Economics and the Problem of Economic Calculation in a Socialist State. *The Quarterly Journal of Austrian Economics* 3 (1 (Spring)): 27–32.

———. 1949. (1998). *Human Action – A Treatise on Economics*. Auburn: The Scholar's Edition. Ludwig Von Mises Institute.

———. 1957. (2007). *Theory and History – An Interpretation of Social and Economic Evolution*. Auburn: Ludwig Von Mises Institute.

———. 1962. *The Ultimate Foundation of Economic Science – An Essay on Method*. New York: Van Nostrand.

———. 1977. Comments About the Mathematical Treatment of Economic Problems. *The Journal of Libertarian Studies* 1 (2, Spring): 97–100.

Wisdom, John. 1968. Proceedings of the Aristotelian Society, Vol. XX. In *Other Minds*. Berkeley/ Los Angeles: University of California Press.

Wittgenstein, L. 1961. *Tractatus Logico-Philosophicus*. Trans. D. F. Pears and B. F. McGuinness. Routledge: London.

Wutscher, Robert. Unpublished. *Foundations in Economic Methodology: The Use of Mathematics by Mainstream Economics and Its Methodology by Austrian Economics*. Available at http://www.mises.org/journals/scholar/Wutscher.pdf. Last visited April 22, 2021.

Zanotti, G. 1990. (2004). *Fundamentos Filosóficos y Epistemológicos de la Praxeología*. Tesis Doctoral. Instituto Acton.

Chapter 2
Microeconomics

Consumer Choice: Contrasting the Austrian Approach with the Neoclassical

> *A judgment of value does not measure, it arranges in a scale of degrees, it grades. It is expressive of an order of preference and sequence, but not expressive of measure and weight. Only the ordinal numbers can be applied to it, but not the cardinal numbers.*
>
> Ludwig Von Mises (1949, 97).

Abstract In this chapter we analyze neoclassical concepts such as utility maximization and indifference, in order to identify their difficulties in explaining consumer choice. Thus, we study the process of human action itself, and the problems of indifference analysis. We provide a critique of the neoclassical view of consumer choice and contrast it with the Austrian approach.

Keywords Neoclassical economics · Consumers · Choice · Utility · Perfect information

JEL Code D11

This chapter is based on our paper Futerman, Alan G. and Block, Walter E. 2021. "A Critique of the Neoclassical Approach to Consumer Choice". *Dialogi Polityczne Political Dialogues*, No. 30, 2021, pp. 201–228. Available at https://apcz.umk.pl/czasopisma/index.php/DP/article/view/DP.2021.011/28729 (last visited April 13, 2021).

A. G. Futerman, W. E. Block, *The Austro-Libertarian Point of View*, https://doi.org/10.1007/978-981-16-4691-1_2

2.1 Introduction[1]

Despite of immense advancements within economic science, microeconomic textbooks have been (essentially) teaching the same models for decades (Boulding 1966; Miller 2013; Nicholson and Snyder 2011; Varian 1992). New advances in behavioral economics[2] and other recent developments complement some of these models and make them more complex. However, others remain almost unchallenged and continue to be presented as the foundation of microeconomic analysis. Since consumer choice is at the very core of economics, indifference analysis has become one of the pillars of the neoclassical approach. Which pillar? The one that attempts to explain how consumers make economic choices.

By studying consumer's preference, neoclassical microeconomics has shifted from cardinal utility theory,[3] where it is assumed that utility can be measured in discrete units named "utils", to ordinal utility theory. The latter consists in comparing baskets of goods, and ordering these according to individual preferences.[4]

Thus, mainstream ordinal utility theory assumes that the individual will act based on how he orders or ranks different combinations of goods, while also finding himself indifferent with respect to any or some of these combinations. The individual ranks such combinations according to their utility, and therefore when he faces two (or more) combinations that he regards as exhibiting the *same* utility, he will then be indifferent with respect to choosing one or the other.

In other words, it is assumed that the individual will act by performing an analysis (previous to his decision) *analogous* to a quantitative calculation, where he will weigh combinations of goods and the utility these exhibit, in order to choose the one that will maximize satisfaction. We will analyze the problems with this approach throughout this work,[5] and therefore try to show in our view why it cannot be regarded as a proper (or, at least, complete) understanding of consumer choice.

It is our intention to focus on the neoclassical approach, and not on the entire modern theory of consumer choice. We do so because we understand that the tools neoclassical economists introduced in consumer choice analysis, although developed and improved more recently, are still in use. As such, we focus particularly on

---

[1] The authors wish to thank three anonymous reviewers for their valuable comments. The usual caveats of course apply; we are responsible for all remaining errors.

[2] Ultimately, though, perpetuating to a large extent the premises of neoclassical economics (Laibson and List 2015).

[3] We will not analyze this approach, since trying to measure valuations and satisfaction is not feasible given the fact that there is no known way of performing such measurement nor of comparing utility. There is no empirical foundation to claim that there is such a thing as "util". See also Rothbard (1962, 267).

[4] See Boulding (1966), Miller (2013), Nicholson and Snyder (2011), Varian (1992). See also Chiang (1984).

[5] For other critiques of this approach, see Barnett II (2003), Block (2009b), Block and Barnett II (2010), Block et al. (2002), Buchanan (1969a, b), Callahan (2003), McChesney (2013), McKenzie and Tullock (1975), and Rothbard (1956).

indifference curves and utility maximization. By doing this, we try to criticize the theory itself, since its assumptions do not coincide with our view on the actual process of consumer choice; rather, this leads to distortion.

Our goal in this chapter is, then, to show why the use of indifference analysis, utility maximization and mathematical analysis obscures our understanding of consumer choice, and therefore creates confusion about the nature of the market process in general. Instead, we propose the Austrian understanding of consumer choice, as presented by Mises (1949) and Rothbard (1962).

In Sect. 2.2 we wrestle with the concepts of utility and perfect knowledge. Our focus in Sect. 2.3 is on the concept of equilibrium in the context of consumer choice. The burden of Sect. 2.4 is to deal with the concept of indifference. In Sect. 2.5 we encounter human action and its standard and conclude in Sect. 2.6.

2.2 Utility and the Qualitative Nature of the Process of Choice

As we have seen in Chap. 1, according to the Austrian tradition (especially in the work of Mises), utility consists in a subjective evaluation of means with respect to ends. It is therefore a relational concept, a judgement based on a means-ends approach. Such analysis is performed on the basis of the expectation of the future state of affairs the individual wishes to attain, by pursuing his goal. In effect, it expresses that state of affairs that the individual desires and values above his other considered alternatives.

In real life, in terms of actual *satisfaction*, the individual does not know *ex ante* the utility (as the concept is used in neoclassical economics) he will *receive*, only the one that he *expects* to obtain. Therefore, he performs a *qualitative* analysis, where he weighs mentally the different possible choices he may make but does not make a quantitative calculation. Thus, equating this process with a mathematical description, or attempting to make exact predictions based on mathematical models or optimization analysis is both incorrect and irrelevant,[6] given that the process is of a different nature than the one treated by mathematics.

Neoclassical micro-economists posit that the process of choosing can best be understood via indifference analysis, which makes possible a legitimate mathematical construction of such process. But the difficulty here exists because the individual

[6] A critic may ask, why is it irrelevant to develop a mathematical model? After all, for instance, Newton's work was indeed not irrelevant even if planets did not know about the law of gravity. Our answer is that it is irrelevant not because it is a model, but because it makes use of mathematical tools in order to explain a process that is better explained (and understood) in qualitative terms. For example, differentiation and integration require smooth curves, based upon infinitesimally small distinctions. But human action is, instead, discrete, and this is the appropriate subject for economics, we contend. As shown in chapter I, it is indeed possible to illustrate theories with mathematics, but we oppose using them if, instead of clarifying a subject, they sow confusion.

does not know what satisfaction he will attain by choosing a specific combination of goods; he only *speculates* about it. Such speculation is conceptual, not mathematical. He analyzes based on previous conceptualizations and experiences about the goods he chooses, which combination will be expected to be more satisfactory. Even if we could construct a model[7] analogous to the actual decision-making process by means of mathematics, it would be a duplication of what we can easily understand by means of words.[8]

Moreover, this theory claims that the individual, in order to maximize his utility function, must allocate resources[9] in such a way that the marginal dollar spent will generate the *same* level of utility. However, this is contradicted by the fact that the only thing the consumer knows is its alternatives and the value judgments he makes of each, but not the *effective* result of any possible choice in terms of utility. In other words, the model could be understood as assuming perfect knowledge, given that this is a necessary condition in order to assure that expected utility[10] (*EU*) would equal received utility (*RU*)[11] (in terms of satisfaction).

---

[7]Any model, whether stated in mathematical terms or not, is indeed a simplification of reality. However, in this case, the models distort reality, and are thus not helpful to advance our understanding of consumer choice.

[8]A critic may say that if it is a duplication of ordinary language, it is not of a *different nature.* However, we do not object to the assertion, that is why we say that *even if*...But we do not endorse the possibility, or at least, the convenience.

[9]That are of course constrained by a budget, as shown graphically by a budget line.

[10]It is true that these authors (Becker 1965, 1968, 1971, 1975, 1981, 1992; Lancaster 1966; Rosen 1974) indeed agree with the Austrian approach. This states that the key to consumer choice is the value the individual expects to get, and not the object itself (Mises 1949, 123). This entire approach affects our understanding from prices to marriage, and the fundamental idea is still the same: expected utility (Schoemaker 1982). However, the mathematical models used induce confusion, in our view. For instance, in the words of Mises (1949, 123): "If a man is faced with the alternative of giving up either one unit of his supply of *a* or one unit of his supply of *b*, he does not compare the total value of his total stock of *a* with the total value of his stock of *b*. He compares the marginal values both of *a* and of *b*. Although he may value the total supply of *a* higher than the total supply of *b*, the marginal value of *b* may be higher than the marginal value of *a*."

[11]Expected value, as presented by Nicolas Bernoulli (1713), assumes that utility functions are linear (or quadratic), and therefore there is no risk aversion. This is demonstrated in the famous St. Petersburg Paradox. However, as Daniel Bernoulli (Nicolas' cousin) explained, the concept of expected utility is more tenable, since it involves both risk aversion and a form of decreasing marginal utility. He stated (Barathalon 2014, 204): "There is no doubt that a gain of one thousand ducats is more significant to the pauper than to a rich man though both gain the same amount [...] The determination of the value of an item must not be based on the price, but rather on the utility it yields [...] the utility is dependent on the particular circumstances of the person making the estimate [...] no valid measurement of the value of a risk [a prospect] can be obtained without consideration being given to its utility". Hence, utility (as later Ludwig Von Mises (1949) definitively explained) is entirely subjective. If the utility function involves risk aversion, and therefore its form is $u = \sqrt{x}$ instead of $u = x$, that may solve the challenge of the St. Petersburg Paradox, but it does not answer the problems entailed in dealing with the subject in a mathematical fashion. This is so because multiple factors enter into consideration when dealing with utility and individual choice. How many factors? All that are relevant for the individual, such as risk, decreasing marginal utility, wealth (as in Friedman and Savage 1948), etc. Moreover, this conceptual framework

Thus, one serious flaw in indifference models[12] is that they can easily be interpreted so as to implicitly assume perfect knowledge.[13],[14] However, since perfect knowledge is an attribute no individual can possess (Hayek 1945, 1974; Kirzner 1963, 1982), no serious model of consumer choice claiming empirical validity may include it as one of it assumptions, either explicitly, or as in this case, implicitly.[15]

Moreover, a critic may argue that (at least) most neoclassical micro-economists think that the individual takes into account only expected utility; not that he knows *ex ante* what utility he will receive.[16] However, even if the model only assumes expected utility, then it would be as useful as any *other* speculation regarding the future, *all* including uncertainty. Utility function maximization and any further mathematical calculation in this regard would be no more rigorous in this context than simply weighing different options mentally. Mathematics, here, only adds an *illusion* of rigorousness.

How should we understand expected utility? Is it not based on subjective probability? And is not probability a quantitative phenomenon that makes use of statistical concepts such as mean, median, standard error and kurtosis? The viewpoint we favor is that when dealing with money prices a consumer indeed considers numerical calculation, but its probability analysis is qualitative.[17] In fact, the consumer

---

has more applications in economics, not just consumer choice. Take the Markowitz (1952) model, which includes two parameters (risk and expected return). If we use expected utility, the only way to render this model useful is by assuming that investors have quadratic utility functions and that the returns of financial assets have normal distributions, so kurtosis and skewness are irrelevant. However, this is far from the truth. We do not pretend to treat financial models in this present chapter, but it is an example of how a specific theory of utility can affect other areas of economic analysis.

[12] See on this Barnett (2003), Block (1980, 1999, 2003, 2007, 2009a, 2009b), Block and Barnett (2010), Callahan (2003), Collingwood (2014), Hoppe (2005), Hülsmann (1999), Machaj (2007), Rothbard (1962 [2009]; 265–267), Sotelo and Block (2014).

[13] True enough, there are many models which focus on decision under uncertainty, but we are dealing here not only with those that assume perfect knowledge, but also with those that *imply* it.

[14] If we must, we could conceive of illustrating the neoclassical perfect knowledge as a limit where C is knowledge which tends to infinity, and therefore, $EU = RU$:

$$\lim_{C \to \infty} EU = RU$$

[15] We do not regard what we say in the text at this point as very controversial. Full knowledge has always been an integral part of the perfectly competitive model. For example, The Economic Times (Undated) defines perfect competition, in part, as: "Consumers have perfect knowledge about the market and are well aware of any changes in the market." Here, we are merely applying this "insight" to indifference curve analysis.

[16] That is, from the point of view of the consumer, he has *some* knowledge of his preferences and how much satisfaction would an extra unit of a good give him.

[17] Although probability is usually stated in a mathematical fashion, e.g., the mean, variance, standard error, etc. when the individual is choosing, he uses a subjective view of probability, although, to be sure, he can make calculations that deal with specific monetary quantities with regard to his decisions.

makes a subjective analysis based on how he understands the relevant factors, all according to his subjectivity.[18] Indeed, he may make any numerical calculations he wants, but the outcome of his action will be subjected to case probability (rather than class probability, as stated by Mises 1949, 107–113), so certainty will not be attained, nor can this result be expected.

Also, individual preferences change, and there is risk aversion. For example, "Prospect theory" (Kahneman and Tversky 1979) divides the analysis of individual alternatives, and their evaluation, where there is a standard of wealth variation that is considered. This, in turn, is affected by the risk aversion of the consumer, which has been studied by behavioral economics (De Pablo 2017, 201–205). For instance, take the asymmetry with which individuals consider certain outcomes with respect to these results subjected to a specific probabilistic component. For instance, there is a preference for a loss of $x + 1$ (with a probability a, where $a < 1$), instead of a certain loss of x. There is also, according to these authors, an asymmetry between loss and gain, where losses are more intensely felt than gains. Therefore, the individual will prefer a certain gain of x, rather than a gain of $x + 1$ (with a probability a, where $a < 1$), but at the same time prefer a loss of $x + 1$ (with a probability a, where $a < 1$), to a certain loss of x. That is, there is a supposed incoherence in behavior in this respect between gain and loss.

What is the praxeological approach on this? It is that gain and loss scenarios are different, and therefore will be analyzed in a different light. It must be remembered, also, that the individual acts according to a value scale, and the cost of any human action is the best discarded alternative (otherwise known as opportunity cost). But observe the following, the best discarded alternative is indeed not the *only* one in the possible alternatives ranked in the value scale. Hence, we may conjecture that the reason for the asymmetry between loss and gain is that when the individual gains

---

In this respect, in relation to Mises' case and class probability, Foss and Klein explain:

"What distinguishes case from class probability, according to Langlois, is the character of the decision-maker's information about the event. Objective probabilities (in the frequentist sense) are simply special cases of subjective probabilities in which the decision-maker structures the problem in terms of classes of events. Entrepreneurship, in Langlois' interpretation, can be described as the act of formalizing the decision problem. To use the language of decision theory, a nonentrepreneur (call him, following Kirzner [1973: 32–37], a Robbinsian maximizer) is presented with a decision tree, a set of outcomes, and the probabilities for each outcome, and simply uses backwards induction to solve the problem. The entrepreneur, as it were, redraws the tree, by noticing a possible option or outcome that other agents failed to see. The key distinction, according to Langlois, is not whether the decision tree is populated with objective or subjective probabilities, but whether the tree itself is exogenous (Knightian risk) or endogenous (Knightian uncertainty)" Foss and Klein (2012, 88).

[18] This could be related to the concept of subjective expected utility (Savage 1954; de Finetti 1970; Pfanzagl 1967; Pfanzagl et al. 1968; Von Neumann and Morgenstern 1944 [1953]) although there are important differences (mainly, the use of mathematical tools). For a critique of this approach in the mainstream of economics, see Allais (1953).

something, that indeed outweighs the rest of the alternatives. However, when there is a loss, it is not just that the individual did not attain the end he intended, but also *lost the opportunity of attaining all other ends in his value scale* (and not only the opportunity cost). Hence, when gaining the individual attains end 1, but when losing, he does not attain end 2 (the opportunity cost), end 3,…, end *n*. Thus, there is an asymmetry between gain and loss, where the probabilistic component is judged according to the degree of certainty about the gain or loss, and therefore is contrasted with this fact.

Moreover, it seems that, when facing a loss, the consumer finds himself in a different context. That is, when preparing for the action *ex ante*, he only considers the evaluation of the ends according to his value scale, where the only relevant ones are the first end he chooses to pursue and the best discarded option (the opportunity cost). But when considering a loss, he does not regard these ends individually. Here, the first end he wished to attain which did not deliver the expected state of affairs is analyzed in comparison with *all* the other possible ends (including the opportunity cost). For example, in the first case the individual chooses an apple (first choice) instead of a banana (second choice), whereas in the second, if the apple is rotten, he has not only experienced a loss in purchasing the apple rather than a banana, but also grapes, oranges, etc., enter the analysis. Anything would have been better than having no food at all. Thus, the asymmetry (although the cost, indeed, is the bananas he did not eat).

In the probability approach, adding a probabilistic factor to the attainment of the end or the loss, which gives rise to their asymmetry, could be explained because of the aforementioned dynamics. We may assume that there is a preference for a loss of $x + 1$ (with a probability a, where $a < 1$), instead of a certain loss of x, because the context is the probability 1-a of *not* losing with respect to the certain loss of x. In the case of gains, the consumer will prefer a certain gain of x, rather than a gain of $x + 1$ (with a probability a, where $a < 1$), because the probability 1-a of losing takes implicitly into account all the other alternatives.

Let us approach this matter in a different way. We are challenged to explain why a loss will weigh more heavily on the consumer than an objectively equal gain. For example, welfare decreases more from the loss of a pen than it increases from a gain of the identical object. But why should we have to explain this at all, any more than would have to account for the fact that at a given time, a person values an apple more than a banana. In both cases it is perfectly acceptable to chalk his up to subjective tastes. Many mainstream economists (particularly some behavioral economists) posit that this ranking is irrational. However, that it is no more irrational than preferring an apple to a banana, or the reverse. *De gustibus non est disputandum*. Not only is there no disputing of tastes, there is no explaining of them either, at least not on the part of the dismal science, where we properly take them as a given.[19]

---

[19] Let us remember here Mises's concept of rationality as presented in our Chap. 1, *supra*. Mathematical rationality of the kind in Allais (1953) or Simon (1955) is not necessarily the only expression of rationality. But behavioral economics seems to take it as such (e.g. Ariely et al. 2003, 2005; Ariely 2008). Hence, any deviation appears as "irrational".

This idea, also, is not new. As Adam Smith explained in his *Theory of Moral Sentiments* (1759 [1853], 311):

> We suffer more, it has already been observed, when we fall from a better to a worse situation, than we ever enjoy when we rise from a worse to a better. Security, therefore, is the first and the principal object of prudence. It is averse to expose our health, our fortune, our rank, or reputation, to any sort of hazard. It is rather cautious than enterprising, and more anxious to preserve the advantages which we already possess than forward to prompt us to the acquisition of still greater advantages. The methods of improving our fortune, which it principally recommends to us, are those which expose to no loss or hazard; real knowledge and skill in our trade or profession, assiduity and industry in the exercise of it, frugality, and even some degree of parsimony, in all our expenses.

Choice does not depend on *ex ante* knowledge of future outcomes, but rather on *previous* conceptualization and identification of goods (those that will be chosen or not by the individual) with such concepts. That is to say, action presupposes evaluation, which depends on identification of concretes by means of concepts. If there were perfect knowledge, then no utility maximization analysis would be required, given that the individual would know the optimum combination *automatically*. Moreover, perfect knowledge is almost never explicitly claimed as a pillar of the model, and even if it were, it neither would correspond with reality, nor would constitute a predictive nor explanatory tool.

For example, if the individual must choose between pizzas or hamburgers, and he gives the nod to the former, the fact that one or all pizzas he consumed in the past had been satisfactory does not imply that it would be the case now.[20] The individual chooses based on his concepts and predilections (of a *qualitative* nature), not because of a specific measurement following quantitative considerations. It cannot be seriously contended that the individual makes a quantitative analysis of the total amount of pizzas he ate in his life and their corresponding received utilities. However, we may assume from the fact that he *chose* pizzas that these may have given him *more* satisfaction than hamburgers (but not how much more). In addition, if a neoclassical micro-economist contended that indifference analysis tries to precisely model the latter fact (or that this is the mathematical counterpart of such process), the refutation is that it is an unnecessary complication (Occam's razor), since this can be easily understood without incorporating mathematics.[21]

Although it could be contended that weighing different options mentally is analogous to making a calculation in order to maximize a utility function, they are categorically different. Otherwise, one would have to accept, for instance, that it would be the same to compare two different colors (e.g. red and green) with two different magnitudes (e.g. fifty-two and seventy-eight). What do we mean by this? This is our attempt to give an example of a comparison between two things that are radically incommensurable, such as color and number: how can we compare the color red with the number 10? The same goes for comparing the mental process of choosing (this is of a qualitative nature), with a calculation in order to maximize a utility

[20] The problem of induction. See Popper (1959).

[21] Or, at least, indifference analysis.

function (this is of a quantitative nature). From our viewpoint, this is incorrect. An objection to this could be that the color red (or any other color) is an attribute of the human vision of wavelength. Thus, it is indeed a concept defined by the length of a wave, and this is a number. But this is a theoretical categorization of the perception, not the perception itself. You can explain to a blind person that color is defined by the length of a wave, but you cannot convey the experience of seeing it from that description, unless you *already know the concrete* that is conceptualized under that description in the first place, which is of course of a qualitative nature. Similarly, utility function maximization pretends to be the theoretical categorization of the process of consumer choice. Naturally, quantity and quality are not the same nor need be so. Consumer choice deals with quantities only insofar as there are magnitudes involved (either with respect to number of goods, or prices), but need not be restricted to it. Consumer preference and choice involve both quantity *and* quality.

Indifference curve analysis is partially predicated upon ordinal utility. The consumer chooses, for instance, between $10x$ units of good X and $20y$ units of Y good, on the one hand, and $30x$ units of X plus $15y$ units of Y on the other hand. Which one is more highly ranked? That is an aspect of ordinality. But the indifference curve analytic tool is also based on cardinal not only ordinal utility. For example, when the budget line is tangent to the indifference curve, the equation describing this point is as follows: $MU_x/P_x = MU_y/P_y$. However, MU_x and MU_y are clearly cardinal, not ordinal numbers as they are being divided by P_x and P_y, respectively. In contrast, ordinal numbers, such as tenth, fifteenth, cannot be divided, or multiplied, added or subtracted. Only cardinal numbers can be so treated. Hence, cardinality. Two for the price of one. Cardinality is therefore not absent from indifference analysis, despite the claim of neoclassic micro-economists to the contrary.[22]

Maximization of utility, therefore, is achieved when the preferred basket of goods presents a marginal rate of substitution (the slope of the indifference curve) that equals the price ratio (the slope of the budget constraint). This is shown in the point where the highest indifference curve is tangent to the budget line (Diagram 2.1). However, the equation allows us to make this analysis, because it is an *equation*.[23] Therefore, cardinality slips in.[24]

---

[22] An objection could be made that this equation does not pretend to assign any numeric value to MU, but only to show that in that case MU is the same for each monetary unit spent. For further analysis of this issue, see Sect. 2.4 below.

[23] In other models, such as the von Neumann-Morgenstern (1944 [1953]) utility function, based on decision under risk, it could be argued that there is cardinality as determined by the use of probability.

[24] Pierre Garello (whom we thank for his valuable comments) has pointed us out that, it is true that according to the von Neumann-Morgenstern framework the cardinality consists in that the utility function representing the preferences of the decision maker are unique up to an affine transformation. Following Celcius, when the temperature goes from 2 °C to 4 °C we cannot claim that it is *twice* as warm, although the temperature recorded is indeed twice as high, numerically. However, the key is what we regard as *affine* transformation. In the equation above, it is cardinality, nonetheless.

Diagram 2.1 Utility maximization point

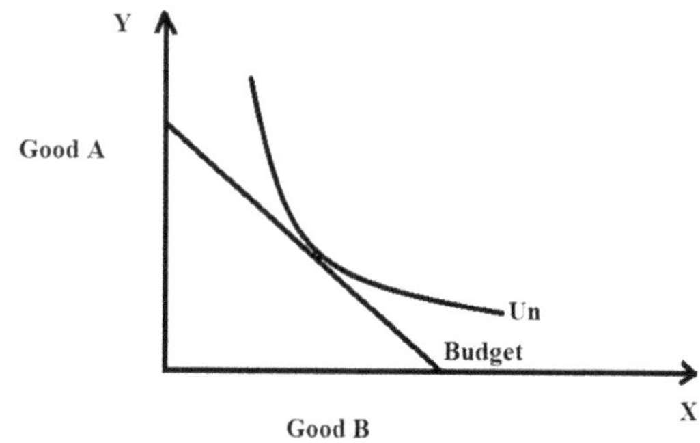

Let us get back to the consumer's choice example mentioned above regarding pizzas and hamburgers. Here are several possibilities of why the outcome was pizzas:

1. The consumer may have never tried hamburgers before, and given that he is highly averse to risk, he prefers to choose what he already knows, i.e. what he had already experienced.
2. It may be the case that both options are equally distasteful for the consumer, but he chooses one because he is having dinner with other friends who would prefer pizza.
3. The consumer may have tried hamburgers before, but not pizzas. However, given that he found hamburgers distasteful, he prefers the unknown.

The possibilities are numerous, but the common denominator is that choice is not performed in a vacuum. Previous conceptualization, evaluation, positive and negative emotions associated with different goods, context, all play a part in consumer choice. In addition, any analysis is contextual, given that the individual takes into account factors that would change the ranking in different circumstances:

4. The individual is on a date, and he prefers to choose something according to the choice of his date, given that he values his date's well-being more than eating something else.

True, there are neoclassical models that include risk aversion and others where one person's utility depends on another's, but in our view the basic method is flawed; not that indifference analysis could be made more complex as to include these considerations.

Yes, the individual chooses one good or combination of goods above others, but this does not imply that he makes any quantitative analysis. In this respect, one (including the individual itself) can only say that he *more highly* values his choice than any other alternative, but neither he nor anyone else can say by how much (quantitatively). Only ordinal utility is legitimate; not the cardinal variety thereof. There is no such measurement as a "util" or unit of happiness. To infer that this is analogous to maximizing a utility function just because both are analyses or comparisons, is the same as to equate the music with the score because both deal with the same subject.

This can be clearly seen once one analyzes how a consumer maximizes utility according to neoclassical microeconomics. In order to find out how the consumer maximizes its utility by consuming optimum quantities of goods (B_1, B_2) of a specific basket, we must employ Lagrange multipliers. This is so because we assume that utility maximization is subject to a restriction, in this case a budget.

Given that the utility function $U = f(B_1, B_2)$, and the restriction (g) is given by the function $\mu B_1 + xB_2 = c$, where μ, x and c are constants, we must maximize U subjected to the aforementioned restriction.

To achieve that, we must first equate the restriction to zero:

$$c - \mu B_1 - xB_2 = 0 \tag{2.1}$$

Later, we proceed to construe the Lagrangian ($\mathcal{L}$) along with the function that we propose to optimize:

$$\mathcal{L} = f\left(B_1, B_2\right) + \lambda\left(c - \mu B_1 - xB_2\right) \tag{2.2}$$

Once we specify it, we proceed to search for the partial derivatives and equate them to zero:

$$\begin{aligned} \frac{\partial \mathcal{L}}{\partial B1} &= 0 \\ \frac{\partial \mathcal{L}}{\partial B2} &= 0 \\ \frac{\partial \mathcal{L}}{\partial \lambda} &= 0 \end{aligned} \tag{2.3}$$

Hence, we can infer from these the values of B_{1i}, B_{2i} y λ_i, where in B_{1i} and B_{2i} we find critical points. To learn if these are maxima or minima, we need to calculate the second derivatives:

$$\partial^2 \mathcal{L} / \partial B_1, \partial^2 \mathcal{L} / \partial B_{2,} \partial^2 \mathcal{L} / \partial B_1 B_2 = \partial^2 \mathcal{L} / \partial B_2 B_1 \tag{2.4}$$

And, also, with these we can construe the Bordered Hessian $|\bar{H}|$, that equals the Jacobian $|J|$. We operate this way because, given the former values, if $|\bar{H}| > 0$ we can state that we found a maximum of U, or vice versa:

$$|J| = \begin{vmatrix} 0 & \frac{\partial g}{\partial B1} & \frac{\partial g}{\partial B2} \\ \frac{\partial g}{\partial B1} & \partial 2\mathcal{L} / \partial B1 & \partial 2\mathcal{L} / \partial B1B2 \\ \frac{\partial g}{\partial B2} & \partial 2\mathcal{L} / \partial B2B1 & \partial 2\mathcal{L} / \partial B2 \end{vmatrix} = |\bar{H}| \tag{2.5}$$

Where, if $|\bar{H}| > 0 \rightarrow (B_{1i}, B_{2i})$ are a maximum; and if $|\bar{H}| < 0 \rightarrow (B_{1i}, B_{2i})$ are a minimum.

Is this process analogous to actual consumer choice? Not in our view.

True enough, the individual, by weighing options that deal with money prices, does indeed resort to calculations of different kinds. However, we object to the idea that these calculations are mathematical in nature, despite the fact that numerical calculations can indeed take place. For instance, the individual may think: 'should I buy one apple at $10, or get an orange and a banana for $10 in total?' He will compare the subjective evaluation he makes of the apple at $10, and the orange and banana at the same price. His calculation considers the price (which is of course numerical) because he compares the value of both options *given* their asked prices, but he does not make anything worth mentioning as a mathematical calculation, or one analogous to it. Money, translated in numerical terms, confuses the issue.[25] Now consider the case of barter: if the individual must choose between exchanging a chair for an apple on the one hand, and a banana and an apple on the other, it is clear that the weighing and calculation he performs is not of a mathematical nature. Rather, it is subjective, qualitative. And, in both cases, the ratio is still 1:1.

There is a sense in which mathematical analysis reproduces the consumer choice process, and that is in the presentation of the options available to the individual. In the example above, he faces two options: an apple at $10, and a banana and orange for $10. So, we can construct ratios between these, and this can be indeed shown in mathematical terms. But this convoluted manner of putting the matter would only be a duplication of what we can easily understand by means of words. However, this is where the analogy ends, because the consumer choice process is not a mathematical calculation, but a subjective evaluation of choices. There is no way to express, in mathematical terms, why an individual chooses one option instead of another without resorting to units of utility. This is not only so in the case of cardinal utility, but also ordinal utility. Why? Because the comparison of $MU_x/MU_y = P_x/P_y$ is not just a presentation of rankings or orders, but an equation that gives the impression of the existence of some kind of numerical difference in utility. That is, between option 1 and option 2, stated in mathematical terms, there is not just the idea that option 1 is more valued than 2, but that there is a differential that consists in a specific quantity (although mathematics does not say, nor need to say, what it is). The actual consumer choice process, in our view, constitutes, instead, a heuristic method.

Utility maximization, it could be argued, is not the most important part of neoclassical theory. The latter consists of the logic behind the ordering of different bundles of goods, and that is indeed based on preference and indifference. The model contemplates certain assumptions that direct such ordering processes, such as transitivity, monotonicity, etc. Insofar as the individual follows such guidelines,

[25] In other words, commercial transactions are predicated upon *inequations*, not equations. If someone buys an apple for $10, and we present the following equation: 1 Apple = $10, that explains nothing about the value that the consumer places on the apple, nor why he is buying it. All we can know is that he values the apple he obtains *more* than the money he pays for it. About the $10 for an apple, we can only say that such was the agreed rate of exchange, in other words, the price.

he will be able to choose, according to his budget and the prices of the goods, the combination of bundles that represents an optimum, that is, a maximization of utility. However, if utility maximization is not the most important part, but the ordinal ranking of different combinations is, then why do we have to resort to maximization analysis and mathematical models in the first place?

Based on the assumptions of the model, let us look closer at the transitivity condition. This concept is unobjectionable when it comes to height and weight. If *A* is taller (heavier) than *B*, and *B* is taller (heavier) than *C*, it follows, logically, that *A* is taller (heavier) than *C*. However, just because baseball team *X* beats *Y*, regularly, and *Y* almost always overcomes *Z*, it by no means follows that *X* will outscore *Z*. Similarly, a person prefers apples to bananas, and bananas to carrots. We are not at all entitled to deduce from this that he will rank apples higher than bananas. The $A > B$ choice is made at time t_1; the $B > C$ decision occurs at time t_2. The person might have changed his tastes in the interim. Even if he did not, we still cannot infer from $A > B$, coupled with $B > C$, that $A > C$. Not every decision pattern is transitive, no matter how conducive to mathematics this might be. We cannot allow the mathematical dog to wag the economic tail, at least not in the dismal science. In our profession, it must be the other way around.

Let us be clear on this. It is perfectly legitimate to construct models in order to understand a specific subject, for example the movement of the leg despite the fact that man need not know nor think about it when moving this appendage of his.[26] But it must be a model *faithful* to the leg's movement. This is precisely what is not present in indifference analysis and utility maximization regarding consumer choice.

Also, the methodological debate concerning the importance of the realism of assumptions is relevant here. Following Friedman (1953 [1966]), the key is not the realism of assumptions, but the capacity to predict that is the standard by which to judge a theory. The problem is that the theory in this case neither helps us properly predict nor understand the process. The assumptions, also, as we see are misleading.

On this methodological problem, Roderick T. Long states as follows:

> "As an empiricist, Friedman takes a theory to explain a phenomenon if it enables us to predict the phenomenon's occurrence; whereas for Austrians, to explain economic phenomena is, in Ludwig Lachmann's phrase, 'to make the world around us intelligible in terms of human action and the pursuit of plans' (Lachmann 1977, pp. 261–62). As philosopher Peter Winch shows, these two conceptions of explanation are radically different:
>
> "'The important question for us is: in what circumstances could one say that one had *understood* this sort of behaviour?... Weber often speaks as if the ultimate test were our ability to formulate statistical laws which would enable us to *predict* with fair accuracy what people would be likely to do in given circumstances.... [But] we might well be able to make predictions of great accuracy in this way and still not be able to claim any real understanding of what those people were doing. The difference is precisely analogous to that between being able to formulate statistical laws about the likely occurrences of words in a language and being able to understand what was being *said* by someone who spoke the language.... [A] man who understands Chinese is not a man who has a firm

[26] Joke: the centipede was asked how he locomotes. He looked down, and couldn't do it anymore.

grasp of the statistical probabilities for the occurrence of the various words in the Chinese language. (Winch 1990, p. 115).'

"Moreover, the Friedmanite position would be on shaky ground even if predictive power were the central point of economics. Suppose it turns out that wildly false assumptions do have some predictive value; from a Misesian point of view, when we find an empirical regularity we still need a correct theory to determine whether this regularity can be expected to hold over a broad or a narrow range of circumstances" (Long (2006, 4).

2.3 The Concept of Equilibrium in the Context of Consumer Choice

The necessary condition for any exchange to take place is that the value of the received goods (*VR*, of the combination of goods) needs to be regarded as higher than the value of those delivered (*VD*, generally in the form of money but may be any other commodity).[27] This is a fundamental point, since here we must take into account the concept of *equilibrium*.[28]

We are accustomed to referring to equilibrium in the Pareto sense (Wagner 2017, 20); that is, in such situations where no individual may improve his condition without worsening that of others'. This occurs also in the individual case, where it is not possible to improve one's own situation given the context where action takes place. Nevertheless, if we must consider as the basis of any exchange that $VR > VD$, then we could say that in any exchange where $VR > VD$ it is true that *an* equilibrium is in fact taking place.[29]

This is so independently of the differential (**δ**) that hypothetically exists between the valuations of both individuals exchanging (given that it cannot be measured), and between the valuations of the goods (or money) delivered and those received by the same individual, i.e. if $VR > VD$ holds, then the exchange will occur. Therefore, as long as it holds, $VR - VD = \boldsymbol{\delta}$**, such that** $\boldsymbol{\delta} > 0$, i.e., it **is positive.**

Thus, *VD* and *VR* are highly relevant, since the following scenarios may take place:

(a) $VR < VD$, in which case no transaction would occur.
(b) $VR = VD$, and therefore no transaction would take place, given that the value placed on the goods received and the money delivered is the same. Exchange would be impossible; why would anyone bestir himself to make such a trade, given that he could not thereby improve his condition, even *ex ante*?
(c) $VR > VD$, being this a case where equilibrium in fact takes place.

[27] Otherwise, no transaction would take place.

[28] And not only optimality or maximization.

[29] See on this a discussion on the concept of equilibrium in the work of James M. Buchanan in Wagner (2017, 20–21).

The problem with the neoclassical model is that it pretends to support the notion that the best way to understand consumer choice is with a model that states (on the basis of certain conditions) that individuals will always maximize utility; that is when $VR - VD = \boldsymbol{\delta}$ **is the highest,** where in reality the individual will always transact as long as $VR > VD$.

At the same time, *only* preference is revealed in action (and not indifference). States Rothbard (1956) in this regard: "The concept of demonstrated preference is simply this: that actual choice reveals, or demonstrates, a man's preferences; that is, that his preferences are deducible from what he has chosen in action. Thus, if a man chooses to spend an hour at a concert rather than a movie, we deduce that the former was preferred, or ranked higher on his value scale. Similarly, if a man spends five dollars on a shirt we deduce that he preferred purchasing the shirt to any other uses he could have found for the money. This concept of preference, rooted in real choices, forms the keystone of the logical structure of economic analysis, and particularly of utility and welfare analysis."

Every exchange creates an equilibrium. Let us again remember that we are using Buchanan's concept of equilibrium (Wagner 2017, 20–21) where as long as individuals exchange, there is an equilibria. Armen A. Alchian's concept of efficiency is also relevant in this regard, since John R. Lott Jr (1997, 186) wrote: "That was when Armen defined the notion of efficiency. He defined efficiency as 'Whatever is, is efficient.' If it wasn't efficient it would have been something different. Of course, if you try to change anything that is there, that is efficient too."

Following this reasoning, let us now consider the cases in which the budget line crosses the two lower indifference curves in Diagram 2.2. The traditional interpretation of such points is that they represent attainable, but inefficient, allocations of resources. Why inefficient? This is due to the fact that within that budget line, higher indifference curves are attainable. Our analysis leads in an entirely different direction. In the days of sailing ships and fortresses meant to repel them, the temperature of a cannon ball was judged too hot if spittle refused to attain contact with it. In like manner, we say that these points *J* and *K* cannot "contact" or, that is, even *exist*. Why not? This is due to the fact that they both depict situations where the consumer (inefficiently, to be sure) purchases a combination of goods with his budget. But, again, we run into the same difficulty: why, ever, would he do (or conceive) any such thing when there is no way he can improve his well-being, not even, once again, *ex ante*.

Diagram 2.2 Utility maximization point and lower indifference curves

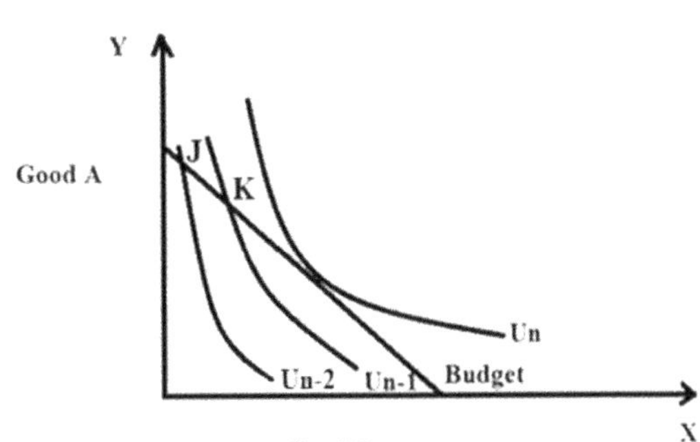

At the same time, equilibrium does not necessarily imply optimality in the sense of maximization. For a transaction to take place, only the condition that *VR* > *VD* needs to hold. To assume that utility maximization as presented in indifference models is the main standard by which individuals choose, gives the impression that if no maximization is possible, the individual will not choose. But individuals may transact even if they don't maximize their utility. The fundamental condition of exchange is *VR* > *VD*, not that *VR* – *VD* = **δ, where δ is the highest level possible. We invite the reader to assess if it is more sensible to assume that transactions take place whenever** *VR* > *VD* (including the cases where utility maximization is achieved), or *only* when utility maximization is present. Moreover, to **assess** if a model pretending to show how the consumer chooses must only consider utility maximization as its standard, or just the simple, universal condition of every exchange: *VR* > *VD*.

Let us emphasize that *VD* and *VR* are not equivalent to the objects that are traded, but rather the subjective evaluation the individual makes of the objects delivered (money or other goods in barter) and received.[30] The use of the word 'value' in *VD* and *VR* can be confusing for this reason. The individual neither delivers nor receives *a* value, but an object that is *valued*. The essence of the exchange is that he gains a value (for him) and delivers a value (that he places below what he gets). The nomenclature of *VD* and *VR* are only shortcuts, abbreviations for this insight. But this important clarification must be taken into account.

That is why the claim that the optimization process is described by a stopping rule is erroneous. The agent, for instance, does not sacrifice one additional unit of what he gives until *VR* = *VD*, because if he reaches that point, he does *not* trade any more. It is precisely because the individual will continue to trade up to the point when the decreasing marginal utility of the object he receives is above the increasing marginal utility of the object he delivers (Cachanosky 1986, 9) that no optimization (in the mathematical sense) takes nor can take place. That is, even if *VR* = *VD* applies at only one point it would be irrelevant.

This concept of equilibrium is better understood if we follow Brennan and Buchanan (1985 [2000], 29):

> The economist, who conceptually observes the trading process and who sees no violations of the basic rules, can assign an 'efficient,' or 'maximum value,' label to the equilibrium result. In so doing, he is not evaluating the result against any scale external to the participants in the trade, nor is he introducing some value scale of his own.

The individual makes choices according to his subjective evaluation in the *ex ante* sense. So, the consumer choice process itself, if it is voluntary, *only* follows the

[30] It is said that peanut butter and jelly are complements, and that beer and wine are substitutes. But even the most thorough chemical analysis of these four items will not yield any such truth. Rather, this situation stems, solely, from the tastes of most people. Nor need this claim be true for all. Some people might like to mix these two beverages and drink them together. In that case, beer and wine would be complements!

equilibrium concept in the sense of Buchanan & Brennan (1985 [2000]), not the neoclassical approach.[31]

Let us apply this concept of equilibrium to neoclassical analysis in order to show the problem in the model. Following Buchanan & Brennan, if no rules are violated, the outcome of the trading process is always efficient. Here, there is indeed a dissociation between the notion of equilibrium and efficiency per se, and "Within the rules, as defined, the trading outcome must always be 'efficient,' and there is no way the economist can define an 'efficient' allocation independent of trade itself. The economist is forced to bring his own evaluative criteria to bear on the rules of trade rather than on the results of trade" (Brennan and Buchanan 1985 [2000], 29). Precisely. The rule that must not be changed is that the exchange be voluntary. The economist cannot judge efficient allocations of resources independent of this fact. This is the meaning of Rothbard's (1956 [1997]) claim that preference is only demonstrated in action (which is partially related to Samuelson's "revealed preference theory"; 1938).

This is not the equilibrium concept used in neoclassical analysis but is the concept that *should* be used, according to our perspective. By avoiding it, neoclassical analysis mistakenly equates mathematical optimization with equilibrium.

Indifference curve analysis, in its mathematical fashion, is also confused with marginal utility. It leads the economist to lose focus on the conceptual framework behind the law of diminishing marginal utility. This, in turn, is derived from the logical structure of the relation between the unit to be acquired or given up and the quantity of stock already available to the actor.[32] Thus, Rothbard (1962, 24–25) explains:

> "The important consideration is the *relation between the unit to be acquired or given up and the quantity of supply (stock) already available to the actor.* Thus, if no units of a good (whatever the good may be) are available, the first unit will satisfy the most urgent wants that such a good is capable of satisfying. If to this supply of one unit is added a second unit, the latter will fulfill the most urgent wants remaining, but these will be less urgent than the ones the first fulfilled. Therefore, the value of the second unit to the actor will be less than the value of the first unit. Similarly, the value of the third unit of the supply (added to a stock of two units) will be less than the value of the second unit. It may not matter to the individual

[31] Buchanan was not an avowed Austrian economist in general, but insofar as praxeological subjectivism is concerned, he could indeed be categorized in this manner. See on this Buchanan (1969a), and Buchanan and Thirlby (1981)

[32] We reject the notion that marginal utility constitutes an additional unit of satisfaction adding to "total utility". To say that is to acquiesce in the concept of cardinal, not ordinal utility. Friedrich Hayek's concept of utility is similar to the one we regard as correct. That is, the services rendered by an object or a person correspond to the use that the consumer thinks of the service he can extract from the object or person. In this respect, if the consumer acts freely, has a stable pattern of preferences and engages in rationality, he will stop his commercial activity as soon as the subjective opportunity cost of an additional purchase exceeds the expected gain from such action. A quantitative analysis, we must add, is an extrapolation from monetary costs (which explains the neoclassical economics derivation of demand curves by resorting to utility functions, and supply curves by using cost functions). But it is not necessary in order to make sense of utility or consumer choice in this respect.

> *which* horse is chosen first and which second, or *which* pounds of butter he consumes, but those units which he does use first will be the ones that he values more highly. *Thus, for all human actions, as the quantity of the supply (stock) of a good increases, the utility (value) of each additional unit decreases*" (emphasis in the original).

2.4 The Concept of Indifference, Transitivity and the Condition of Utility Maximization

Another relevant point, often claimed by Austrian School economists (e.g., Block 1980, 2009a; Rothbard 1956, 1962), is that it is not only the case that the model presents problems, but that it is also based on (in our view) an incorrect assumption, given that there is no such thing as indifference in the field of human *action*. Quite the opposite, preference and only preference is revealed through action.[33]

The concept of indifference with regard to human choices lacks *economic* sense.[34] In this context, Callahan (2003) explains that,

> [...] only preferences revealed in action are relevant to the economist. Those are the preferences that played a role in actual economic activity. A psychologist or an epistemologist might have something to say about preferences not acted on, but the economist does not. No Austrian of which I am aware has ever held that the only thing going on in a person's head during the day are his preferences as revealed in his choices.

Moreover, a purely random choice in a given context may suffice, that is, the standard for choosing a unit in that context is the convenience of taking the first one at hand, since any unit of a given good is deemed good enough. However, observe that this is different from saying that the agent is indifferent between the units, because he effectively chose one, and not the others (even if the explanation for this is that the chosen unit was the one that was closest at hand).

Also, regarding the concept of utility as used in the neoclassical model, a difference between the utility that corresponds to the budget line and the utility that corresponds to indifference curves is that the former is in an *accomplishment*, an aspect of wealth already attained, whereas the utility of indifference curves represents only *potential* utility. The latter depends on the individual exchanging and acquiring the combination of goods corresponding to the indifference curve. Thus, actual and potential utility are different, which renders the model even more unrealistic,[35] because both utilities are treated equally in the mathematical formulation.

---

[33] For an analysis of "Revealed Preference Theory" (which is quite different than the Austrian sense of "preference reveals itself through action"), see Samuelson (1938). For a critique of the Austrian approach to microeconomics, see Caplan (Undated, 1999, 2001, 2003), and their rebuttals by Block (1999, 2003, 2007).

[34] On the concept of indifference in the context of specific classes of goods, see Zanotti (1990, 22).

[35] For an analysis of Utility and Price, see Kirzner (1963, 45–141).

Let us now take another look at transitivity. It is a common mistake to equate exchange of goods *at market prices* with direct exchange of *goods*. Murray Rothbard (1962, 236) explains:

> "It is evident that, with money being used for all exchanges, money prices serve as a common denominator of all exchange ratios. Thus, with the above money prices, anyone can calculate that if one horse exchanges for five ounces and one barrel of fish exchanges for 1/20 ounces, then one horse can, indirectly, exchange for 100 barrels of fish, or for 80 dozen eggs, or 5/3 of an hour of X's labor, etc. Instead of a myriad of isolated markets for each good and every other good, each good exchanges for money, and the exchange ratios between every good and every other good can easily be estimated by observing their money prices. Here it must be emphasized that these exchange ratios are only *hypothetical*, and can be computed at all only *because of the exchanges against money*. It is only through the use of money that we can hypothetically estimate these 'barter ratios,' and it is only by intermediate exchanges against money that one good can finally be exchanged for the other at the hypothetical ratio. Many writers have erred in believing that money can somehow be *abstracted* from the formation of money prices and that analysis can accurately describe affairs 'as if' exchanges really took place by way of barter. With money and money prices pervading all exchanges, there can be no abstraction from money in analyzing the formation of prices in an economy of indirect exchange" (emphasis added).

As an example, if someone buys a banana at $10, and an apple has a market price of $5, this does not mean that he will be able to exchange a banana for two apples, or vice versa. Market prices indicate relative prices, but you cannot deduce all possible exchanges from them. The person who pays $5 for an *A* may not pay $10 for a *B*, and vice versa.[36] The standards of value will be different in both situations, and *therefore* the transactions will be different (given that the utilities of the items are different).

Yet another explanation is that these initial transactions took place at time t_1. It is now time t_2, and all sorts of relevant considerations might have changed. Further, there is the issue of profit. Contrary to fact conditional coming up so beware, if a banana were worth exactly two apples, there would be no gains to be made from trading them at par, even *ex ante*.

Now let us get back to the point of tangency of the highest indifference curve possible and the budget line, i.e. the equilibrium of the consumer:

$$\frac{MUx}{MUy} = \frac{Px}{Py} \rightarrow \frac{MUx}{Px} = \frac{MUy}{Py}$$

This equation presumes to show that, at the aforementioned point the marginal utility garnered by the last unit of the budget spent on each good is the same. Therefore, it is contended, there is an equilibrium and utility maximization is attained.

---

[36] And even if we would concede that this should *logically* be the case, this would only occur at equilibrium (in the sense of the "general equilibrium model"), but in the real world we are never at equilibrium, only always tending in that direction.

According to the Austrian School, this is not the proper way of explaining consumer choice. The individual does not maximize utility when the marginal utility of a unit of the budget is *equal* to the marginal utility of the final unit of good acquired, but rather "…when he buys even the last unit whose decreasing marginal utility exceeds the increasing marginal utility of the good delivered in exchange (for example, money)" (Cachanosky 1986, 9[37]). The former is the case where $VR = VD$ (and where as we have seen there would be no exchange), whereas the latter is the case of $VR > VD$, i.e. the *last* case where such condition holds (and therefore exchange may take place).

2.5 Human Action and Its Standard

Indifference curve analysis also assumes that human behavior follows patterns that could be modeled by means of differential calculus and involve continuous functions (being the most relevant example the case of the indifference curve that presents the same utility).

However, reality is the opposite: human beings only choose and act by taking into account subjectively relevant units, i.e. discrete units. It is not the case that the individual acts according to continuous variables, but that *because* he chooses and acts with regard to variables whose units are *able* to be divided (on many occasions), it is mistakenly *inferred* that the consumer's decisions and actions take into account continuous intervals of such variables. Nevertheless, this deduction is only used as a premise in order to develop models and use differential calculus as to build curves and be able to derivate (with the purpose of analyzing the options of the acting agent and determine, identify and predict utility maximization points, etc.). However, it is not implicit *in* human action.

This is so because the individual does not obtain satisfaction or utility[38] based on infinitesimally small proportions of the same unit, given that there are no units of utility per se and received satisfaction or utility is obtained from the consumption of the *relevant* unit, *as* a unit (not of its non-registerable fragments).[39] The only thing actually identified in human action are specific points in the Cartesian plane, where action effectively takes place (e.g., the acquisition of a specific quantity of goods obtained by means of the exchange of a determinate amount of money).

The fact that it is intended to identify other points in the plane on the basis of the one (or ones) that effectively take place only implies that the intention is to justify the *model*, not to accurately depict human action. And with regard to indifference curves themselves, these are implicitly built based on imaginary units such as those

[37] Translated from the original in Spanish by the first mentioned author of the present chapter.

[38] Using the concept here in that sense.

[39] Although the consumption of a unit implies the consumption of all the parts of such unit, this is not relevant to the individual at the time of making *economic* decisions.

of utility[40] and the existence (or *relevancy*) of fragments of such units are merely assumed. Such units are abstractions impossible to quantify and merely descriptive of a pretended identification of human behavior. We cannot continue the reasoning and assimilate to such non-existent, unquantifiable and abstract units, fragments of itself in order to build a theory by using mathematical tools, differential calculus, and planes with continuous functions, and pretend to be making *real* analyses of human action.[41]

The fundamental mistake is to take human behavior as quantifiable based on hypothetical abstract units, as if these were real.[42] This error repeats itself both in the theory of cardinal utility and in that of ordinal utility (as presented in Neoclassical Microeconomics).[43] This is so because the satisfaction or utility received by baskets of goods, or units of goods, only shows the utility attained. And this utility is received *ex post* of choosing the acquisition of the goods in specific (discrete) quantities. We cannot deduce from this fact the existence of fragments of such utility or that these necessarily exist only because utility was received through consumption, given that such consumption may not be separated nor could be made so under certain circumstances (some goods cannot be divided in order to consume them).

For instance, if a person eats a slice of pizza, it is not that the satisfaction or utility received came separately from the cheese and the bread, but rather from both at the same time, in combination with one another.[44] If he ate them separately, they would be two different goods, and no longer a slice of pizza.[45] We face a *non sequitur*, because from the fact that satisfaction or utility is received through the consumption of a combination of goods we cannot deduce that such utility is quantifiable, comparable in numerical terms nor much less explained in its nature by continuous functions and able to be modeled through differential calculus.

The Austrian approach has been criticized by none other than Robert Nozick (1977), who claimed that the Law of Marginal Utility requires "indifference" among

---

[40] We refer here to our discussion of the implicit use of cardinality in the model, as discussed above.

[41] A critic may say that this type of analysis does not pretend to be realistic, but rather useful to understand some aspects of reality. However, we reject both claims.

[42] According to Friedman (1953 [1966]), unrealistic assumptions should be no bar to economic theories; prediction, not accuracy, is the desiderata. One would be hard pressed, however, to come up with a prediction based on indifference curve analysis. In this regard, even when public finance literature uses this technique to make predictions, such as that people save more given higher interest rates, this is hardly a conclusion that can be reached only by means of indifference analysis. For support of Friedman, see Boland (1979). For a critique, see Rappaport (1986).

[43] The Austrian approach on ordinal utility is different. See Klein (2012), Menger (1871), Menger (1973), Mises (1933), and Rothbard (1962).

[44] The consumer may indeed say that he enjoyed the cheese more than the bread of the pizza, but he cannot quantify it by separating their "utilities". Only an ordinal analysis is correct, coherent, not a cardinal one.

[45] Another example is to assume that the utility reported by the use of a pair of shoes implies that, if only one shoe would be used then it will report half of the latter's utility, when it most likely be useless without the other shoe. Therefore, it would provide low or zero utility.

each unit. This is so, he claimed, because in order to substitute one unit for another, one needs to be "indifferent" among them.

However, this is a mistake, as Zanotti (1990, 22) explains:

> Nozick has objected that from the fact that one person chooses *a* does not imply that it does not want nor prefer *b*. It is true. But our contention that every action implies choosing between *a* and *b* does not mean deducing that the person does not prefer *b*, rather that since not every necessity could be satisfied at the same time, then the acting agent must create a value scale and set his priorities, according to which he will option. Perhaps, respect to this observation by Nozick we may say that every action implies to choose between *a* and *non a*.[46]

Indifference (although having psychological implications), has no economic relevancy whatsoever.

2.6 Conclusion

As we tried to show throughout this chapter, the neoclassical model of consumer choice is highly problematic in properly explaining human action or decision-making processes. In the spirit of lending rigorousness to its conclusions by adding mathematics, it only ends up confusing the student of economics and obscuring the proper understanding of social phenomena.

While it could be unwise to rule out mathematics as a tool in order to explain phenomena in the social sciences, it is equally unwise to over-mathematize the science of economics in order to bring an illusion of certainty to it (Herbener 1996; Leoni and Frola 1977; Miss 1938, 1949, 1953). Economic theory can certainly be expanded and illustrated by the use of mathematical models (Moorhouse 1993), but this does not mean that mathematics can *replace* theory presented in discursive reasoning altogether.

Indifference curves and budget constraints models deal with unquantifiable abstractions such as utility, pretending to mathematize it through utility maximization analysis. They also make use of the concept of indifference, which has no economic relevancy. All these (in our view) mistakes appear due to the obsession of neoclassical economics with mathematics. An alternative explanation is what Fritz Machlup (1956) correctly defined as the "inferiority complex of the social sciences".

Since consumer choice is at the core of economics, it is of the utmost importance to renew its study *as* economic theory, and overcome the mistakes of the past. Economics is not a branch of mathematics, but mathematics is a tool in order to *aid* economic theory.

What should replace the neoclassical model? As is the goal of this book to present, the best candidate is the Austrian School, with its understanding of the heuristics of the consumer choice process, that is of a qualitative, and not quantitative,

---

[46] Translated from the original in Spanish by the first mentioned author. Other critics of Nozick on this matter include Block (1980). Hoppe (2005) reject's Block's analysis. Block (2009a) and Barnett and Block (2010) respond to Hoppe (2005).

nature. The evaluation phase of the decision is the key to understanding consumer choice, and this is an entrepreneurial dimension that neoclassical economics does not consider. As entrepreneurs, consumers make decisions in the *ex ante* sense in order to attain the highest end possible in their value scale, given the means at their disposal. However, also as entrepreneurs, they check *ex post* to determine if the outcome was gainful, or if they experienced a loss, and then act accordingly in the next iteration. That is, consumer choice is a process of trial and error, guided by the ordinal ranking of ends and a continuous process of checking profit and loss. Preferences are continually tested in the market, and utility is not a fixed unit. This is why the consumers tend to be open to new products and services, and why they sometimes regret their previous choices.

Mathematics may try to build models to emulate the choice process, but it is incapable of transmitting the essential of consumer choice: a non-quantitative process that is guided by conceptual evaluation and contextual considerations, where the key is that the consumer will try to achieve the best outcome on the basis of his means, but not as the result of an analysis analogous to a utility function maximization.

The decision process consists of two phases, setting the problem and evaluating what course of action to take.[47] The former is the one that involves the entrepreneurial dimension, and neoclassical economics takes it as a given. The latter is the one analyzed by neoclassical economics, and which has all the problems we have reviewed in this work. Hence, this approach does not help us understand consumer choice, neither its context nor its evaluation process.

It is of the utmost importance to bring back theory[48] to the center of economic science, and use mathematics only for its proper role: as a subservient tool.

Bibliography

Allais, Maurice. 1953. Le Comportement de l'Homme Rationnel devant le Risque: Critique des Postulats et Axiomes de l'Ecole Americaine. *Econometrica* 21 (4 (October)): 503–546.

Ariely, Dan. 2008. *Predictably Irrational: The Hidden Forces that Shape Our Decisions*. New York: HarperCollins.

Ariely, Dan, G. Loewenstein, and D. Prelec. 2003. Coherent Arbitrariness: Stable Demand Curves Without Stable Preferences. *The Quarterly Journal of Economics* 118 (1): 73–105.

———. 2005. Tom Sawyer and the Construction of Value. *Journal of Economic Behavior & Organization* 60: 1–10.

Barathalon, Eric. 2014. *Uncertainty, Expectations, and Financial Instability*. New York: Columbia University Press.

Barnett, William, II. 2003. The Modern Theory of Consumer Behavior: Ordinal or Cardinal. *The Quarterly Journal of Austrian Economics* 6 (1): 41–65.

Becker, Gary S. 1965. A Theory of the Allocation of Time. *The Economic Journal* 75 (299 (September)): 493–517.

[47] We owe this distinction to Pierre Garello.

[48] See Rothbard (1957, 1997), Selgin (1988) and Smith (1999).

———. 1968. Crime and Punishment: An Economic Approach. *Journal of Political Economy* 76 (2 (March–April)): 169–217.
———. 1971. *The Economics of Discrimination*. 2nd ed. Chicago: University of Chicago Press.
———. 1975. *Human Capital*. 2nd ed. Columbia University Press: New York.
———. 1981. *Treatise on the Family*. Chicago: University of Chicago Press.
———. 1992. Human Capital and the Economy. *Proceedings of the American Philosophical Society* 136 (1 (March)): 85–92.
Block, Walter E. 1980. On Robert Nozick's 'On Austrian Methodology'. *Inquiry* 23 (4, Fall): 397–444.
———. 1999. Austrian Theorizing, Recalling the Foundations: Reply to Caplan. *Quarterly Journal of Austrian Economics* 2 (4): 21–39.
———. 2003. Realism: Austrian vs. Neoclassical Economics, Reply to Caplan. *Quarterly Journal of Austrian Economics* 6 (3, Fall): 63–76.
———. 2007. Reply to Caplan on Austrian Economic. *Methodology, Corporate Ownership & Control* 4 (2, November): 312–317.
———. 2009a. Rejoinder to Hoppe on indifference. *Quarterly Journal of Austrian Economics* 12 (1): 52–59.
———. 2009b. Rejoinder to Machaj on Indifference. *New Perspectives on Political Economy* 5 (1): 65–71.
Block, Walter E., and I.I. William Barnett. 2010. Rejoinder to Hoppe on Indifference, Once Again. *Reason Papers* 32: 141–154.
Block, Walter, William Barnett II, and Stuart Wood. 2002. Austrian Economics, Neoclassical Economics, Marketing and Finance. *The Quarterly Journal of Austrian Economics* 5 (2 (Summer)): 51–66.
Boland, Lawrence. 1979. A Critique of Friedman's Critics. *Journal of Economic Literature* 17 (2): 503–522.
Boulding, K. 1966. *Economic Analysis*. 4th ed. New York: Harper & Row.
Brennan, Geoffrey, and James M. Buchanan. 1985. The Reason of Rules: Constitutional Political Economy. In *The Collected Works of James M. Buchanan*, vol. 10. Indianapolis: Liberty Fund.
Buchanan, James M., and G.F. Thirlby. 1981. *L.S.E. Essays on Cost*. New York: New York University Press.
Buchanan, James M. 1969a. Is Economics the Science of Choice? In *Roads to Freedom: Essays in Honor of Friedrich A. Von Hayek*, ed. E. Streissler, G. Haberler, F. Lutz, and F. Machlup, 47–64. London: Routledge and Kegan Paul.
———. 1969b. *Cost and Choice: An Inquiry into Economic Theory*. Chicago: Markham.
Cachanosky, J. C. 1986. La Ciencia Econ6mica vs. La Economía Matemática II. *Revista Libertas* 4. Mayo.
Callahan, G. 2003. Choice and Preference. *Mises Daily*. February 10. Available at https://mises.org/library/choice-and-preference. Last visited February 18, 2019.
Caplan, Bryan. 1999. The Austrian Search for Realistic Foundations. *Southern Economic Journal* 65 (4, April): 823–838.
———. 2001. Probability, Common Sense, and Realism: A Reply to Hulsmann and Block. *Quarterly Journal of Austrian Economics* 2 (4, summer): 69–86.
———. 2003. Probability and the Synthetic A Priori: A Reply to Block. *Quarterly Journal of Austrian Economics* 6 (3, Fall): 77–83.
———. Undated. *Why I Am Not an Austrian Economist*, Available at http://www.gmu.edu/depts/economics/bcaplan/whyaust.htm
Chiang, A.C. 1984. *Fundamental Methods of Mathematical Economics*. 3rd ed. New York: McGraw-Hill.
Collingwood, Robin G. 2014 (1945). *The Idea of Nature*. Martino Fine Books.
de Finetti, Bruno. 1970. *Theory of Probability*. New York: Wiley.
De Pablo, Juan C. 2017. *Nobelnomics: Vida y Obra de los Ganadores del Nobel de Economía*. Buenos Aires: Sudamericana.

Foss, Nicolai J., and Peter G. Klein. 2012. *Organizing Entrepreneurial Judgment*. Cambridge: Cambridge University Press.
Friedman, Milton, and L.J. Savage. 1948. The Utility Analysis of Choices Involving Risk. *Journal of Political Economy* 56 (4 (August)): 279–304.
Friedman, Milton. 1953 (1966). The Methodology of Positive Economics. In *Essays in Positive Economics*, pp. 3–16, 30–43. University of Chicago Press: Chicago.
Hayek, Friedrich A. 1945. The Use of Knowledge in Society. *The American Economic Review* 35 (4 September): 519–530.
———. 1974. The Pretense of Knowledge. Friedrich A. Hayek's Nobel Prize Lecture, Nobel Prize in Economics, Stockholm, Sweden. In *A Free Market Monetary System and The Pretense of Knowledge*, Auburn: Ludwig Von Mises Institute, 2008.
Herbener, Jeffrey M. 1996. Calculation and the Question of Mathematics. *Review of Austrian Economics* 9 (1): 151–162.
Hoppe, Hans Hermann. 2005. A Note on Preference and Indifference in Economic Analysis. *The Quarterly Journal of Austrian Economics* 8 (4, Winter): 87–91.
Hülsmann, Jörg G. 1999. Economic Science and Neoclassicism. *The Quarterly Journal of Austrian Economics* 2 (4): 1–20.
Kahneman, Daniel, and Amos Tversky. 1979. Prospect Theory: An Analysis of Decision under Risk. *Econometrica* 47 (2 (March)): 263–292.
Kirzner, Israel M. 1963. *Market Theory and the Price System*. New York: D. Van Nostrand Co.
———. 1973. *Competition and Entrepreneurship*. Chicago: University of Chicago Press.
———. 1982. *Method, Process, and Austrian Economics, Essays in Honor of Ludwig Von Mises*. Lexington: Lexington Books.
Klein, P. G. 2012. Austrian and Neoclassical Concepts of Marginal Ulitity. *Mises Wire*, Sep. 28. Available at https://mises.org/blog/austrian-and-neoclassical-concepts-marginal-ulitity. Last visited February 18, 2019.
Lachmann, Ludwig M. 1977. Sir John Hicks as a Neo-Austrian. In *Capital, Expectations, and the Market Process*, ed. Walter E. Grinder. Kansas City: Sheed Andrews and McMeel.
Laibson, David, and John A. List. 2015. Principles of (Behavioral) Economics. *American Economic Review* 105 (5, May): 385–390.
Lancaster, Kelvin J. 1966. A New Approach to Consumer Theory. *Journal of Political Economy* 74 (2, April): 132–157.
Leoni, B., and E. Frola. 1977. On Mathematical Thinking in Economics. *The Journal of Libertarian Studies* 1 (2, Spring): 101–110.
Long, Roderick T. 2006. Realism and Abstraction in Economics: Aristotle and Mises Versus Friedman. *The Quarterly Journal of Austrian Economics* 9 (3, Autumn): 3–23.
Lott, John R., Jr. 1997. In Celebration of Armen Alchian's Eightieth Birthday. In *Uncertainty and Economic Evolution – Essays in Honor of Armen A. Alchian*, ed. John R. Lott Jr. New York: Routledge.
Machaj, Mateusz. 2007. A Praxeological Case for Homogeneity and Indifference. *New Perspectives on Political Economy* 3 (2): 231–238.
Machlup, Fritz. 1956. The Inferiority Complex of the Social Sciences. In *On Freedom and Free Enterprise, Essays in Honor of Ludwig Von Mises*, ed. Mary Senholz , 161–172. Alabama: The Ludwig Von Mises Institute.2008
Markowitz, Harry M. 1952. Portfolio Selection. *The Journal of Finance* 7 (1): 77–91.
McChesney, Fred S. 2013. Behavioral Economics: Old Wine in Irrelevant New Bottles? *Supreme Court Economic Review* 21 (January): 43–76.
McKenzie, Richard B., and Gordon Tullock. 1975. *The New World of Economics*. 6th ed, 2012. New York: Springer.
Menger, Carl. 1871. *Principles of Economics*. Auburn: The Ludwig Von Mises Institute. 2007.
Menger, Karl. 1973. Austrian Marginalism and Mathematical Economics. In *Carl Menger and the Austrian School of Economics*, ed. J.R. Hicks and W. Weber. Oxford: Clarendon Press.
Miller, R.L. 2013. *Economics Today: The Micro View*. 17th ed. Pearson.

Mises, Ludwig V. 1933 (2003). *Epistemological Problems of Economics*. Auburn: Ludwig Von Mises Institute.
———. 1938. (2000). The Equations of Mathematical Economics and the Problem of Economic Calculation in a Socialist State. *The Quarterly Journal of Austrian Economics* 3 (1, Spring): 27–32.
———. 1949. *Human Action – A Treatise on Economics*. San Francisco: Fox & Winkles, 1996.
———. 1953. Comments About the Mathematical Treatment of Economic Problems. Trans. from German Bemerkungen iiber die mathematische Behandlung national konomischer Probleme, in *Studium Generale* VI No 2. 1953, Springer Verlag, Berlin-Goettingen-Heidelberg, by Helena Ratzka. *Journal of Libertarian Studies*, *1*(1), 1977. Great Britain: Pergamon Press, pp. 97–100.
Moorhouse, J.C. 1993. A Critical Review of Mises on Mathematical Economics. *History of Economics Review* 20 (1): 61–74.
Nicholson, W., and C. Snyder. 2011. *Microeconomic Theory: Basic Principles and Extensions*. 11th ed. Mason: South-Western, Cengage Learning.
Nozick, Robert. 1977. On Austrian Methodology. *Synthese* 36: 353–392.
Pfanzagl, J. 1967. Subjective Probability Derived from the Morgenstern-von Neumann Utility Theory. In *Essays in Mathematical Economics In Honor of Oskar Morgenstern*, ed. Martin Shubik, 237–251. Princeton: Princeton University Press.
Pfanzagl, J., in cooperation with Baumann, V, and H. Huber. 1968. Events, Utility and Subjective Probability. In *Theory of Measurement*, 195–220. Wiley.
Popper, Karl R. 1959. *The Logic of Scientific Discovery*. New York: Basic Books.
Rappaport, Steven. 1986. What is Really Wrong with Milton Friedman's Methodology of Economics. *Reason Papers* 11 (Spring): 33–62.
Rosen, Sherwin. 1974. Hedonic Prices and Implicit Markets: Product Differentiation in Pure Competition. *Journal of Political Economy* 82 (1 (January–February)): 34–55.
Rothbard, M. N. 1956 (1997). Toward a Reconstruction of Utility and Welfare Economics. In *On Freedom and Free Enterprise: The Economics of Free Enterprise*, May Senholz. Princeton, N.J.: D. Van Nostrand; reprinted in "The Logic of Action" Vol. I. Lyme, NH: Edward Elgar. pp. 211–254. Available at http://www.mises.org/rothbard/toward.pdf. Last visited January 30, 2018.
Rothbard, M.N. 1957. In Defense of Extreme Apriorism. *Southern Economic Journal* 23: 314–320.
Rothbard, M. N. 1962. *Man, Economy and State*. Scholar's Edition, Second Edition. Ludwig Von Mises Institute. Auburn, 2009.
Rothbard, M.N. 1997. Praxeology: The Methodology of Austrian Economics. In *The Logic of Action One: Method, Money and the Austrian School*. Cheltenham: Edward Elgar.
Samuelson, P.A. 1938. A Note on the Pure Theory of Consumer's Behaviour. *Economica. New Series* 5 (17, February): 61–71.
Savage, Leonard J. 1954. *The Foundations of Statistics*. New York: Wiley.
Schoemaker, Paul J.H. 1982. The Expected Utility Model: Its Variants, Purposes, Evidence and Limitations. *Journal of Economic Literature* 20 (2 (January)): 529–563.
Selgin, George A. 1988. Praxeology and Understanding: An Analysis of the Controversy in Austrian Economics. *Review of Austrian Economics* 2: 19–58.
Simon, Herbert. 1955. A Behavioral Model of Rational Choice. *The Quarterly Journal of Economics* 69 (1): 99–118.
Smith, Adam. 1759 (1853). *The Theory of Moral Sentiments*. London: Henry G. Bohn.
Smith, Vernon. 1999. Reflections on Human Action After 50 Years. *Cato Journal* 19 (2, Fall): 195–209. Cato Institute.
Sotelo, Jose A.M.A., and Walter E. Block. 2014. Indifference Curve Analysis: The Correct and the Incorrect. *Oeconomia Copernicana* 5 (4): S7–S43.
The Economic Times. Undated. *Definition of 'Perfect Competition.'* Available at https://economictimes.indiatimes.com/definition/perfect-competition. Last visited January 9, 2018.
Varian, H.R. 1992. *Microeconomic Analysis*. 3rd ed. New York: Norton.

Von Neumann, John & Morgenstern, Oskar. 1944 (1953). *Theory of Games and Economic Behavior*. 3rd edn. Princeton University Press: Princeton.

Wagner, Richard E. 2017. *James M. Buchanan and Liberal Political Economy. A Rational Reconstruction*. Lanham: Lexington Books.

Winch, Peter. 1990. *The Idea of a Social Science and Its Relation to Philosophy*. 2nd ed. Routledge: London.

Zanotti, G. 1990 (2004). *Fundamentos Filosóficos y Epistemólogicos de la Praxeología*. PhD Dissertation. UNSTA, Tucumán.

Chapter 3
Labor Economics

A Brief Exposition of the Economics of Minimum Wages

> *There is only one efficacious way towards a rise in real wage rates and an improvement of the standard of living of the wage earners: to increase the per-head quota of capital invested.*
>
> Ludwig Von Mises (1912, 424)

Abstract This chapter offers a critique not only of raising government enforced minimum wages, but allowing them to continue in existence. This law makes it impossible for some unskilled workers to obtain employment, and raises no one's wage in the long run. Minimum wages are defended, primarily, on the basis of an ethical (in our view, mistaken) point of view, not on economic grounds. Here we analyze the economics of wage determination, and explain why minimum wages thwart the process of increasing capital formation and thus real wages. Hence, since wages are the result of discounted marginal revenue products, any intervention to artificially increase them not only ends up harming workers on the margin (those whose productivity is below levels mandated by law), but also distorts the labor market, capital allocation, and economic growth and development.

Keywords Minimum wage law · Unemployment · Justice

JEL Code J64

This chapter is based on our paper Aguilar, Kevin; Futerman, Alan G., and Block, Walter E. 2020. "On Legally Enforced Minimum Wages". *MEST Journal*, Vol. 8 No. 1, January, pp. 1–6. Available at https://mest.meste.org/MEST_1_2020/15_01.pdf?fbclid=IwAR1rfRDfc4XqltqoImIBOtMnCwNhv9zmJTqKYiCjC_NZmMZtvssliPEfIi8 (last visited April 22, 2021).

A. G. Futerman, W. E. Block, *The Austro-Libertarian Point of View*, https://doi.org/10.1007/978-981-16-4691-1_3

3.1 Introduction

Minimum wage laws have been, are, and most likely will continue to be a burning issue. As politicians look forward to attaining voters, and responding to their demands, minimum wage laws are a preferred policy. Essentially, it puts them in a suitable position: for those industries where employees' wages effectively go up, politicians can take credit; and for those who remain unemployed, that is explained as just a market phenomenon that entails the requirement of even more intervention, that is, policies supposedly aimed at promoting more work. However, are minimum wage laws *really* beneficial? This is the question we will try to answer in this chapter.

Hence, Sect. 3.2 looks at this law from an ethical perspective while Sect. 3.3 touches upon the corporate/private minimum wage and its characteristics. Section 3.4 deals with the minimum wage on a theoretical level. We conclude in Sect. 3.5.

3.2 Appeal to Ethics

Minimum wage laws are primarily defended as a *good* policy. Hence, opposing them is usually seen as immoral and unsensitive. Therefore, since this debate is surrounded by ethical considerations, it is important to discuss them and their appeal to emotion.

A growing trend among the comparatively unskilled and unexperienced is that large corporations represent an evil and lead to growing wage inequality in the nation. How can it be just that a corporate CEO earns over a thousand times more than the struggling factory worker who has to support his family? Is this great disparity not an example of the failings of the capitalist state?

The proper way of analyzing the subject is by resorting to methodological individualism. Instead of decrying such a disparity, we should focus first and foremost on what factors determine salary. And that, as is clearly shown by economic theory, is productivity. The reason LeBron James earns so much money is that, due to his efforts, his employer adds substantively to his bottom line. How much money does LeBron James make? Easily the equivalent of a well-paid CEO, or more. And, yet, for some strange reason, no one ever complains about the multiple of his pay vis a vis the man who sweeps the basketball court after the game. Maybe it is not so strange. Perhaps this is due to the fact that even the meanest intelligence can appreciate his contribution to society. Or, more specifically, the basketball fan can appreciate this splendid athlete's contribution to *him*. That of the CEO is possibly more difficult to appreciate.

The reason a CEO is worth so much is because according to the market, he, too, brings home the bacon. Both contribute great value to a company, and if their salaries did not reflect that primordial fact, competitors would snap them up, the both of them, and pay them well. Yet, the comparatively rich CEO is not the person we are concerned about earning a living wage. A living wage being defined as the minimum amount that an individual would need to sustain themselves with housing and food.

So, let's introduce two characters who will help us demonstrate the value of the individual to the market. Sam and Max are both 18 years old and work at a generic store. We know nothing of their work ethic and neither have any previous experience so they are both hired at the minimum wage,[1] for this example we will say $8 dollars an hour. Two years later Sam makes $8.50 an hour and Max makes $16 dollars an hour. Is this unjust? What makes Max so special? Could it be that Max was always at work on time, was cleanly dressed, satisfied customers, cheerfully obeyed the manager's instructions? What if Sam was a decent employee but just didn't do anything to stand out? The generic store has to have valued Max more and raised his wages in order to reflect his increased productivity. Now let us change the scenario so that after a year of the two being employed, a new $10 minimum wage was enacted. At the end of year two Max still earns $16 dollars an hour while Sam has lost his job. This is no fault of Sam's and the generic store would still like to have him employed at the $8.50-hour price.

Some might argue that the owner is being stingy and that he could surely pay Sam that $1.50 an hour from his own funds, or, at least from Max's pay. However, if he does the former, once too often, he will go broke, and not be in a position to hire anyone. If he does the latter, his competitor will offer Max $16 an hour and woo him away from his present employer. The company must do what is competitively best in order to remain in business. And, also, there is the phenomenon of opportunity cost: the return on the company's invested capital needs to be comparatively higher than the other considered investment alternatives, otherwise it would be liquidated, and the capital invested somewhere else. Labor costs affect, just like any other cost, the company's net profit. Artificially increasing them only reduces return on invested capital and may end up affecting the entire operation altogether.

From a libertarian perspective, a minimum wage policy also violates the rule of freedom of association. If an employer and employee agree on a deal, it should not be the government's role to intervene. If at $6 an hour an employer wants to hire someone to sit in chair to stare at paint drying and an employee accepts, it should be a legitimate decision. At $7.25 the employer will no longer value someone staring at the wall; he will then have to deal with looking at an empty chair. Sam would rather work for $6.50 or even $6 dollars again if it means he still would be employed. Jobs are lost that would have been created or retained if the government did not interfere in the interaction of these two consenting parties.

From a utilitarian perspective it also makes sense to allow for freedom of contract enforced by the ethics that is upheld by society. If the majority of customers of a business are upset at a decision in the company, there will tend to be repercussions. There will be critical news articles, people in the industry cutting ties,

[1] The idea that the minimum wage does not have negative effects on employment can be traced in its modern form to Card and Krueger (1994). A critique can be seen in Neumark and Wascher (2000). This debate continued in several works, among which can be seen in Dube et al. (2010), Neumark et al. (2014), Jardim et al. (2017), Harasztosi and Lindner (2019), Allegretto et al. (2018).

consumers who boycott the product/service, and investors who start disinvesting, and even to trade against[2] and thus devalue the stock of the company.

We invest heavily in private charity and help those who are downtrodden in a community. This is done for the benefit and good feeling that is created and supported thereof (as Adam Smith (1759 [1853]) explained, by *sympathy*). Employers want to keep their employees happy and productive, this is why we see other forms of payment in addition to wages. Hence, companies will hold retreats, buy comfortable chairs, put in a fish tank, etc. They do so in order to retain talented employees. To be sure, there are also miserable unhappy dead-end jobs that physically and emotionally drain their employees. For instance, picking up the garbage. But it is not the case that these jobs will cease to exist anytime soon. To the extent these job slots are considered onerous, additional pay will be offered to compensate workers.

3.3 Corporate/Private Minimum Wage

There are politicians who point to large corporations providing their own private minimum wage as indicative of support for legislation mandating this state of affairs. The difference between a privately undertaken minimum wage and publicly enforced one is significant for multiple reasons. Whereas the latter creates unemployment for unskilled workers, the former creates *competitive* benefits for a company. Additionally, and with respect to the ethical implications involved (especially from the perspective of libertarian philosophy) the public minimum wage is forced upon a corporation, while a private one is voluntary.

Let us look at an example. Ikea freely decided to incorporate a minimum wage of $10.76 for all its U.S. employees (Hellman 2014; Jamieson 2015). Now, that is just one way of putting the matter. A more accurate one would be merely to say that this company engaged in a wage *increase*. In contrast, a real minimum wage is compulsory. To violate it is to incur criminal penalties. On the other hand, if Ikea lowered its wage, as long as it remained above the level required by law, it would suffer no legal punishment.

Moreover, unlike the public counterpart this private minimum wage may have lucrative effects for the company. A higher base wage for the company renders present and potential employees more eager to work there. This could mean a more motivated staff which would attain for itself a competitive advantage. The marginal productivity of the workers employed might possibly rise as a result of this practice. Hence, the reasons for establishing a voluntary floor for wages inside a company do *still* take into account the essential factor at work when determining wages: discounted marginal revenue products.

In contrast, a mandatory law entails none of these benefits, because it has no effect on the incentive structure implicit in the change of compensation. This is the

---

[2] Sell short.

answer to the common charge that the same beneficial effects of a private voluntary wage increase would be registered if it is instead mandated by law.

3.4 Wages and the Minimum Wage

Market prices guide a rational allocation of resources (Mises 1949 [1996]). Minimum wages are, indeed, a price. If they are imposed on, labor, in this case, they do not rationally allocate society's resources.

As the price of a factor of production, the analysis of wages is not different than that of other factors. That is, their price responds to the theory of imputation. In other words, the level of wages depends on the service produced by the employee. The more homogeneous a specific work is, then the less scarce, and the less valuable in relative terms it is. Thus, the wage is lower. The opposite happens when it is extremely specialized, and highly scarce, again, other things equal.

In technical terms, wages are a reflection of discounted marginal revenue products (Block 1990). As such, the key is which product they produce. To dissociate the final product (hence, the marginal revenue product) from the work of labor, is to turn the concept of wage meaningless in economic terms. Where does the value of labor come *from*? If it is not arbitrary, then it stems from marginal revenue product. Since productive processes take time, and time preference is indeed relevant, then, we need to discount it.[3] And what, in turn, is this based upon? Discounted marginal revenue product (DMRP) is predicated upon the quantity and quality of the capital equipment with which labor works.

For instance, Mexicans, *in* that country, have low DMRPs, and hence low wages, since the sophistication, and quantity of the capital with which they work is low. When they arrive at the US, their internal human capital (Becker 1964) changes not one whit, but the machinery and tools available certainly does. And why, in turn, is there more and better capital available north of the Rio Grande rather than south? This is explained by the different level of economic freedom prevailing in the two countries (e.g., Gwartney et al. 1996).

Proponents of minimum wage laws often claim that workers and business owners do not negotiate on the basis of equal power. However, in reality, workers do not face any such asymmetric situation. It is not, as the cartoons like to show, the fat capitalist facing a poor wage earner. The real situation is that workers compete with other workers for a specific position, and at the same time, employers compete with other employers in order to employ a given worker. In that sense, in terms of Böhm Bawek's (1888 [1930]) price formation dynamics, wages are the result of, like any other market price in this context, bilateral competition and marginal pairs.

The only counter argument to this is labor monopsony or oligopsony. This is a very weak argument, with the possible exception for highly skilled scientists,

[3] That is an important difference between the neoclassical and Austrian approach (Block 1990).

engineers, chemists, who have only one or a very few potential employers in their narrow fields. However, their salaries are way above and beyond minimum wage levels, so this possible counter example is not apropos.[4]

Therefore, the relative scarcity of labor supply in a specific industry, with respect to its demand elsewhere, is one determinant of wage rates. And the bidding by employers takes into account, then, discounted marginal revenue products.

More specifically, the supply of labor in any industry depends on the demand for labor of competing industries. Thus, when a worker can earn *x* in industry *A*, while industry *B* now offers $x + 1$, then he will tend to leave *A* for *B*. The impetus for this can either be a "push" from the employee's side, who seeks greener fields, or a "pull" from other employers, who are now "raiding" the firm that pays inordinately low wages.

So, if *B* wants to attract workers, it will have to increase wages. And, of course, the higher the quantity and quality of capital in any area, the greater the wages, other things equal, due to competition for workers among employers. This is why cities tend to have higher wages, in relative terms, than the countryside.

Why would *B* increase wages in the first place? This is because they see a profit opportunity: the gap between production costs and sale price, always suitably discounted.

If industry *B* produces 100 units of product *z*, and has one worker whose wage is $100, then each unit of *z* costs $1 of labor. However, *B* acquires capital in order to enhance its production process. Now, the worker produces 200 units. Posit that labor costs associated with the production of *z* were reduced by 50%! Hence, industry *B* may very well increase the wages it pays to its worker, in order to preclude him from going elsewhere. It may attract another worker in order to produce more with the new capital, for instance 400 units. How does it attract another worker? By increasing its wage to $x + 1$ or more (*x* is the wage of the new worker in the non-*B* industry).

Observe that everyone wins, when capital accumulation takes place. But minimum wage laws disrupt this process, since they negatively impact every step of the previously explained virtuous circle. It creates fewer jobs available (workers' DMRPs do not justify higher wages), fewer companies are created since they cannot sustain themselves (or returns are deemed too low relative to alternatives), job benefits decrease because employers tend to reduce non-monetary compensations (vacation, health insurance, etc.), and job desirability is reduced, because of other cheaper labor conditions apart from wage are established in order to sustain the company.

Further, there is an incentive to invest in automation, because this law renders it *relatively* cheaper. Minimum wages, then, paradoxically (although logically) end up

[4] For a critique of monopsony in general, see Block and Barnett (2009).

benefiting the highly skilled, rather than those with lesser skills, precisely those who the minimum wage was presumably[5] set to protect.

Minimum wage supporters often resort to the argument that those jobs which pay low wages are bad from a moral perspective. Not so, not so. These laws will rather create a *lower* wage, of *zero*, for all those workers whose productivity falls below the level stipulated by this legislation. If by pure enactment we could actually raise wages, why not advocate $100,000 an hour? Then, we would all be rich, beyond the dreams of avarice. Supporters of minimum wage laws fail to respond to this objection. Subconsciously, they do know and understand that there is a relation between productivity and wage rates, although they believe that small, compulsory marginal changes to low wages (thus establishing minimum wages) barely affect the employment situation of low scale workers. In reality, because it affects precisely those on the *margin*, legislators do not pay attention to those who are rendered unemployable.

3.5 Conclusion

As we have seen throughout this chapter, minimum wage laws are harmful both in theory and practice. They are neither moral nor practical. As a matter of libertarian philosophy, they override and set aside otherwise voluntary associations between consenting adults. And as a matter of Austrian economics, they intervene in prices, thereby affecting resource allocation and the incentive structure of wages in the labor market, thus creating unemployment for those that need work the most.

What is then the best way to increase real wages? Reduce taxes and regulations, which in turn increases capital accumulation, production and ultimately reduces prices. Eliminate taxes on labor. Abolish the welfare state, that distorts incentives to work, accumulate capital, and produce. In sum, free markets, not minimum wage laws.

Bibliography

Allegretto, S., A. Godoey, C. Nadler, and M. Reich. 2018. *The New Wave of Local Minimum Wage Policies: Evidence from Six Cities*. Center on Wage and Employment Dynamics. Available at https://irle.berkeley.edu/the-new-wave-of-local-minimum-wage-policies-evidence-from-six-cities/. Last visited September 23, 2019.

Becker, G. 1964. *Human Capital*. New York: The National Bureau of Economic Research.

[5]There is a heavy emphasis on this word, since in point of fact, the most vociferous supporters and beneficiaries of this pernicious legislation are labor unions, who are in competition with low wage labor. How better to drive them from the labor market than to reduce, by law, their ability to compete with higher skilled union labor?

Block, W.E. 1990. The Discounted Marginal Value Product – Marginal Value Product Controversy: A Note. *Review of Austrian Economics* IV: 199–207. Available at http://www.mises.org/journals/rae/pdf/rae4_1_7.pdf. Last visited September 23, 2019. Reprinted as Block, W. E., (1994). On Marginal Productivity Theory. In *The Elgar Companion to Austrian Economics* (Peter Boettke, ed., Hants, England: Edward Elgar, pp. 123–130).

———. 2015. Abolish the Minimum Wage. *Lew Rockwell*, September 7. Available at https://www.lewrockwell.com/2015/09/walter-e-block/abolish-the-minimum-wage/. Last visited September 23, 2019.

Block, W.E., and W. Barnett. 2009. Monopsony Theory. *American Review of Political Economy* 7 (1/2): 67–109. Available at https://sites.bemidjistate.edu/arpejournal/wp-content/uploads/sites/2/2015/12/v7n1-2-block-barnett.pdf. Last visited September 23, 2019.

Böhm Bawerk, E.V. 1888 [1930]. *The Positive Theory of Capital*. G.E. Stechert & Co: New York.

Card, D., and A.B. Krueger. 1994. Minimum Wages and Employment: A Case Study of the Fast-Food Industry in New Jersey and Pennsylvania. *The American Economic Review* 84 (4): 772–793.

Cooper, D., and D. Hall. 2012. How Raising the Federal Minimum Wage Would Help Working Families and Give the Economy a Boost. *Economic Policy Institute*, August 14. Available at https://www.epi.org/publication/ib341-raising-federal-minimum-wage/. Last visited September 23, 2019.

Dube, A.T., W.T. Lester, and M. Reich. 2010. Minimum Wage Effects Across State Borders: Estimates Using Contiguous Counties. *The Review of Economics and Statistics* 92 (4): 945–964.

Gwartney, J., R.W. Lawson, and W.E. Block. 1996. *Economic Freedom of the World, 1975–1995*. Vancouver: The Fraser Institute.

Harasztosi, P., and A. Lindner. 2019. Who Pays for the Minimum Wage? *The American Economic Review* 109 (8): 2693–2727.

Hellman, M. 2014. IKEA Is Going to Raise Minimum Wages in All Its U.S. Stores. *Time*, June 26. Available at https://time.com/2926270/ikea-minimum-wage-living-wage-calculator/. Last visited September 23, 2019.

Jamieson, Dave. 2015. Ikea's Minimum Wage Hike Was So Successful, It's Raising Wages Again. *HuffPost*, June 24. Available at https://www.huffpost.com/entry/ikea-minimum-wage_n_7648804. Last visited April 23, 2021.

Jardim, E., M.C. Long, R. Plotnik, E. van Inwegen, J. Vigdor, and H. Wething. 2017. *Minimum Wage Increases, Wages, and Low-Wage Employment: Evidence from Seattle*. NBER, Working Paper No. 23532.

Mises, Ludwig Von. 1912 [1953]. *The Theory of Money and Credit*. New Haven: Yale University Press.

———. 1949 (1996). *Human Action – A Treatise on Economics*. San Francisco: Fox & Winkles

Neumark, D., and W. Wascher. 2000. Minimum Wages and Employment: A Case Study of the Fast-Food Industry in New Jersey and Pennsylvania: Comment. *The American Economic Review* 90 (5): 1362–1396.

Neumark, D., J.M.I. Salas, and W. Wascher. 2014. Revisiting the Minimum Wage Employment Debate: Throwing Out the Baby with the Bathwater? *Industrial and Labor Relations Review*, ILR Review, Cornell University, ILR School, 67 (2.5): 608–648.

Smith, Adam. 1759 (1853). *The Theory of Moral Sentiments*. London: Henry G. Bohn.

Chapter 4
Macroeconomics

Austrian Business Cycle Theory: Traditional and Fiscal

> *Austrian capital theory amounts to a theory of intertemporal coordination; Austrian business-cycle theory (that is, the analysis of the effects of an exogenous monetary expansion in the light of Austrian capital theory) amounts to a theory of intertemporal discoordination.*
>
> Roger Garrison (1989, 24)

Abstract When governments accounted for a small proportion of the economy, the Austrian *Business* Cycle theory (ABCT) was apropos because private enterprises comprised the lion's share of commercial interactions. But, of late, in more and more countries, the share of the economy accounted for by the state has increased, and that by business firms, less and less. Thus, it is time, it is past time, to introduce a new concept, Austrian Government Cycle Theory (AGCT). The present chapter is an attempt to move us in that direction.

Keywords Business cycle · Austrian economics · Inflation · Depression

JEL Code E14

This chapter is based on our paper Futerman, Alan G.; Barnett II, William and Block, Walter E. 2020. "Austrian Government Cycle Theory". *World of Ideas and Politics*, Vol. 19, pp. 9–28. Available at https://www.ukw.edu.pl/download/58278/01._Alan_G._Futerman,_William_Barnett_II,_Walter_E._Block.pdf (last visited April 22, 2021).

A. G. Futerman, W. E. Block, *The Austro-Libertarian Point of View*, https://doi.org/10.1007/978-981-16-4691-1_4

4.1 Introduction

Cycle theory is a fundamental subject within economic theory and analysis. Particularly since it is the greatest malady the economic science can be used to prevent, cycles have been studied from a wide range of different perspectives. As defenders of the Austrian business cycle theory, we support the idea that it is the government, through the manipulation of money and credit via a central bank, that is primarily to blame for boom and bust cycles.

However, when Ludwig von Mises and Friedrich Hayek developed this theory, governments had a relatively small weight with respect to GDP. Now, this proportion (taking into account federal, state and city governments) often rises above 50% in the developed world.

We present in this chapter the theory that, although ABCT is still valid, in the sense that manipulation of money and credit remains the fundamental cyclical factor, a government of such a scale and scope has a similar impact. Hence, business is no longer the main character in cycles, but the government now is.

We explain our position in Sect. 4.2. Section 4.3 deals with government interventions into the macro-economy. We conclude in Sect. 4.4.

4.2 Government, Not Business

In order to better present our main hypothesis, let us first briefly review ABCT.[1] This theory is, as its name indicates, a *business* cycle theory. Not just a theory on cyclical economic fluctuations. As such, the main question it purports to answer is: Why do businesses err in their investment decisions, first generating a boom, and then a bust? Why is it that all (or most) of them fail at the same time? And why is this a cyclical reality of economic history? To answer this question, ABCT focuses in that which is the core of any business: resource allocation. But what does this mean?

Capital is the blood of the economic system. As such, its investment in specific projects implies that, due to its scarcity, other alternatives will not be pursued. What is it that indicates which projects to pursue or not, then? Naturally, it is the rate of return. But a required return is a function of alternative investments. In other words, it depends upon the opportunity cost. Why invest capital in project *A* if project *B*, of a similar matirity and risk, yields a higher return? That would be economically

---

[1] For more on this see Bagus (2003), Bagus et al. (2013), Barnett and Block (2005, 2008, 2009a), Baxendale (2010), Block and Caplan (2008), Block and Garschina (1996), Block and Posner (2008), Davidson (2008), Davidson and Block (2011), French (1992 [2009]), Hanke (2008), Hayek (1931, 1933 [1966]), Hazlitt (1979), Hollenback (2013, 2014), Hoppe (1994), Hoppe et al. (1998), Howden (2013), Huerta de Soto (1995, 1998, 2006, 2010, 2012, 2014, 2018), Hülsmann (1996, 1998, 2000, 2002; 2003; 2008), Kirzner (1990), Machlup (1940), Mises (1912), Mulligan (2006), Murphy (2010), Oppers (2002), Polleit (2010), Reisman (1996, 2009), Rothbard (1962 [1991]; 1963 [2008]; 1962 [2009]; 1962 [1991]), Salerno (2010a, b; 2011, 2012), White (2008a, b; 2010).

irrational. In turn, entrepreneurs can bid for capital in the market at the pervailing rate of interest. Any project that yields a higher return than the interest rate will be viable, whereas those below the rate of interest will not. Hence, the purpose of entrepreneurs allocating capital to investment projects is to obtain return maximally higher than the prevailing interest rate.

Interest rates, in turn, are the price that coordinates intertemporal consumption and investment decisions by economic agents. They will therefore indicate not only what investments are to be made, but also for which time horizons. A reduction (increase) in consumption and increase (reduction) in savings will promote a lower (higher) interest rate that will in turn incentivize longer (shorter) term projects. This can be easily seen by analyzing the reaction of different investment projects when the interest rate changes. For instance, when it falls, longer term investment projects will see their present values increase more than proportionally than shorter term projects.[2]

But what happens when interest rates are set by a central bank, instead of being determined by market phenomena? This essential price will then diverge from that which would have prevailed in the unhampered market (the natural rate of interest). Hence, it will no longer reflect consumption and saving decisions by economic agents, and hence properly coordinate resource allocation in time. Thus, an artificial reduction in interest rates creates an expansion of money and credit and makes longer term projects (more capital intensive[3]) more attractive. The structure of production will therefore change. But the key to the entire analysis is that the underlying consumption and saving preferences *do not* alter.

Eventually, the divergence between longer and shorter term projects is evident when different projects compete for the same resources, bidding up the prices of the factors of production. Money and credit expansion also creates either bubbles that will burst (as in the housing market before the Great Recession), or an increase in prices at the consumer level (as during the 70s in the US, or in the most extreme cases, hyperinflations of the kind of the Weimar Republic during the 20s). But essentially, any inflation of the money supply will create distortion of relative prices. Therefore, waste and malinvestment will occur.

But if entrepreneurs have the *alertness* (Kirzner 1999) of identifying and creating profit opportunities, why are they not aware of this process? That is because, as with any other relevant variable treated by economic analysis since 1871 (Menger), the key is what goes on at the *margin*. It is not necessary that all entrepreneurs get caught in these dynamics, but only those that, at the margin, will act on the basis of the artifically low interest rates and allocate resources and capital based on the basis of it.[4] Hence, the pernicious effects of the manipulation of money and credit cannot

---

[2] Duration and convexity are of course relevant for this financial dimension. See also Cwik (2008).

[3] Or higher order.

[4] An alternative explanation is provided by Block (2001). It is based on the claim that the government, in artificially lowering interest rates, is in effect subsidizing entrepreneurs into investing in more roundabout methods of production than would be warranted by the unchanged saving and consumption ratios of the public.

be stopped, and history itself repeats over and over again. As Kindleberger (1989) characterizes this phenomenon: manias, panics and crashes. The cause of the business cycle, then, is the manipulation of money and credit, i.e. government intervention.

With this introduction, we are now ready to introduce our present hypothesis. At a time when the government accounts for so large a portion of the economy, it is no longer appropriate to talk strictly about a *business* cycle. The scope of this section of the economy has become more and more marginal compared to the gargantuan size and operation of the government. Of course, when such boundary is crossed[5] is a difficult question to answer. However, we can easily see[6] that when the government accounts for 50% and more of GDP, then its influence becomes beyond doubt of extreme importance.

In this situation, the private sector that still exists is affected by the government in both a direct and an indirect way. Thus, the government is the main character in the cycle, not business. It channels the resources from debt and taxes to the sectors determined by the bureaucracy, and the distortion of relative prices and the structure of production no longer comes solely from monetary manipulations which are channeled to the private sector through the financial system (although this could also happen at the same time, via the monetary expansion of the Central Bank in order to finance government deficits, or by the nature of fractional reserves[7]), but through this very same allocation of resources directed by the government (Block 2019).

It could be said that such distortion always comes from the government, whether through monetary expansions or contractions, price controls of various sorts, or public spending sustained by taxes. But the central point we are now making is that in the classical case of the Austrian business cycle theory, the government is the *exogenous* agent that promotes the distortion of relative prices through the manipulation of money (Salerno 1987), credit and interest rates (Salerno 2016) which in turn impacts the private sector. In sharp contrast in the second case (bigger government spending), it is the very same *government* that promotes such distortion and channels it, therefore leaving the private sector as a marginal agent certainly with a *less* considerable importance than years gone by or the government on this regard. The government thus turns into the most relevant spending agent, because of the magnitude of its direct influence in the market, thus presenting itself as an *endogenous* agent.

In this regard it is important to highlight that both Mises and Hayek developed their main cycle theories in the context of government spending of 5–15% of GDP, with far less direct regulation and allocation of resources than at present. Moreover, in the case of the earlier economy, all sectors often make mistakes in their

[5] See on this Block and Barnett (2008).

[6] Easily, at least, in comparison to when Mises and Hayek developed their theory. With a government weight of 10% in GDP, that means (for a weight of 50% now) a 400% increase.

[7] See Bagus and Howden (2010; 2011).

commercial decisions at the same time,[8] as the result of central bank interest rates manipulation. This, in turn, in the modern era is also due to the fact that a large part of the productive and the consumption sectors depends directly or indirectly on government resource allocation. The central point is the same: the distortion of relative prices and the structure of production. In this case we characterize the situation as a *Government Cycle Theory, with an Austrian Base*. Let us examine its role in more detail.

4.3 Real Interventions by Government

The purpose of the interventions falling into the real category is not, in general, overall stability, but rather, the reallocation of resources to politically favored uses and the redistribution of wealth to powerful and/or politically-favored groups; that is, these interventions are of the types of government activity associated with the concept of "rent-seeking."[9] Although it is true that there are still some who would maintain that the governmental budget; i.e., fiscal policy, is the primary tool of stabilization (Lee and Sung 2007), and that the levels of governmental expenditures and taxes, and the consequent deficits and surpluses, are the primary determinants of such things as inflation, interest rates, and unemployment, etc., because the evidence of the real world seems to refute it, the credibility of this position among professional economists continues to be in decline.

These real interventions are essentially microeconomic; that is, they consist of governmental actions which are intended to cause more or less specific results in particular markets and/or for specific groups of people. Such governmental actions can work only to the extent that they cause individuals to alter their actions to conform to the pattern of behavior necessary to bring about the intended results. The specific actions people take depend on their individual (subjective) values and perceptions of the alternatives available to them. As a result, real interventions take the form of alterations of, and succeed to the extent that they do "correctly" alter, the set of alternatives available in the particular markets or targeted groups of people intended to be affected.[10]

Thus, any attempt to understand the (re)allocational/(re)distributional ramifications of such interventions requires a detailed examination of the particulars of each case. Real interventions, however, and, for the purposes of this chapter, of more importance, also affect the macro-stability of the economic system. But analysis of

---

[8] Rothbard (1969) refers to this as the "cluster of error."

[9] For a critique of this appellation, but certainly not of the phenomenon it represents, see Block (2000a, b, 2002, 2015), DiLorenzo and Block (2017).

[10] The matter of governmental attempts to alter people's actions by attempting to alter their values raises difficult issues of moral and political philosophy; and, the consequences of such actions for the most fundamental of human values and rights are of the first magnitude of importance. This is particularly relevant for the libertarian philosophy.

the consequences for business cycles of such interventions does not require, fortunately, a detailed examination of each one. Rather, for this purpose, real interventions may be analyzed according to the way they interfere with the functioning of the market process.

There is a strong parallel between ABCT and AGCT. In the former case, government artificially lowers the interest rate (in relation to the natural rate), moving the market in the direction of more roundabout projects than would be justified by the time preference of the marginal person. But, this phenomenon[11] has not changed, certainly not as a result of the exogenous activities of the central bank in artificially lowering interest rates from the levels that would otherwise have prevailed. Instead, the people's saving and loan decisions are as they were before this state intervention into the economy. Thus, there is a "tension" between market prices, the interest rate in this case, and the desires of the populace.

A parallel situation takes place with regard to AGCT. Here, let us suppose, the government places its big fat thumb not in the direction of longer-term projects vis a vis shorter run ones, but in favor of coal (Block 2019), and thus against all other goods and services. The bureaucrats either subsidize coal, and or penalize alternative energy sources. But the demand conditions have not changed. The market still demands coal in the old proportions, compared to other products. Thus, there is a similar "tension" in the AGCT case as well. And, since coal is a capital-intensive industry, resource allocation to it certainly implies more capital invested in longer-term, more roundabout processes of production. The structure pf production changes here, then, too.

Real interventions affect both phases of the cycle: they impact the duration and intensity of the boom by changing the volume of fiat money/credit created and the specific uses to which it is put; they also affect the duration and severity of the contraction by interfering with the adjustment process (determining which adjustments take place and when they occur).

Real interventions do not "just happen". Rather they are governmental responses to perceived problems. The causes of the problems are perceived, virtually always and everywhere, to be the same: for sellers, insufficient demands for their goods or resources; and, for buyers, insufficient supplies of the goods or resources sought. Insufficient demands are the cause of sellers' problems in the sense that they think that their problems would be eliminated if they could but sell their goods or resources in greater volumes and/or at higher prices. Similarly, insufficient supplies are the cause of buyers' problems in the sense that they think that their problems would be solved if they could but buy goods or resources at lower prices.

Of course, these are the real problems only if one takes the odd positions that: (1) re sellers' problems, buyers should act not in accordance with their own values and the opportunities available, but in the interests of the sellers; and, (2) re buyers'

[11] Let us make a clarification here. This is often called a time preference "rate" in the scholarly literature of ABCT. But we eschew this verbiage since there is no real "rate" of preference here, any more than there is a "rate" of preference for vanilla vis a vis chocolate ice cream. Nevertheless, this is the way the concept is presented. See on this Barnett and Block (2011).

problems, sellers should act not in accordance with their own values and the opportunities available, but in the interests of the buyers. If these positions are rejected, the real difficulties are seen to be: for sellers, mismatches between their supplies and buyers demands, requiring for their correction changes in the sellers' actions; and, for buyers, mismatches between their demands and sellers supplies, requiring for their correction changes in the buyers' actions. The requisite changes for buyers are changes in their demands; the requisite changes for sellers are alterations in their supplies, which usually involve changes in production.

But most people are more concerned about the markets in which they sell their goods and/or resources, especially their labor services, than about the markets in which they are buyers. That is, for most people, the role of producer is more important than that of consumer, in the sense that the events in the markets in which they sell their goods or resources dominate the events in other markets in terms of the impacts upon their material well-being. Thus, most people perceive the key problem to be one of insufficient demand (Shades of Lord Keynes! Where is Major Douglas when we need him?). We all tend to be more concentrated as sellers (of labor services) than as buyers. In our latter role, we consume literally tens of thousands of items. Just take a stroll through a modern supermarket. In contrast, most of us hold one job in a single occupation; it is the rare person who is spread more thin than that.

Although from each seller's perspective the problem is insufficient demand for his goods and or resources, in reality it is the mismatch between what the seller is producing and what the buyers want. Nevertheless, each thinks the solution is increased demand for his own goods and/or resources. Of course, even if producers' problems did consist of insufficient demand, this would be relative, not absolute. Thus, no general solution would exist as it is impossible for every producer to experience an increase in demand relative to the other sellers. Thus, any governmental intervention that "solves" the problem for one individual or group of people necessarily makes the problems of at least some others worse. That is, state intervention creates a zero-sum game.

Nevertheless, people do seek the assistance of governments to solve these sorts of problems, and the bureaucrats do respond. Attempts to diminish the (perceived) demand problems of particular groups of producers affect the course of the business cycle because they inevitably hinder the adjustment process whereby the mismatches between demands and production are eliminated. Here, then, mismatches are enhanced.

The producers' problems arise when the pattern of demand changes. This occurs when the monetary/credit expansion decelerates, and resource owners attempt to spend their decreased incomes in accord with their unchanged values.[12] If a monetary/credit expansion has reached significant proportions the consequential adjustments will have to be large, involving great losses for many producers. For those experiencing a reduction in demand, the only alternatives available in the market are painful: price and/or quantity reductions, and the acceptance of the attendant losses.

[12] We are now back to ABCT.

Each such producer thinks that an increase in demand for his goods and/or resources would solve the problem. But this is precisely the opposite of what is required on a systemic level.

Of course, a systemic effect takes place during this phase. Since the reduction in prices affects the price level downward, the real value of debt and liabilities increase. This, in turn, exposes companies and households to a greater financial burden, and in relation to their assets, it worsens their situation, i.e. what they sell is valued less. While their debts are nominally unaltered, they increase in real terms.

Hence, this dynamic feedback: the downward path of the cycle during the bust. It is, however, necessary. This is so because the process of liquidation forces companies and households to reduce the prices of their assets, and hence accommodate their values to the new situation. In other words, the price of assets needs to reflect their new discounted future cash flows.[13] Once this process takes place, assets get cheaper and it is profitable again to invest and allocate capital, which takes the economy out of the crisis.

There is, of course, another alternative: governmental intervention. With great regularity, producers finding themselves in such a position seek, and, also with great regularity, receive public sector assistance (bailouts constitute real intervention). Such assistance is designed to maintain or increase the incomes of the favored producers. Although the details vary greatly from one such assistance program to the next, the primary approach used is to artificially bolster demand for the favored groups' goods and/or resources, and/or artificially reduce their costs. Such interventions take diverse forms, the most important of which are: direct and indirect purchases by governments, e.g., the food stamp program; direct subsidies to producers; indirect subsidies to producers, e.g., bail-outs of producers' creditors; subsidized credit for customers; and, restriction of competition (with regulations at the local level, or with tariffs and quotas on international trade). Such interventions make it possible for the affected producers to avoid the market alternatives: price and/or quantity reductions. This prolongs the agony.[14]

Because in the real world supplies are not perfectly elastic, sound adjustments involve, sooner or later, some price changes. Thus, real interventions slow down the structure of prices from adjusting to people's unchanged time, goods and services preferences values.

Of course, such interventions thwart the real demands of the people based upon their values, substituting instead, artificial demands predicated upon political power. This process allows vendors to maintain the misallocation of resources begun in the boom. The longer the boom continues due to successive, and more rapid, increases in money/credit, the greater the misallocations, this is an ABCT insight. But the nature of the assistance is, precisely, the thwarting of the adjustments required to return the economy to a sound basis (correct allocation of resources); here, we

---

[13] These decrease for two reasons, a reduced cash flow, and a higher interest (discount) rate.

[14] Woods (2009) points out that the depressions of 1921 and 1929 were initially roughly equal in terms of severity. However, there was little government intervention in the former case, and the depression phrase was shallow and of short duration. The opposite occurred in the latter case.

wheel in the AGCT counterpart analysis: the greater the number of producers seeking and receiving assistance, also the more misallocation.

In the context of a government that accounts for 50% of GDP, the (mis)allocation of resources is mainly performed by it and perpetuated by it. The change between ABCT and AGCT is not the dynamics or the origin of the "cluster of error", but the focus on the main agent that carries it out. In other words, it is not the same to distort investment signals (as in the ABCT with interest rates) and then inducing business to err in its investment decisions, that the government directly misallocating capital (as in the AGCT). In both cases relative prices are distorted and the production structure changes (hence, there is still an Austrian type business cycle), but the main agent directing the process is different.

Thus far, we have been considering what Rothbard (2004) characterizes as triangular intervention. G, the government compels, or prohibits, acts between A and B, buyers and sellers in this case. But, there is also what he calls binary intervention: the state compels or prohibits commercial endeavors regarding just one person under its control, A. For example, G taxes A; compels A to render funds to it. Or G prohibits A from entering a specific industry, or paying his employees less than the mandated minimum wage. These, interventions, too, when G looms *large* in the economy, can also significantly misallocate resources, and contribute to set up an AGCT.[15]

How is the AGCT triggered by binary intervention? Precisely by the allocation of resources to areas that the market would not have underwritten. However, the necessary condition to distinguish *simple* binary intervention from an AGCT would be, for the latter, to identify government as comprising a relatively high proportion of the economy. That is, when the public sector represents, for instance, 50% or more of GDP. In this sense, AGCT not only comes into being due to the government's role in allocating huge amounts of resources, but also from its necessarily high taxation, debt, and/or inflation to finance it. The latter distorts the structure of production in much the same way as occurs with ABCT due to the artificial lowering of interest rates. Hence, AGCT is a possible, but not a necessary, outcome of binary intervention.

Another way in which large scale government affects the economic system is through its public financing operations. For instance, if the issuance of short-term debt is preferred to that of a longer duration, then it is likely that short term rates will increase. If that happens, it is also relevant to see what the situation is for long term debt yields. That is important because if short term interest rates increase above long-term rates, it means the yield curve inverts (and this is a signal of future recessions[16]). Of course, the central bank could also intervene by purchasing treasury securities (directly or through primary dealers) to try to stabilize their prices (hence,

[15] Government prohibiting individuals of smoking marijuana, or drinking alcohol, are also instances of binary intervention, but not economy-wide enough to count as business cycle related.

[16] See Cwik (2004, 2008). In terms of ABCT, a reason for yield curve inversion anticipating recession could be that it signals investment projects progressively shifting from more to less roundabout (hence, the change upward in short term yields compared to long term).

their yields), thereby expanding its balance sheet. Or, it could do so by directly imposing some sort of yield curve control. Now, this discussion is beyond the scope of this chapter and it is not nor need be as linear as presented here.[17] But, in any case, this is a relevant subject in the context of AGCT.

If the state wants to extend the duration of the boom, it can also choose to finance its operations through the issuance of long-term debt, which will likely push long rates upward, hence reinforcing a positive yield curve. However, if the government cannot get enough buyers for its bonds, there is no other way but to finance the deficit through debt monetization, that later exacerbates inflation. In any case, relative prices (especially interest rates) are distorted. True enough, the Central Bank can hardly directly affect long term rates, but the Treasury policy can indeed influence it. This is indeed a link between the fiscal policy and the interest rate, that in turn has systemic effects.

Where the government (in terms of GDP) is so big, its direct interventions in the market through "public investment", subsidies, etc.[18,19] distort relative prices in such a way as to emulate price distortions from monetary causes (as in the classical ABCT). And, most importantly, it is no longer business, or the private sector, the one that channels malinvestment, but rather the state itself.[20] The structure of production will also change, according to the specific government interventions in channeling resources. If it channels more resources to "public investment",[21] then more roundabout processes of production will take place, whereas if it focuses on subsidies to consumption, or direct consumption spending, then the economy will shift to the production of goods closer to consumption.

As we can see, government replaces business as the main character in the cycle play, but the Austrian analysis remains the same: distortion of relative prices and malinvestment.

The major effect of real intervention is that the distortion of the structure of prices away from peoples' values persists indefinitely. It is as if these interventions form a "wedge" between people's values and the structure of prices which prevents the latter from adjusting to, and conforming with, the former. This condition manifests itself in the form of massive and persistent misallocations of resources: the boom and the bust.

Economic cycles need a general explanation of their occurrence. As such, the key is to identify why is it that business errs periodically in its resource allocation decisions. As the ABCT explains, the source is government's monetary and interest rate

---

[17] For instance, central bank's influence on long term rates is much lower (if not non-existent) than on short term rates (that it directly affects).

[18] A new form could be "Fiscal QE", see Selgin (2020).

[19] The type of economy we have in mind may be more similar to that of the economic system of fascism.

[20] Directly, or through government sponsored enterprises (GSEs). See Gjerstad and Smith (2014), Norberg (2009) and Pinto (2010a, b).

[21] Rothbard (1962 [2009]) took the position that the state could only engage in consumption, never in production. For an alternative view, see Barnett and Block (2009b).

policy. Here, we present the idea that, although business is the traditional agent that misallocates resources due to government manipulation of money and credit, it can also be the case that the government itself does this job. Hence, a government-based cycle, AGCT. The central factor in the recurrence of errors in resource allocation, and therefore economic cycles, is the source of errors itself: the government (Hülsmann 1998).

4.4 Conclusion

The consequences for business cycles of the confluence of important new categories of borrowers (households, domestic governments, and foreigners) in the monetary/credit system and massive increases in governmental intervention, both financial and real, are: (1) longer, more diffuse booms; and, (2) more severe contractions; (3) persistent, but erratic, inflation; (4) massive, persistent misallocations of resources; (5) stagnant productivity; (6) attenuated economic growth; and (7) deteriorated standards of living, compared to what otherwise would have been the case.[22]

We note that the essentials of Austrian Business Cycle theory are still relevant for understanding macroeconomic booms and busts. All that is required to enable ABCT to be used to gain key insights into current macroeconomic events is to extend it to account for significant alterations in economic institutions; e.g., AGCT. In other words, the interest rate is not the only channel to create an Austrian type business cycle. A fiscal[23] involvement of enough magnitude operates in a similar way.

Hence, it is important to distinguish between a government cycle and a business cycle. The distinction also has a psychological effect: although economic cycles are, in our view, to be blamed always on government intervention, the use of the word "business" may implicitly give the impression that there is some sort of failure or malfunctioning in the market economy itself. It is important, at least when business is not the main character, to recognize the state apparatus as the key factor in play. Thus, a government cycle theory is coupled with an Austrian analysis.

The present chapter is only a preliminary discussion of this possible new extension of the Austrian approach to business cycles in the context of the scale and scope of modern states (especially in the developed world). Theorizing about business cycles requires first a basic understanding of the operations of both the market process and of government intervention in general. This is why, according to Mises, Bohm-Bawerk said, "A theory of the trade cycle, if it is not to be mere botching, can

[22] Continuing technological progress can often mask this phenomenon. The US was far freer, but poorer, in 1870 than in 2019. Does this mean the economic freedom reduces prosperity? Of course not. The difficulty here is that ceteris paribus conditions are not met. The latter period enjoys far better technology than the former.

[23] See also on this Chapter 5 of Garrison (2001).

only be written as the last chapter or the last chapter but one of a treatise dealing with all economic problems", a dictum with which he "fully agreed."[24]

Bibliography

Bagus, Philipp. 2003. The Commons and the Tragedy of Banking. *Mises Daily*, November 12. Available at http://mises.org/story/1373. Last visited June 13, 2019.

Bagus, Philipp, and David Howden. 2010. Fractional Reserve Free Banking: Some Quibbles. *The Quarterly Journal of Austrian Economics* 13 (4): 29–55.

———. 2011. Unanswered Quibbles with Fractional Reserve Free Banking. *Libertarian Papers* 3 (18): 1–24.

Bagus, Philipp, David Howden, and Walter E. Block. 2013. Deposits, Loans and Banking: Clarifying the Debate. *American Journal of Economics and Sociology* 72 (3): 627–644. Available at https://onlinelibrary.wiley.com/doi/abs/10.1111/ajes.12023. Last visited June 13, 2019.

Barnett II, William, and Walter E. Block. 2005. In Defense of Fiduciary Media—A Comment; or, What's Wrong with "Clown" or Play Money? *Quarterly Journal of Austrian Economics* 8 (2): 55–69. Available at http://mises.org/journals/qjae/pdf/qjae8_2_4.pdf. Last visited June 13, 2019.

———. 2008. Time Deposits, Dimensions and Fraud. *Journal of Business Ethics*. Available at https://link.springer.com/article/10.1007/s10551-008-9976-9. Last visited June 13, 2019.

———. 2009a. Crash and Carry: Financial Intermediaries, the Intertemporal-Carry Trade, and Austrian Business Cycles. *Ethics & Politics* XI (1): 455–469.

———. 2009b. Investment and Consumption: A Critique of Rothbard's Claim that There Can Be No Such Thing as Governmental 'Investment'. *Journal of Public Finance and Public Choice* 27 (2-3): 183–188. Available at http://www.walterblock.com/wp-content/uploads/InvestmentConsumption.pdf. Last visited May 29, 2021.

———. 2011. The Rate of Time Preference: A Praxeological Oxymoron. *Dialogue* 4: 38–47.

Baxendale, Tony. 2010. Free Banking, the Balance Sheet and Contract Law Approach. *The Cobden Centre*, March 15. Available at http://www.cobdencentre.org/2010/03/free-banking-the-balance-sheet-and-contract-law-approach/. Last visited June 13, 2019.

Block, Walter E. 2000a. Watch Your Language. *Mises Daily*, February 21. Available at https://mises.org/library/watch-your-language. Last visited July 16, 2019.

———. 2000b. Word Watch. *Mises Daily*, April 20. Available at http://www.mises.org/fullstory.asp?control=414&FS=Word+Watch. Last visited April 6, 2020.

———. 2001. Yes, We Have No Chaff: A Reply to Wagner's 'Austrian Business Cycle Theory: Saving the Wheat While Discarding the Chaff'. *The Quarterly Journal of Austrian Economics* 4 (1): 63–73. Available at www.mises.org/journals/qjae/pdf/qjae4_1_4.pdf. Last visited May 21, 2021.

———. 2002. All Government Is Excessive: A Rejoinder to 'In Defense of Excessive Government' by Dwight Lee. *Journal of Libertarian Studies* 16 (3): 35–82. Available at https://mises.org/library/all-government-excessive-rejoinder-dwight-lees-defense-excessive-government. Last visited July 16, 2019.

———. 2015. The Rent Seeker. *Romanian Economic and Business Review* 10 (3): 7–14. Fall. Available at http://www.rebe.rau.ro/REBE_10_3_2015.pdf. Last visited July 16, 2019.

[24] L. v. Mises, "The Trade Cycle and Credit Expansion: The Economic Consequences of Cheap Money," 1946, in *On the Manipulation of Money and Credit*.

———. 2019. Stop Trying to Make Coal Great Again. When It Comes to Coal, President Trump Seems to Care More About Politics Than Free-Market Principles. *The New York Times*, June 4. Available at https://www.nytimes.com/2019/06/04/opinion/trump-coal.html. Last visited July 16, 2019.

Block, Walter E., and William Barnett II. 2008. Continuums. *Journal Etica e Politica/ Ethics & Politics* 1 (June): 151–166. Available at http://www2.units.it/~etica/2008_1/ BLOCKBARNETT.pdf. Last visited July 16, 2019.

Block, Walter, and Bryan Caplan. 2008. Walter E. Block Versus Bryan Caplan on Fractional Reserve Banking. *Lew Rockwell*, November 1. Available at http://www.lewrockwell.com/ block/block110.html. Last visited June 13, 2019.

Block, Walter, and Kenneth M. Garschina. 1996. Hayek, Business Cycles and Fractional Reserve Banking: Continuing the De-Homogenization Process. *Review of Austrian Economics* 9(1): 1995, 77–94. Available at http://www.mises.org/journals/rae/pdf/rae9_1_3.pdf. Last visited June 13, 2019.

Block, Walter Versus Eric Posner. 2008. Posner vs. Block on Fractional Reserve Banking. *Lew Rockwell*, November 29. Available at http://www.lewrockwell.com/block/block114.html. Last visited June 13, 2019.

Cwik, Paul Francis. 2004. An Investigation of Inverted Yield Curves and Economic Downturns. PhD Dissertation, May 14. Auburn University.

———. 2008. Austrian Business Cycle Theory: A Corporate Finance Point of View. *The Quarterly Journal of Austrian Economics* 11: 60–68.

Davidson, Laura. 2008. Fractional Reserve Banking Is Indeed Fraudulent. *Lew Rockwell*, November 17. Available at http://www.lewrockwell.com/orig9/davidson-l1.html. Last visited June 13, 2019.

Davidson, Laura, and Walter E. Block. 2011. The Case Against Fiduciary Media: Ethics Is The Key. *The Journal of Business Ethics* 98 (3): 505–511. Available at http://www.springerlink. com/content/j76323752648720g/. Last visited June 13, 2019.

DiLorenzo, Thomas J., and Walter E. Block. 2017. *An Austro-Libertarian Critique of Public Choice*. New York: Addleton Academic Publishers.

French, Douglas E. 1992 [2009]. *Early Speculative Bubbles and Increases in the Supply of Money*, 2nd ed. The Ludwig Von Mises Institute: Auburn.

Garrison, Roger W. 1989. The Austrian Theory of the Business Cycle in the Light of Modern Macroeconomics. *The Review of Austrian Economics* 3 (1): 3–29.

———. 2001. *Time and Money: The Macroeconomics of Capital Structure*. London: Routledge.

Gjerstad, Steven D., and Vernon L. Smith. 2014. *Rethinking Housing Bubbles*. Cambridge: Cambridge University Press.

Hanke, Steve. 2008. Banking Crises: Plus Ça Change…. *Globe Asia*, November, pp. 168–169. https://www.cato.org/publications/commentary/banking-crises-plus-c-change. Last visited June 13, 2019.

Hayek, Friedrich A. 1931. *Prices and Production*. London: Routledge.

———. 1933 [1966]. *Monetary Theory and the Trade Cycle*. The Ludwig Von Mises Institute: Auburn.

Hazlitt, Henry. 1979. Gold Versus Fractional Reserves Part 1. *Mises Daily*, in *The Freeman*, May. Available at https://mises.org/library/gold-versus-fractional-reserves. Last visited April 6, 2020.

Hollenback, Frank. 2013. Insuring Deposits, Ensuring Insolvency. *Mises Daily*, July 24. Available at http://mises.org/daily/6487/Insuring-Deposits-Ensuring-Insolvency. Last visited June 13, 2019.

———. 2014. The Fraud in Fractional Reserve Banking. *Mises Canada Daily*, November 26. Available at http://us2.campaign-archive2.com/?u=7e6cc2f6072b7ebfaa847047f&id=189c14 aa12&e=53fc31c1bb. Last visited June 13, 2019.

Hoppe, Hans-Hermann. 1994. How Is Fiat Money Possible? Or, the Devolution of Money and Credit. *Review of Austrian Economics* 7 (2): 49–74.

Hoppe, Hans-Hermann, with Guido Hülsmann and Walter E. Block. 1998. Against Fiduciary Media. *Quarterly Journal of Austrian Economics* 1 (1): 19–50. Available at http://www.mises.org/journals/qjae/pdf/qjae1_1_2.pdf. Last visited June 13, 2019.

Howden, David. 2013. A Simple Math Question for Bankers. *Mises Canada Daily*, December 28. http://mises.us2.list-manage1.com/track/click?u=7e6cc2f6072b7ebfaa847047f&id=b10182ff5e&e=cb339c58df; http://www.economicpolicyjournal.com/2013/12/the-best-critique-i-have-ever-read.html?utm_source=feedburner&utm_medium=email&utm_campaign=Feed%3A+economicpolicyjournal%2FKpwH+%28EconomicPolicyJournal.com%29. Last visited June 13, 2019.

Huerta de Soto, Jesús. 1995. A Critical Analysis of Central Banks and Fractional-Reserve Free Banking from the Austrian Perspective. *Review of Austrian Economics* 8 (2): 25–38.

———. 1998. A Critical Note on Fractional-Reserve Free Banking. *The Quarterly Journal of Austrian Economics* 1 (4): 25–49.

———. 2006. *Money, Bank Credit and Economic Cycles*. Auburn: Ludwig von Mises Institute.

———. 2010. Economic Recessions, Banking Reform, and the Future of Capitalism. *Mises Daily*, November 1. Available at http://mises.org/daily/4817. Last visited June 13, 2019.

———. 2012. Recesiones Económicas, Reforma Bancaria y el Futuro del Capitalismo. *Procesos de Mercado: Revista Europea de Economía Política* IX (2): 431–456.

———. 2014. Crisis Financiera: El Fracaso de la Reforma Contable. *Mises Hispano*. Febrero, 3. Disponible en http://www.miseshispano.org/2014/02/crisis-financiera-el-fracaso-de-la-reforma-contable/. Visitado por última vez el 18 de Marzo de 2018.

———. 2018. What Free-Banking Advocates Get Wrong. *Mises Wire*, February 26. Available at https://mises.org/wire/what-free-banking-advocates-get-wrong. Last visited June 13, 2019.

Hülsmann, Jorg Guido. 1996. Free Banking and the Free Bankers. *Review of Austrian Economics* 9 (1): 3–53. Available at http://www.mises.org/journals/rae/pdf/rae9_1_1.pdf. Last visited June 13, 2019.

———. 1998. Toward a General Theory of Error Cycles. *The Quarterly Journal of Austrian Economics* 1 (4): 1–23.

———. 2000. Banks Cannot Create Money. *The Independent Review: A Journal of Political Economy* 5 (1): 101–110. Available at http://www.independent.org/pdf/tir/tir_05_1_hulsman.pdf. Last visited June 13, 2019.

———. 2002. Free Banking Fractional Reserves: Reply to Pascal Salin. *Review of Austrian Economics* 1 (3). Available at http://www.mises.org/journals/qjae/pdf/qjae1_3_8.pdf. Last visited June 13, 2019.

———. 2003. "Has Fractional-Reserve Banking Really Passed the Market Test?". Independent Review 73, 399-422. Available at http://www.independent.org/publications/tir/article.asp?a=90. Last visited June 13, 2019.

———. 2008. *The Ethics of Money Production*. Auburn: Ludwig von Mises Institute.

Kindleberger, Charles P. 1989. *Manias, Panics and Crashes. A History of Financial Crisis*, 2nd ed. London: MacMillan.

Kirzner, Israel M. 1990. The 'Austrian' Perspective on the Crisis. *Austrian Economics* 1: 191–202.

———. 1999. Creativity and/or Alertness: A Reconsideration of the Schumpeterian Entrepreneur. *Review of Austrian Economics* 11: 5–17.

Lee, Young, and Taeyoon Sung. 2007. Fiscal Policy, Business Cycles and Economic Stabilisation: Evidence from Industrialised and Developing Countries. *Fiscal Studies* 28 (4): 437–462.

Machlup, Fritz. 1940. *The Stock Market, Credit and Capital Formation*. London: William Hodge & Co.

Menger, Carl. 1871 [2007]. *Principles of Economics*. Auburn: The Ludwig Von Mises Institute.

Mises, Ludwig Von. 1912 [1953]. *The Theory of Money and Credit*. New Haven: Yale University Press.

Mulligan, Robert F. 2006. An Empirical Examination of Austrian Business Cycle Theory. *The Quarterly Journal of Austrian Economics* 9 (2): 69–93.

Murphy, Robert P. 2010. The Fractional-Reserve Banking Question. *Mises Daily*, June 14. Available at http://mises.org/daily/4499. Last visited June 13, 2019.

Norberg, Johan. 2009. *Financial Fiasco: How America's Infatuation with Home Ownership and Easy Money Created the Economic Crisis*. Cato Institute: Washington, DC.

Oppers, Stefan E. 2002. *The Austrian Theory of Business Cycles: Old Lessons for Modern Economic Policy?*. IMF Working Papers. January.

Pinto, Edward J. 2010a. Sizing Total Federal Government and Federal Agency Contributions to Subprime and Alt-A Loans in U.S. First Mortgage Market as of 6.30.08. *AEI Online*, October 11. Available at www.aei.org/docLib/PintoGovernmentHousingPoliciesintheLead-uptotheFinancialCrisis3Memoranda2511.pdf. Last visited March 6, 2018.

———. 2010b. Government Housing Policies in the Lead-up to the Financial Crisis: A Forensic Study. *AEI Online*, November 4. Available at www.aei.org/docLib/GovernmentHousing-Policies-Financial-Crisis-Pinto-102110.pdf. Last visited March 6, 2018.

Polleit, Thorsten. 2010. The Faults of Fractional-Reserve Banking. *Mises Daily*, December 23. Available at http://mises.org/daily/4880. Last visited June 13, 2019.

Reisman, George. 1996. *Capitalism*, 954–963. Ottawa: Jameson Books.

———. 2009. A Pro-Free-Market Program for Economic Recovery. *Mises Daily*, November 20. Available at http://mises.org/daily/3870. Last visited June 13, 2019.

Rothbard, Murray N. 1969. *Economic Depressions: Their Cause and Cure*. Lansing: Constitutional Alliance. Available at https://www.lewrockwell.com/1970/01/murray-n-rothbard/what-causes-an-economic-depression/. Last visited April 6, 2020.

———. 1983 [2008]. *The Mistery of Banking*. Auburn: The Ludwig Von Mises Institute.

———. 1962 [1991]. The Case for a 100 Percent Gold Dollar. In *Search of a Monetary Constitution*, ed. Leland B. Yeager, 94–136. Cambridge, MA: Harvard University Press and Auburn: Ludwig von Mises Institute. See also *The Logic of Action One*, pp. 364–384. Available at http://mises.org/story/1829; http://mises.org/rothbard/100percent.pdf. Last visited June 13, 2019.

———. 1963 [2000]. *America's Great Depression*. Auburn: The Ludwig Von Mises Institute.

———. 2004. *Man, Economy, and State: A Treatise on Economic Principles with Power and Market*, Scholar's edition. Auburn: Ludwig von Mises Institute.

———. 1963 [2008]. *What Has Government Done with Our Money*. Auburn: The Ludwig Von Mises Institute.

———. 1962 [2009]. *Man, Economy and State*. Scholar's edition, 2nd ed. Auburn: Ludwig Von Mises Institute.

Salerno, Joseph T. 1987. The True Money Supply: A Measure of the Supply of the Medium of Exchange in the US Economy. *Austrian Economics Newsletter*, Spring.

———. 2010a. *Money, Sound and Unsound*. Auburn: Ludwig von Mises Institute.

———. 2010b. White contra Mises on Fiduciary Media. *Mises Daily*, May 14. Available at http://mises.org/daily/4389. Last visited June 13, 2019.

———. 2011. Dr. Joseph Salerno Explains Everything You Ever Wanted to Know About Money (But Were Afraid to Ask). *The Daily Bell*, July 3. Available at http://www.thedailybell.com/2602/Anthony-Wile-Dr-Joseph-Salerno-Explains-Everything-You-Ever-Wanted-to-Know-About-Money-But-Were-Afraid-to-Ask. Last visited June 13, 2019.

———. 2012. A Reformulation of Austrian Business Cycle Theory in Light of the Financial Crisis. *The Quarterly Journal of Austrian Economics* 15 (1): 3–44.

———. 2016. The Fed and Bernanke Are Wrong About the Natural Interest Rate. *Mises Wire*, June 26. Available at https://mises.org/wire/fed-and-bernanke-are-wrong-about-natural-interest-rate. Last visited March 19, 2018.

Selgin, George. 2020. *The Menace of Fiscal QE*. Washington: Cato Institute.

White, Lawrence H. 2008a. How Did We Get into This Financial Mess?. *Cato Institute Briefing Papers*, N° 110, November 18. Available at http://object.cato.org/sites/cato.org/files/pubs/pdf/bp110.pdf. Last visited March 6, 2018.

———. 2008b. What Really Happened? *Cato Unbound*, "What Happened? Anatomies of the Financial Crisis", Lead Essay, December 2. Available at http://www.cato-unbound.org/2008/12/02/lawrence-h-white/what-really-happened. Last visited March 6, 2018.

———. 2010. Credit-Rating Agencies and the Financial Crisis: Less Regulation of CRAs Is a Better Response. *Journal of International Banking Law and Regulation* 25 (4): 170. Available at https://www.stern.nyu.edu/sites/default/files/assets/documents/con_039549.pdf. Last visited March 6, 2018.

Woods, Thomas E., Jr. 2009. *Meltdown: A Free-Market Look at Why the Stock Market Collapsed, the Economy Tanked, and Government Bailouts Will Make Things Worse*. Washington, DC: Regnery Publishing.

Chapter 5
International Economics

Abstract This chapter is divided in two sections, both dealing with different aspects of international trade from an Austrian perspective. In Sect. 5.1, we analyze Ricardo's Law of Comparative Advantage (also known as "Law of Association") in order to critically respond to the analysis offered by Taleb (Antifragile: things that gain from disorder. Random House, New York, 2012). The latter points to the invalidity of the model, since it does not assume price variability, thus exposing it to grave systemic consequences due to abrupt changes in relative prices. Our critique is based on the approach taken by Ludwig Von Mises (Human action – a treatise on economics. The Scholar's edition. Ludwig Von Mises Institute, Auburn, 1949) on the same subject. The Ricardian model is viewed from a praxeological perspective. We maintain that Taleb's critique, although correct in invalidating Ricardo's analysis, not only does not harm but even reaffirms Ricardo's original conclusion pointing to the advantages of cooperation in general, and international free trade in particular.

In Sect. 5.2, we offer a critique of the theory of the deterioration in the terms of trade, developed by Raúl Prebisch and Hans Singer. As an example of the theory's shortcomings, the case of Argentina's import substitution model is analyzed. Thus, we demonstrate how a misunderstanding of the influence of price variability in international trade may lead to the mistaken conclusion that protectionist measures must be adopted and enforced in order to achieve growth and prosperity.

Keywords Taleb · Mises · International trade · Comparative advantage · Ricardo · International trade · Terms of trade · Argentina · Prebisch · Singer

JEL Code F19

> Foreign trade differs from domestic trade only in so far as goods and services are exchanged beyond the borderlines separating the territories of two sovereign nations. (Ludwig Von Mises 1949, 662)

A. G. Futerman, W. E. Block, *The Austro-Libertarian Point of View*,
https://doi.org/10.1007/978-981-16-4691-1_5

5.1 Taleb and Ricardo: Defending the Theory of Comparative Advantage[1]

5.1.1 Introduction

David Ricardo's Theory of Comparative Advantages, originally presented in his work *On the Principles of Political Economy and Taxation* (1817), has been criticized throughout the last two hundred years for multiple reasons. As a theory that extols the advantages of unrestricted international trade, its main critiques come from those authors who hold protectionism as a mechanism for progress.

Among the various critiques on this regard, we can find not only the Neo-Mercantilists derived from the works by Keynes (1936 [2013]) since the publication of his *General Theory of Employment, Interest and Money*, but also by other more sophisticated developments, such as the Stolper-Samuelson Theorem (that could be read in this light), in the context of the Heckscher-Ohlin model (Stolper and Samuelson 1941).

Among the most recent critiques, there is Nassim Nicholas Taleb's work *Antifragile* (2012), where he focuses in what he identifies as the fundamental mistake in Ricardo's analysis: the non-inclusion of price variability.

In the present work, we will first proceed to a brief presentation of Ricardo's theory (Sect. 5.1.2), and afterwards to Taleb's critique (Sect. 5.1.3). Then, we will analyze the theory from the perspective of Ludwig Von Mises (Sect. 5.1.4), in order to show why Ricardo's contribution is still valid, Taleb to the contrary notwithstanding. We end with our conclusions (Sect. 5.1.5).

5.1.2 The Theory of Comparative Advantage

Adam Smith, when analyzing the negative effects of Mercantilism in *The Wealth of Nations* (1776, IV. ii), develops the concept of *absolute advantage*. Basically, this demonstrates that given two countries, *A* and *B*, both can improve their situations by trade, given that *A* is more efficient in producing some goods, while this applies to *B* for others. Thus, with free trade, global production increases, and they both benefit.

However, Smith did not analyze the case in which, given two countries, *A* and *B*, what happens if *A* has an absolute advantage in the production of *every* good in

[1] This section of the present chapter is based on our paper Futerman, Alan G., and Block, Walter E. 2019 "On Taleb on Ricardo: A Clarification." *Revista Procesos de Mercado, Revista Europea de Economía Política*, Vol. XVI, N° 2, Autumn, pp. 81–102. Available at http://www.procesosdemercado.com/wp-content/uploads/2020/01/02_ART%C3%8DCULO.pdf (last visited May 8, 2021).

relation to *B*. David Ricardo (1817, 81–93) treated this scenario by developing the theory of *comparative advantage*.[2]

In the famous example of two countries, *A*'s cost structure is lower than that of *B* for the production of both goods in a two-good world, and therefore possesses an absolute advantage with respect to both.

Nevertheless, they can still benefit from trade. Given that product *x* is relatively less costly in *A* and product *z* is relatively less costly in *B*, it is in both countries interest (based on these comparative advantages), that *B* specializes in *z* and *A* in *x*.

Hence, if *A* produces less *z* and more *x*, and *B* produces less *x* and more *z*, it is possible that both benefit at the same time that global production increases.

Hence, it is also true that both countries benefit *even* if one of them has an absolute advantage in the production of both goods over the other.

For example, suppose the following; there are two countries, two goods, two seasons. If there is no trade, Japan can produce 100 TV sets and 50 units of wheat, devoting half of its inputs into each, while Canada can manufacture 5 TVs and 10 wheat units, with the same allocation of inputs. With no trade, the world, consisting of these two countries, boasts 105 TVs and 60 bushels of wheat. The Japanese GDP is 150, while that of Canada is 15, for a total of 165. Then, trade occurs. Each country apportions its entire endowment to the product which exemplifies its comparative, not absolute advantage. Japan produces only TV sets, doubling its production to 200 of them, while Canada does the same with wheat, harvesting 20 units instead of 10.[3]

World GDP, consisting of the annual production of both nations, rises from 165 to 220. Both countries gain. See Table 5.1.

Now assume trade, in which Japan specializes in its comparative advantage in TV sets, while Canada focusses on its comparative advantage in wheat (Table 5.2).

In addition, this happens[4] while factor allocation has not changed, and the assumptions of the model apply:

(a) There is perfect mobility of factors inside each country.
(b) There are only two countries and two products.

Table 5.1 World GDP with no trade

(Assume no trade)	Japan	Canada	Both
TV sets	100	5	105
Wheat	50	10	60
GDP	150	15	165

[2]An accurate exposition can be seen in Krugman et al. (2012). Indeed, virtually every economic textbook properly explains this brilliant insight of Ricardo's.

[3]We assume these two products are additive.

[4]It is true that, in our example, wheat production ends up being lower. But what we are trying to show is that *global* production increases. That is the main point of the theory, and multiple examples could be shown where no product's quantity ends up being lower than it was before producing (and trading) on the basis of comparative advantages.

Table 5.2 World GDP with trade

(Assume no trade)	Japan	Canada	Both
TV sets	200	0	200
Wheat	0	20	20
GDP	200	20	220

(c) There are constant returns to scale (the slope of the production possibilities frontier does not vary between the two countries, thus constituting a linear function).
(d) There are no transport costs.
(e) There are no barriers to trade.
(f) There is *stability* in marginal costs and the factors of production.

The basis for the analysis is point (f). This is the target of Taleb's critique, which we will present next.

5.1.3 Taleb's Critique: Price Variability

Taleb (2012, Appendix II) contends that, in the previous example, there is serious a problem. Price variability is not considered, therefore disregarding possible systemic risks.

It is true, the *apparent* optimum strategy in the example ~~is~~ seems to be specialization and trade on the base of comparative advantage. In effect, Taleb recognizes that there are advantages derived from trade and, as presented in the example of the doctor and the secretary: even when the former can very well do the work of the latter, it is preferable that the doctor focuses in his specialty and leaves the work of the typist to the assistant. Even so, here Taleb notes that comparative advantage is not the only variable to take into account (for the doctor to choose to work as such), but there are others equally relevant such as:

(a) Labor stability associated with the work of a doctor, derived from the fact that people will continually get sick.
(b) Superior social status derived from the prestige of the profession of doctor in relation to secretary.

More importantly, Taleb points to what he interprets as the fundamental mistake in the theory: it is based in the assumption that unitary costs of production assume a *normal distribution*, where extremes have no significant influence. In other words, there are no large changes in costs and prices, and therefore variability is irrelevant (or inexistent). In addition, he criticizes Krugman (1998) given that in one of his essays defending Ricardo's theory he does not include tail risks and risk management. Taleb thinks that this must be taken as a central part of the theory since it is not possible nor reasonable to talk about returns or profits without contemplating that these must be discounted by the risks involved (as any reasonable portfolio analysis would do).

According to Taleb (2012, 449), "... Traditional Ricardian analysis assumes the variables are endogenous, but does not add a layer of stochasticity". Moreover, even if we assume that costs are variable, but these values do represent the unbiased long-term average, if these follow a "fat tail" distribution (thus with a higher probability of occurrence of extreme events),[5] then if everything goes well, important profits are registered. However, if the worse scenario occurs, the results can be negative and of a "massive" magnitude. Thus, "There are concavities to the exposure—severe concavities" (2012, 449).

In other words, Taleb is telling us that the absolute costs affecting the determination of relative costs are not stationary. Moreover, they often do not follow a normal distribution. In terms of Ricardo's theory, this undermines the assumption of constant returns of scale, or stable marginal costs.

Taleb (2012, 450) states that "Indeed, we have had problems in history with countries specializing in some goods, commodities, and crops that happen to be not just volatile, but extremely volatile. *And disaster does not necessarily come from variation in price, but problems in production*: suddenly, you can't produce the crop because of a germ, bad weather, or some other hindrance. A bad crop, such as the one that caused the Irish potato famine in the decade around 1850, caused the death of a million and the emigration of a million more... It is very hard to reconvert resources—unlike the case in the doctor- typist story, countries don't have the ability to change. Indeed, monoculture (focus on a single crop) has turned out to be lethal in history—one bad crop leads to devastating famines" (emphasis added by present authors). Although there is no reason why free trade in general or the law of association in particular would lead to monoculture, it is true that history, then, can work contrary to what the theory indicates.

The author continues (2012, 450): "The other part missed in the doctor-secretary analogy is that countries don't have family and friends. A doctor has a support community, a circle of friends, a collective that takes care of him, a father-in-law to borrow from in the event that he needs to reconvert into some other profession, a state above him to help. Countries don't. Further, a doctor has savings; countries tend to be borrowers."

Finally, Taleb contends that Ricardo's theory is analogous to the strategy of "probability matching", that is, to predicting the membership in a class according to unconditional class probability. In other words, if one extracts (with replacement) a black ball from an urn 60% of the time, and a white one 40%, then to predict these percentages for the next ball would be to engage in a "probability matching" strategy. Even if decision theory literature, says this NYU professor, considers it mistaken given that probabilities are unstable or unknown, to use this strategy operates as a regulator. Yet, nothing renders Ricardo's model free of the problems entailed by price variability. Taleb (2012, 450) concludes:

---

[5] Presents leptokurtosis, above normal.

> The reader should not interpret what I am saying to mean that specialization is not a good thing—only that one should establish such specialization after addressing fragility and second-order effects. Now I do believe that Ricardo is ultimately right, but not from the models shown. *Organically, systems without top-down controls would specialize progressively, slowly, and over a long time, through trial and error, get the right amount of specialization—not through some bureaucrat using a model.* To repeat, systems make small errors, design makes large ones. So the imposition of Ricardo's insight-turned-model by some social planner would lead to a blowup; letting tinkering work slowly would lead to efficiency—true efficiency. The role of policy makers should be to, *via negativa* style, allow the emergence of specialization by preventing what hinders the process (emphasis added).

Hence the fundamental distinction, between criticizing Ricardo's *model*, and doing so to Ricardo's *insight*.

5.1.4 **A Priori** *Vision of Ricardo's Theory*

Taleb criticizes Ricardo's model not because it is incorrect with respect to the idea by which it is construed (based on the fact that trade benefits all economic agents), but because it omits price variability. Moreover, it makes it possible to arrive at a mistaken conclusion: one can determine the optimum specialization for a country by means of central planning, *given that* the relevant variables are known in advance (and presumed to be normally distributed; so it is assumed that extremes are not relevant). Therefore, we can see why Ricardo's insight is correct, even though the model illustrating it is not.[6]

Yet, Ricardo's development, construed by another methodology, can yet be shown to be useful. We will now make use of praxeology[7] to do just that. We choose to follow the praxeological approach to the law of association since it is a more refined version of the Ricardian analysis. Let us begin by identifying the underlying logic behind the law of diminishing returns, such as it was presented by Ludwig Von Mises (who called it "law of returns"), in his *magnum opus*, *Human Action* (Mises 1949, 127–130).

Mises contends that such a law does not derive from experience (and its accuracy in describing reality in the context of specific technical processes of production is irrelevant for it being true), but it is an *a priori* deduction, implicit in the category of human action.

Mises begins by stating that in the case of first order goods, a quantity a produces a quantity α of *effect* (instantaneously or after some time). In the case of higher order goods, a quantity b of the good B produces a specific quantity of the effect β, while a specific quantity c of the good C produces a quantity of effect Υ. The

[6] Or, at least, it is incomplete.

[7] The science of human action, based on the action axiom and its logical implications. For a full description of this science, see Mises (1949), and our Chap. 1, *supra*. However, this is not the only *a priori* methodology that could state such a law. For instance, see Stigler (1966), and even, to some extent, Krugman (1998).

combined effects of β and ϒ of both complementary goods produce the quantity *p* of the first order good *D*. If *b* is fixed, the optimum value of *c* is such where the relation *p*/*c* is the biggest. Thus, the largest return occurs when both factors are used in optimum proportions. An increase in the quantity of one of the factors generates a boost in the return, but at a decreasing rate as more input is added, otherwise we could not talk of an optimum in the former relation.

For example, if fewer units of *B* could be replaced with more of *C* at the same time that production of *p* is held constant, then *B* would be a good of unlimited production (always assuming that there are enough units of *C* available), and therefore it would no longer be regarded as an economic good, since it would no longer be scarce. Thus, it would be a free good.

On the other hand, if the quantity of *B* rises but the production of *p* remains the same, then the previous increase of *p* would have to be entirely created by the increase of *C*, in which case *B* no longer is regarded as an economic good.

The law of diminishing returns states that in the case of higher order goods there are optimum combinations of factors that produce a greater quantity of product, and after that point whenever there is an increase in the use of one of the factors then the growth in the quantity produced will decrease, or increase less than proportionally to the surge in the consumption of the factor of production (higher order good) used. The key to this reasoning is that the quantitative effects of the consumption of the factor in relation to the produced quantity of *p* must be limited, and therefore these must receive the name of economic goods.

We now turn our attention again to trade. Mises (1949, 158) analyzes the law of absolute advantage in this way:

> If *A* is fit to produce in 1 unit of time 6 *p* or 4 *q*, and *B* only 2 *p*, but 8 *q*, they both, when working in isolation, will produce together *4* p + *6* q; when working under the division of labor, each of them producing only that commodity in whose production he is more efficient than his partner, they will produce 6 *p* + 8 *q*.

Let us now see how this author presents the law of comparative advantage (1949, 159):

> If *A* is in such a way more efficient than *B* that he needs for the production of 1 unit of the commodity *p* 3 hours compared with *B*'s 5, and for the production of 1 unit of *q* 2 hours compared with *B*'s 4, then both will gain if *A* confines himself to producing *q* and leaves *B* to produce *p*. If each of them gives 60 hours to producing *p* and 60 hours to producing *q*, the result of *A*'s labor is 20 *p* + 30 *q*; of *B*'s, 12 *p* +15 *q*; and for both together, 32 *p* + 45 *q*. If, however, *A* confines himself to producing *q* alone, he produces 60 *q* in 120 hours, while *B*, if he confines himself to producing *p*, produces in the same time 24 *p*. The result of their activities is then 24 *p* + 60 *q*, which, as *p* has for *A* a substitution ratio of 3/2 *q* and for *B* one of 5/4 *q*, signifies a larger output than 32 *p* + 45 *q*.

Observe that numbers could be changed according to the example employed, but as long as quantitative relations are the same, this analysis will be valid for any possible world where the conditions of the model apply. Mises contends that (1949, 160):

> If and as far as labor under the division of labor is more productive than isolated labor, and if and as far as man is able to realize this fact, human action itself tends toward cooperation and association [...] Experience teaches that this condition—higher productivity achieved

> under the division of labor—is present because its cause—*the inborn inequality of men and the inequality in the geographical distribution of the natural factors of production*—is real (emphasis added).

The theory, as presented by Mises, constitutes an *a priori* truth. It is true that we must not confuse the place of the law of comparative advantage within praxeology with the demonstration and validity of the law of comparative advantage as a praxeological theorem. But we treat these subjects together here because our goal is to analyze Taleb's approach, not the law of association itself.

As we can also see, the theory refers to reality as well, because men *are* unequal, and therefore will have different capabilities and wishes, and also the factors of production *are not* necessarily homogeneous geographically.

Does this affect the validity of the subjective theory of value? Not in our view, because the law of returns, as well as the law of association, deal with objective aspects of the external world (such as the geographically unequal distribution of resources). But the relations among human beings and their evaluations of the external world (Mises 1949, 92) continue to be compatible with the subjective theory of value. The law of returns and the law of association, however, correspond (in our view) to what Böhm-Bawerk (1888 [1930], 10) called "the theory of the Production of goods". This addresses the cases of real constraints and objective variables affecting production. Thus, praxeology deals with both aspects, the subjective evaluation of human beings of their fellow men and of the world, and the conditions of the world (as in the case we analyze here). Let us also note that the *a priori* methodology of praxeology is not the relevant factor here, but instead that the law of returns and the law of association are praxeological theorems because they explain aspects of man's conduct with regard to his external world. The real constraints and objective variables that the law of returns and the law of association deal with have to be discovered by the human mind, i.e. they are, as everything else, not automatically understood, but require a theory (a conceptual framework) to be identified.

Why, then, is the law of association attacked? Mises explains (1949, 160):

> This law is an offense to all those eager to justify protection and national economic isolation from any point of view other than the selfish interests of some producers or the issues of war-preparedness.
>
> Ricardo's first aim in expounding this law was to refute an objection raised against freedom of international trade.

Therefore:

> But Ricardo deals with a world whose conditions are determined by settlement in earlier days, a world in which capital goods and labor are bound to the soil by definite institutions. In such a milieu free trade, i.e., the free mobility of commodities only, cannot bring about a state of affairs in which capital and labor are distributed on the surface of the earth according to the better or poorer physical opportunities afforded to the productivity of labor. Here the law of comparative cost comes into operation. Each country turns toward those branches of production for which its conditions offer comparatively, although not absolutely, the most favorable opportunities. For the inhabitants of a country it is more advantageous to abstain from the exploitation of some opportunities which—absolutely and technologically—are more propitious and to import commodities produced abroad under conditions

> which—absolutely and technologically—are less favorable than the unused domestic resources (1949, 161).

Let us remember here the distinction that Taleb makes between the case we analyzed and that of the doctor-secretary. However, we can still say that both cases are analogous because they focus on just *one* aspect: comparative advantage. And abstract from the others. Mises contends that (1949, 162):

> If we do not want to deal with the law of comparative cost under the simplified assumptions applied by Ricardo, we must openly employ money calculation. We must not fall prey to the illusion that a comparison between the expenditure of factors of production of various kinds and of the output of products of various kinds can be achieved without the aid of money calculation [...] In comparing the conditions of two countries we must say: If conditions are such that in England the production of 1 unit of each of the two commodities *a* and *b* requires the expenditure of 1 working day of the same kind of labor, while in India with the same investment of capital for *a* 2 days and for *b* 3 days are required, and if capital goods and *a* and *b* are freely movable from England to India and vice versa, while there is no mobility of labor, wage rates in India in the production of *a* must tend to be 50 percent, and in the production of *b* 33 1/3 per cent, of the English rates. If the English rate is 6 shillings, the rates in India would be the equivalent of 3 shillings in the production of *a* and the equivalent of 2 shillings in the production of *b*. Such a discrepancy in the remuneration of labor of the same kind cannot last if there is mobility of labor on the domestic Indian labor market. Workers would shift from the production of *b* into the production of *a*; their migration would tend to lower the remuneration in the *a* industry and to raise it in the *b* industry. Finally Indian wage rates would be equal in both industries. The production of *a* would tend to expand and to supplant English competition. On the other hand the production of *b* would become unprofitable in India and would have to be discontinued, while it would expand in England. The same reasoning is valid if we assume that the difference in the conditions of production consists also or exclusively in the amount of capital investment needed.

Thus, we can see that the particular conditions where such a theory could apply are not relevant at judging its general validity. Moreover:

> Ricardo, however, starts from the assumption that there is mobility of capital and labor only within each country, and not between the various countries. He raises the question what the consequences of the free mobility of products must be under such conditions. [...] The theory of comparative cost answers this question. [...]
>
> However, the teachings of the classical theory of interregional trade are above any change in institutional conditions. *They enable us to study the problems involved under any imaginable assumptions* (1949, 163) (emphasis added).

In other words, it is certainly true that the real conditions in specific time and space may imply that some of the assumptions of the model do not apply (such as the normality in the distribution of the costs of production and prices), *but this does not mean that economic agents must no longer guide their choices based in their comparative advantages*. In fact, if they changed their conduct in this regard, they would abstain from obtaining the benefits derived thereby.

How is this related to the law of returns? Mises (1949, 161–2) explains[8]:

---

[8] We must state that the place of the law of comparative advantage within praxeology, the validity of the law of comparative advantage as a praxeological theorem, and the relation between a praxe-

> The law of comparative cost is as independent of the classical theory of value as is the law of returns, which its reasoning resembles. In both cases we can content ourselves with comparing only physical input and physical output. With the law of returns we compare the output of the same product. With the law of comparative costs we compare the output of two different products. Such a comparison is feasible because we assume that for the production of each of them, apart from one specific factor, only nonspecific factors of the same kind are required.

Taleb's critique refers to the likely negative implications of central planning with respect to Ricardo's model and its assumptions, but not necessarily to the idea of comparative advantage itself, such as Mises explains with the use of praxeology. This is so because the formal analysis of the theory permits to identify, *ceteris paribus*, how convenient it is to guide oneself by the theory *only in the context of the market process*.

We can conclude from these considerations that, as even Taleb recognizes, the mistake is not to support the theory as such, but to do so based on central planning schemes. Due to the absence of spontaneous and dynamic information, these will likely create a structure of production allegedly based in comparative advantages, but subject to systemic risks due to ignorance (mainly, of price variability and its risks). This problem derives, in part, from the exposition of a model where prices are a given, when in reality this is far from true. As Taleb (2012, 450) says, "systems make small errors, design makes large ones".

Moreover, the analysis presented by Taleb could render Ricardo's model as refuting the advantages of free trade whether we accept it (because by ignoring the relevance of price variability it expounds the system to catastrophic risks), or if we reject it (since its assumptions are unrealistic). This is why it is important to point out that what is *being criticized is the model, and not the theory that inspires it*. In addition, such a theory can be presented as well under Mises' approach.

Scott Gordon (1993, 208) explained:

> Any theory, whether in natural or social science, must employ *ceteris paribus*. Otherwise every theory, no matter how small, would have to take everything in the universe into account. So there cannot be any serious criticism of classical political economy simply on the ground that it constructed *ceteris paribus* theories. However, Ricardo and other classical economists were not as clear about this matter as they should have been. Ricardo sometimes spoke of the conclusions he had arrived at as 'tendencies' and sometimes as if they were certain. Properly stated, the conclusions were *analytically certain* under the conditions of *ceteris paribus*, but they could be construed only as *empirically probable*, because in the real world 'other things' are not constant (emphasis in the original).

In this respect, any theory could be refuted if the assumptions on which it stands do not apply. Nevertheless, according to Gordon (1993, 208) there are four different meanings of *ceteris paribus*:

ological law with the advocacy of free trade are different subjects. Nevertheless, Mises (1949) treats them together to defend a free market economy. Since we are following Mises' approach here, we also conform to his treatment of these subjects.

1. When the exact formal conditions, which allow the application of a proposition, hold.
2. When the variables not included in the theory are irrelevant or constant.
3. When the latter variables are neither relevant nor constant but have been made so in a laboratory.
4. The variables not included in the theory are neither constant nor irrelevant nor made so in a laboratory, but we accept the current hypothesis, until we can make a new one that includes them.

Mises's praxeology, according to him grounded in the synthetic *a priori*,[9] can be interpreted as belonging to category 1. This is so because we take praxeology to be a formal science; however, if this is denied then it equally applies to 4 as a set of simple assumptions.

But, at the same time, the *ceteris paribus* of Ricardo's model, that assumes price stability, would deprive it of the empirical reality that makes it possible to recognize, for example, the relevant part of Taleb's critique, which would include it in classification 4.

In addition, we can recognize that by including price variability in the theory, we not only do not refute it but rather enrich it. Therefore, instead of assuming that this theory refutes the advantages of trade or free markets, it reaffirms them by showing that if there is price and cost variability, central planning would be disastrous for the economy, and even more so if such prices and costs follow a "fat tail" distribution.

To conclude this section, we can say that comparative advantage theory is valid, but it is true that the model usually used to illustrate it does not reproduce its foundations faithfully. Moreover, due to the absence of price variability in its assumptions, it may allow the unwary to assume that specialization and division of labor could be centrally planned without a market process,[10] which in turn makes it impossible to permit the efficient transfer of information via the price system.

Taleb contends that price variability may have a huge and negative impact on international trade relations. Nevertheless, it does not follow that:

(a) Prices are the only guides to identify comparative advantage.
(b) Crises should necessarily correspond to price changes.[11]

Comparative advantage is identified and refined through the market process, over time and by means of trial and error, in the context of entrepreneurial ventures. It is not due to self-evident facts (even when, as Mises declares, geographical dotation of

[9] See Chap. 1 *supra* for a discussion of alternative interpretations.

[10] Since prices are a given in the real world, it can be thought that all the planner needs to do is to identify comparative advantages and promote the production of the relevant goods. This is mistaken.

[11] With respect to the case of Ireland in the XIXth century, see Thornton (2000, 2008). About the source of economic crises, see Hayek (1931), Mises (1912 [1953]), and Rothbard (1963 [2000], 1963 [2008], 1983 [2008]).

factors and individual conditions are heterogeneous). Were this the case, there could only be profits, never losses, a non-existent situation.

Therefore, we can see that, following Taleb's critique (but also building on it), to focus on price variability is certainly relevant, but focusing *only* on this variable is mistaken.

Taleb's critique could be read as maintaining that Ricardo's model of comparative advantage mistakenly (and implicitly) allows us to think that it is possible to centrally plan specialization and the division of labor. But to focus only on price variability as the fundamental factor when analyzing international trade can also lead to mistaken conclusions. Among these paradoxically, is the idea that specialization must be centrally planned but from a different perspective.

For example, the theory of the "deterioration in the terms of trade" by Raúl Prebisch and Hans Singer[12] held that, since the terms of trade of periphery countries (such as Latin American countries like Argentina[13]) increasingly worsen with respect to those of the core countries (Europe and the US), it is convenient for the former to develop government subsidized import substitution industries. In Latin and South America, these policies have been an abject failure. As they would be if Kansas, Iowa, or Missouri, were to compel the substitution of manufactured for agricultural products.

This error was based on the premise that the law of comparative advantages, one of the most profound laws in all of economics, is false. And the focus was price variability. To conclude, *the mistaken interpretation of Ricardo's theory under an excessively simplified model may imply the application of policies that would lead to disastrous failures*. Such disasters must not be blamed on the theory, but to a mistaken interpretation of it due to both placing excessive emphasis on price variability and interpreting such a factor as the fundamental one.

5.1.5 Conclusion

As we have argued throughout this section, Taleb's critique is valid insofar as it identifies Ricardo's model as too simplistic and that it does not allow us to fully understand the fundamental importance of price variability in the development of international trade, specialization and the division of labor processes. Ricardo's mistake, also, resides in what can be called methodological nationalism. Countries do not benefit from specialization, the division of labor and trade. Rather, this applies, only, to *individuals* within the nation. The doctrine of methodological individualism of the Austrian school is definitive in this regard (Boettke and Coyne 2005; Hayek 1948; Hoppe 1992, 1995; Infantino 1998; Mises 1962, 1949 [1998];

[12] See Toye and Toye (2003), Etchebarne (2008), Ocampo and Parra (2003), and Ocampo (2015, 352–3). See also the next section for a full treatment of this theory.

[13] For an economic history of Argentina in the twentieth century, see Cortés Conde (2009).

Selgin 1988; White 1977). Moreover, as Taleb holds, antifragility is indeed relevant. There could be producers of commodities or products with characteristics that do not show simple comparative advantages with other competitors, but which are useful in certain scenarios (for instance, the proximity of the producer in a natural disaster, such as a wheat producer in Japan, although Canadians are better at this endeavor).[14] Despite this, it is incorrect to view price variability as the only relevant factor when analyzing international trade.

We have also analyzed Ricardo's theory and showed that it is valid in the light of Praxeology. In addition, it promotes an understanding of how countries benefit from trade, *as an instance of the more general law that any individual can benefit from such cooperation*.[15]

In this sense, Taleb's excessive focus on price variability can be seen as supporting the belief that free trade can lead to inefficient results, despite his own defense of the Hayekian (1944) spontaneous orders vis a vis central planning. Although his critique is valid, it is so only in the context of the exposition of a more important factor: specialization, such as any other criteria for resource allocation in the market, must be performed organically, and not by means of central planning. And this is true *even if price variability did not exist*. But even more so because it does exist.

Moreover, price variability will continue to occur under a system of free prices and unhampered markets. Milton Friedman (1982, 36) was once asked about the future course of the stock market: "Sir, to continue on that—in a general sense, what is the matter with the stock market now where virtually all of the good companies are substantially undervalued in terms of their real assets?". Came the answer: "If you think they are substantially under-valued in terms of their real assets you have an opportunity to make some money. I am not going to second guess the stock market. I have a very simple answer that I always give when people ask me what is going to happen to the stock market. I repeat the answer John Pierpont Morgan used to give and his answer was, '*It will fluctuate*.' I think that is a very good answer don't you?" (emphasis added).

Under anything even approaching laissez faire capitalism, the effects of price variability will be more readily seen as beneficial, since they would help allocate resources more effectively and contain poor results in specific sectors of the economy. In contrast, under a centrally planned system, *its effects can be systemic*, and thus negative for the economy as a whole.

In sum, Taleb's critique does not undermine the truth of the law of comparative advantage itself but does so for some of the assumptions of the model. The mistake, then, lies in Ricardo's *analysis*, not in Ricardo's *law*. Price variability is neither an argument *against* free markets, nor *for* interventionism.

---

[14] Moreover, some customers may prefer locally produced products, rather than imported, despite comparative advantages. In any case, *this* would be the comparative advantage of the product in the eyes of local customers, i.e. that they are locally produced.

[15] This is necessarily true in the ex ante sense, and almost always so ex post as well.

To conclude, Taleb's critique, in the present context, ultimately offers more justifications for, and therefore strengthens, Ricardo's fundamental insight: that free trade, and cooperation in the context of a free market, brings benefits for all agents.

Despite this, Taleb excessively focuses on price variability, although he does offer an important insight in favor of sound economics. That, unfortunately, may encourage the belief that free trade can lead to bad results, despite his own undoubted support for the spontaneous order argument against central planning.

Although this author does not oppose free markets, his implicit view that Ricardo's mistaken model affects in a way the validity of Ricardo's law, may lead to the very opposite of what he intends to defend, interventionism. This is so because some interventionist economist[16] can argue, "look, price variability is too important and free trade will not work because of it". This may well occur despite Taleb's view that free trade should be based on an organic process, on the market, precisely because of price variability.

Also, price variability is not often the cause of crises; these regularly happen due to monetary and fiscal interventions.[17] So, our critique of Taleb is more a *clarification* than a rebuttal, but, hopefully, an important and relevant one.

5.2 The Benefits of World Trade: A Critique of Prebisch-Singer[18]

Imports are in fact paid for by exports and not by money. (Ludwig Von Mises 1912, 252)

5.2.1 Introduction[19]

The theory of the deterioration in the terms of trade was developed independently by Hans Singer and Raúl Prebisch, mainly during the 1950s. It became the source of problematic economic policies throughout the world, particularly in Latin

---

[16] Such as Raúl Prebisch and Hans Singer's theory of the "deterioration in the terms of trade" (Ocampo 2015).

[17] See Hayek (1931), Mises (1912 [1953]), Rothbard (1963 [2000]; 1963 [2008]; 1983 [2008]).

[18] This section of the present chapter is based on our paper Futerman, Alan G., and Block, Walter E. 2020. "An Austrian Critique of the Prebisch-Singer Theory of the Deterioration in the Terms of Trade." *The Journal of Financial Economic Policy*, Vol. 12 No. 4, pp. 721–735. Available at https://www.emerald.com/insight/content/doi/10.1108/JFEP-09-2019-0181/full/html (last visited April 23, 2021).

[19] We are grateful to William Barnett II for helpful suggestions regarding an earlier version of this essay. The usual provisos of course apply: the authors are solely responsible for all errors and infelicities.

America. These programs consisted, primarily, in the development of import substitution industries reinforced by a series of protectionist measures.

Such policies were adopted because the theory claimed that there was a deterioration in the terms of trade between the export products by "periphery" countries with respect to those of the "core". The former consisted mainly of primary commodities, while the latter, were industrial. These policies were an attempt to change this dynamic. They ended in resounding failures due to the fact that the Prebisch-Singer hypothesis was erroneous.

In this work, we analyze why this was the case, and why the theory is wrong, from an Austrian economic perspective. The theory is reviewed in Sect. 5.2.2. Next, in Sect. 5.2.3, we present a concrete example, by focusing on the case of Argentina. We end with our conclusions in Sect. 5.2.4.

5.2.2 *The Theory of the Deterioration in the Terms of Trade*

The core-periphery scheme is a theory of economic analysis that makes a fundamental distinction between certain countries (the core, and the periphery). It claims a uni-directional cause and effect relationship: The former heavily impacts the latter, while the latter has little influence on the former, and often none.[20] The dog wags the tail; the tail does not wag the dog. The core "wags" the periphery, while the periphery does not "wag" the core.

According to this theory, the typical goods of periphery countries are low-income elasticity (commodities), with a specialized productive structure. For the core, they are high income elasticity (capital goods, etc.), with a diversified economic structure (Ocampo 2001, 26). Hence, Singer and Prebisch held that, over time, as income rose, the terms of trade of the latter increase with respect to the former, and therefore harm the periphery. This is so because with a low-income elasticity, as wealth increased there would not be much of a boost in demand for farm goods; in contrast, with high income elasticities, there would be for industrial goods. As a result, there is a need for an increasing volume of exports from the periphery in order to acquire the same volume of products from the core.

This dynamic, in turn, further afflicts the periphery, which eventually cannot pay its debts. Not surprisingly, the concept of "exchange terms" was also used for the development of fallacious theories such as "Dependence Theory" (Cardoso and Faletto 1969), and others, which claimed that the periphery ends up being politically controlled by the core through the latter's economic influence on the former.

According to the Prebisch-Singer theory, therefore, developing countries focused on the production of commodities would need to export a growing volume of the latter in order to import the same number of industrial products (from developed countries). Ocampo (2015, 352–3) explains:

[20] See Hoffmann and Schnabl (2011); Ballardini et al. (2011); Tejera et al. (2012).

> By incorporating some ideas of Schumpeter and in opposition to Malthus, two economists – the Argentine born Raul Prebisch and the German-British Hans Singer – in the 1950s independently developed the hypothesis of the secular deterioration of the relative commodity price. According to this hypothesis, in the long run the prices of *commodities* in relation to industrial goods show a declining trend. A corollary of this hypothesis is that developing countries are in a disadvantage facing industrialized countries, given that they export the former and import the latter. In a simplified fashion, this implies that they have to produce more wheat in order to buy a car or industrial machinery.
>
> The Prebisch-Singer hypothesis is based in two assumptions. First, that the demand for food is not very sensitive to increases in income. This means that, when industrial countries grow, in relative terms they demand less food (i.e., as they grow rich they expend less in food with respect to their level of income). Secondly, technological innovation is asymmetrical: while technological advances in industrial countries benefit the workers of those countries, technological advances in the food-exporting countries tend to benefit the consumers in industrial countries and not their own workers.
>
> Singer expanded this hypothesis based on the Schumpeterian theory of the business cycle and postulated that standardized industrial products prices would tend to deteriorate with respect to those which appear through innovation. This means that even if developing countries industrialize, they will keep being harmed because they will concentrate their efforts in the former, since innovation only happens in advanced countries. From this perspective, during the boom phase of the cycle the terms of trade of developing countries improve, while in the bust phase of the cycle, when recession and stagnation appears, these deteriorate.
>
> Prebisch and Singer developed their hypothesis not based on a sophisticated statistical analysis, but through the simple observation of the evolution in the terms of trade of England from 1870 to 1938. During this period, the prices of the products which England exported (mainly industrial) increased more than those which it imported (mainly agricultural). Prebisch and Singer concluded that for countries such as Argentina the opposite situation should have applied and they developed the hypothesis of the secular declining trend of the price of commodities appeared.
>
> However, there are several reasons for which their analysis was incorrect. Today, the academic world would not even consider this hypothesis, but in 1950, econometrics was yet in its infancy. Nevertheless, the Prebisch-Singer hypothesis was adopted as dogma in many Latin American countries, especially in Argentina, where it was used to justify unsuccessful import substitution policies. The use of statistical analysis – which has improved a lot in the last sixty years – does not support this hypothesis as an explanation of the evolution of the terms of trade during the XX century.[21]

What is wrong with this theory? First, the concepts of core and periphery are vague and diffuse. In other words, they are not clear enough to be used as tools of economic analysis. For instance, A. Hoffmann and G. Schnabl (2011, 6), define them as follows:

> One economy is the center economy, in which monetary policy decisions are exogenous (for instance based on domestic inflation and growth). The other economy is (a group) of periphery countries. The model does not pre-impose a restriction on which is the center and

---

[21] Translation from the original in Spanish by Emilio Ocampo. Republished with permission by the author.

which the periphery. But we will elaborate it assuming that the economy with higher saving preferences is the center economy. Further, we assume a similar size of the center economy and an aggregated group of periphery countries.

But, if there are no restrictions on which is the center and which the periphery, how should we determine this without *ad hoc* justifications? Moreover, why choose a higher saving preference as the standard for a core country? How should we judge size?

Also, a core can be a periphery and *vice versa*, depending on the context and standard by which it is compared; which means that a country could be the core of a smaller one, and also be the periphery of another one bigger than itself. Hence, the concepts are neither clear nor precise.

Moreover, there is no tight link between a country's level of economic development and its status as an exporter of primary commodities.[22] Second, the theory implicitly ignores services. International transportation services are provided overwhelmingly by core countries, and the prices of these services have been declining significantly because of technological innovations. This improves the terms of trade for countries in the periphery. Third, it does not account for the transfer of production, based on imports of technology and capital goods as producers in the core seek to reduce costs by moving production. Fourth, it flies in the face of rising standards of living in the periphery.

Further, this theory[23] does not take into account the possibility that there could be both boom and bust commodity cycles. Either could reverse the terms of trade. This could invalidate conclusions with respect to the alleged growing tendency for the need of a higher volume of agricultural exports to acquire the same volume of industrial imports. And it has been refuted by the empirical experience (Etchebarne 2008) of the XXth century, where both increases and decreases in the terms of trade have been registered.

Moreover, it does not incorporate technological evolution in both types of countries, where crops not only improve in quality, but also in quantity due to the use of agrochemicals, direct seeding, etc. In addition, it ignores the fact that imports of industrial goods may include capital goods which improve commodities productivity.

Also, it does not analyze other factors apart from price variability, such as monetary and fiscal influences, etc.

If this core exploits the periphery theory were correct, it would not apply, only, internationally. It would also explain intra national economic effects as well. After all manufacturing in the core, and farming in the periphery, is by no means limited to countries; if this thesis has validity, it should apply to areas within a given country. Consider the U.S. as a case in point. Detroit, Baltimore, Chicago, may

---

[22] For instance, both Argentina and Australia export commodities, but the latter is a developed country while the former is not. Iowa sends corn abroad as does Kansas, wheat. Neither is exactly impoverished.

[23] For a detailed analysis see Ocampo and Parra (2003), and Toye and Toye (2003).

reasonably be considered "core" areas. Where, then, lies the U.S. periphery? Clearly, in Iowa, Nebraska, South Dakota, and other "fly-over" terrain. We do not need anything like careful statistical analysis to demonstrate that the bread basket of this nation is not at all reeling in poverty, as it would be if the terms of trade were continually turning against agricultural output.[24] Nor are those major cities exactly fountainheads of wealth. Rather, great poverty prevails there. If this does not refute the Prebisch-Singer hypothesis, then nothing can.

Moreover, the same would apply to a city, and to a neighborhood, and then to specific families. The mistaken essence of the theory is that it assumes wealth as a zero-sum game.

However, it is telling that Prebisch developed a theory of the business cycle based on his conception of the core-periphery scheme, where the core countries influence, by means of their fiscal and monetary policies,[25] the periphery, but not vice versa. As such, he explained:

> Until before the First World War, London was the center of the international system featuring the gold standard. Great Britain was connected to the rest of the world, to the countries in the periphery, by strong commercial and economic ties and constituted the main financial center of the globe. Therefore the expansion and contraction movements that were generated there, had an impact on the economic activity in the rest of the world[26] Prebisch (1944 [1991], 320).

In this analysis, he not only treats the monetary impact, but also the fiscal impact in their relation.[27] Prebisch fundamentally identifies that the periphery depends on the core with respect to exports, and therefore once a crisis appears in the latter, it affects the former in an asymmetrical way. He contended:

> The characteristics of the Argentine cycle differ from those that are common to industrial and creditor countries. But although the process is different, our cycles are actually a reflex of the cycles in those countries, mainly Great Britain before the First World War, and then the United States, because of the important part that both countries, in their periods, have had in the economic activities of the world Prebisch (1944 [1991], 319).[28]

And,

> But the functioning of the gold standard was not the same in the core of the system that in the periphery. In the core, in London, the banks and financial institutions acted with entire freedom to expand credit and to increase their loans when an abundance of gold existed in the market. And they did it without the fear of causing an excessive reduction of their monetary reserves that could take them to the abandonment of the gold standard, because

---

[24] We abstract, here, from transfer payments. To ascertain which geographical areas are net beneficiaries of these transfers would take us too far from the subject of this work.

[25] This assumes that cycles are the result of fiscal and monetary policies in the core, whereas there are a number of cycle theories that do not maintain that, e.g., ABCT (monetary/credit, but not fiscal policy; yet, see Chap. 4), Keynes – real factors ("animal spirits" of businessmen re profit expectations and investment), and Schumpeter (innovation regarding production).

[26] Translated from the original in Spanish by the first mentioned author.

[27] See Ballardini et al. (2012).

[28] Translated from the original in Spanish by the first mentioned author.

> London had the supreme resource to stop and revert the movement when the time was judged as critical. The banks in the countries of the periphery – like our experience shows – also had the freedom to expand credit when metal entered during the boom, and their natural desire of not having unproductive funds in their balances stimulated this expansion. However, when gold outflowed in the form that we have seen, there was no other means in order to correct the situation and avoid the metal from going out than the contraction of credit, as much intense as the stronger the prior expansion had been. It was not conceived, of course, the possibility of acting by increasing the discount rate in competition with the London monetary core. The gold standard was, then, an automatic mechanism for the periphery countries but not for the core. The financial oligarchy of London had the organization, flexibility and required capabilities in order to manage the international gold standard system according to its own objectives, and monetary stability could only be achieved successfully at the expense of monetary shocks in the periphery countries Prebisch (1944 [1991], 322).[29]

Thus, this author claimed that the functioning of the banking system under fractional reserves was a factor that increased the crisis in *both* the periphery and the core:

> If the bank only lends the funds it gets by its clients and does not goes beyond, its economic function would only be to concentrate scattered savings and distribute them; it would not create any currency, but it would throw back again to the market the funds that it has been trusted with Prebisch (1921 [1991], 182).[30]

This way, periphery countries increase their exports, thereby growing their dependence on the core, in the boom phase of the cycle; but when a financial crisis afflicts the core, the latter then diminishes its imports, thus generating a negative impact in the capacity of the periphery to pay back both its debts and imports:

> ... it is on imports where the prod presents itself with the highest momentum and effect, not only because on them there is an impact as a consequence of the increase in inner businesses when a higher demand of external capital goods and consumption goods is created, but also because its enlargement is one of the factors that matters most in the transformation of the balance of payments ... Prebisch (1930 [1991], 613 and 618).[31]

And again:

> ... an important part of direct consumption of the country, or of the machinery and commodities for its industries, come from abroad, the increase in the purchasing power finally impacts on an increase of imports Prebisch (1932b [1991], 74).[32]

Moreover, the government increases its size in the boom phase of the cycle, and its accounts register a deficit, which, when the crisis arrives, worsens the previous consequences:

> The budget deficit is a primary factor in credit inflation and finally in the artificial stimulus to imports, with the consequent disequilibrium in the balance of payments. If the government spends above its real resources, it is forced to resort to credit, and thus compels its

[29] Translated from the original in Spanish by the first mentioned author.

[30] Translated from the original in Spanish by the first mentioned author.

[31] Translated from the original in Spanish by the first mentioned author.

[32] Translated from the original in Spanish by the first mentioned author.

> creditors to do the same, due to its lack of payment. In both cases, there is an expansion of loans, creation of bank fiduciary media, which its effects on businesses are the same, in substance, to those of the issuance of paper money. Thus, the population has an artificial purchasing power, originated in credit, which lets it increase its consumption or, according to the circumstances, remain its level despite of the economic depression. And because one important part of the goods that the country consumes come from abroad, as finished products or commodities and energy, that increase in purchasing power tends in turn to increase imports or prevents them to contract in the necessary proportion, as demanded by the decrease in exports Prebisch (1932a [1991], 45-46).[33]

> [...] after the bonfire of external financial markets, [...] a monetary tension more or less intense follows. Capital inflows are interrupted, and thus it is necessary to use the previously accumulated gold in order to pay both the imports and financial services that increased during the boom. The metal is exported, and therefore the amount of bank reserves fall, thus bringing familiar shocks because portfolios are immobilized due to the previous private and fiscal excesses during the boom Prebisch (1932a [1991], 64).[34]

Hence, according to Prebisch himself, price variability and terms of trade could be understood ultimately as a *consequence* of monetary and fiscal factors, and not as a primary.

In this sense, the application of the core-periphery concepts is closely linked to the monetary sector. Building on this, we could define the core as the countries that operate strong currencies which represent and act as monetary standards or patterns at a global scale, and therefore are the core, by the manipulation of money and interest rates, of economic cycles; and where the periphery depends, for saving, reserves and the external sector through the exchange rate, on the monetary standard from such core countries.

Of course, there are questions to be raised about this definition of core countries. Certainly, the U.S. is a core country, today (and one would probably say the same about certain European countries), but the USD, euro, GBP, etc. are not strong currencies on any absolute basis, only relatively. The only reason they may look strong at times is because that which they are being compared to is even weaker. Against assets, on a long-term basis, they are weak. A century ago, $20 would buy approximately one ounce of gold; today $20 will buy about 1/90th of an ounce of gold.[35] It might well be that core countries are better defined in terms of per capita GDP, and maybe population (this latter to eliminate countries such as Macau, Qatar, and a number of others).[36]

Therefore, the cycle in the core countries (if we follow this interpretation in the Austrian tradition)[37] is transmitted[38] to the periphery by its effect on prices and

33 Translated from the original in Spanish by the first mentioned author.

34 Translated from the original in Spanish by the first mentioned author.

35 If we take a price of around USD 1800.00 for an ounce of Gold, at the time of this writing.

36 We owe this point to William Barnett II.

37 On the Austrian business cycle theory, see Barnett and Block (2012), Garrison (2001), Hayek (1931), Mises (1912, 1949), Rothbard (1962 [2009]; 1963 [2000]), Woods (2009); see also Chap. 4.

38 On this transmission phenomenon, see Block et al. (2018).

interest rates. Also, the manipulation of the exchange rates and monetary policies of the periphery countries can have a feedback effect on the policies of the core.

Hence, the transmission of the problems from the financial system of the core to those of the periphery can be channeled through the private sector (such as by debts from banks and companies from the periphery to those of the core) or public sector (through the holdings by the private sector and central banks, of titles, notes, bonds and the like by treasuries of core countries), or via the increase of interest rates in the core, which in turn raises both the public and private debt's burden of the periphery nations (and reduces the value of their assets in the market).

Thus, disequilibrium and reversal of "terms of trade" arise as a result of the latter factors. This can occur both in a positive or negative way for periphery countries, depending on the phase of the business cycle.

The main point explained by the Austrian business cycle theory is the distortion of relative prices due to artificial government monetary manipulation exogenous to the market, later channeled through the financial system.

This business cycle approach can theoretically apply to core countries, and be transmitted to those of the periphery in essentially four ways:

1. Central banks in the core manipulate interest rates downward, their currencies weaken, and therefore prices of periphery exportable goods rise, thus generating in the latter countries a resource allocation towards those sectors that appear as artificially profitable because of such monetary policy in the core. The new saving from those periphery sectors is channeled to other sectors in the periphery economy. When foreign investment is incorporated into the analysis the expansion is channeled in those sectors and a bubble tends to form there.
2. Central banks from the core manipulate interest rates in a downward direction, and periphery governments start to borrow money (thus increasing debt) so as to increase public spending, which channels to several sectors. In this case the bubble is government growth.
3. A combination between the last two. Plus, the "profitable" sector (due to 1) is subject to high taxes; as a result the state collects more revenue and exacerbates the cycle. In this case the bubble appears in both sectors.
4. This is like the third case, but in addition the central banks from the periphery artificially lower interest rates and monetize public deficits in order to extend the boom. This Central Bank policy allows the central banks from the core to extend their cycle, because, as the old aphorism has it, "Currencies do not float, they sink at different rates" (Schiff 2006). So, the policy of monetary expansion by the periphery countries counterbalances the impact of the expansion by those in the core (in the sense that the currency from the core weakens less than otherwise), thus allowing the process to continue still further.

These are several different possible cases for open periphery economies, with fiat money and subject to a sub-cycle of the core cycle.

During the bust in the core countries, capital flows to the periphery fall. Faced with a reduction in foreign capital flows (known as "sudden stop"[39]), this is reflected in a decrease in the current account deficit and/or a reduction in international reserves. This situation puts upward pressure on the exchange rate of the periphery country.

Therefore, those sectors that did expand in the periphery because of long-term investment (in capital goods), such as housing, mining and industrial sectors, stop expanding and their revenue decline, which causes a fall in the value of assets. In consequence the crisis begins and since the government sector does not tend to decrease sufficiently, higher taxes, regulations and even larger public deficits appears. When interest rates fall again in the core during the new boom, the sub-cycle starts again.

Thus, the situation is different in the two sets of countries. Such a crisis creates an immediate impact on interest and exchange rates, which affect the prices of exports from the periphery and also entail a reduction in capital flows to the periphery (with a decreased possibility of accruing new debt). The current account collapses and/or the capital and financial account (both of the balance of payments) follows the same pattern. Whatever the source of capital, the system tends to collapse. The government and/or private sector bubbles explode due to lack of financing, and therefore the crisis is transmitted to the entire economy. This is the bust phase of the sub-cycle, attached to the bust of the core cycle.

However, in the context of the cycle, even when the core continues in the boom stage, a periphery country may still collapse due to inner causes. This may happen because of the problems involved with fractional reserve banking (under a Central Bank), which multiplies credit to an unsustainable boom.[40] Also, the quantity of money in circulation may not be consistent with the amount of reserves of foreign currency held by the central bank at the prevailing exchange rate (if the demand for local currency decreases in the face of a higher supply), thus forcing a devaluation. The system may collapse from within because of a massive capital flight due to distrust of uncontrolled public spending, forecast of devaluation, or a bank run in a closely related periphery country that affects trust (Ávila 2010, 65–68), etc.

This entire analysis works, arguendo, if we accept the concepts of core and periphery as *useful* economic tools of analysis. But even so we do not need to resort to terms of trade as a fundamental or primary aspect of it. Terms of trade, in this respect, are a derivative of monetary influences.

[39] See Calvo (1998), Edwards (2004), Reinhart and Calvo (2000).

[40] For more on this see Bagus (2003), Bagus et al. (2013), Barnett and Block (2005; 2008, 2009), Baxendale (2010), Barnett II and Block (2008), Block and Caplan (2008), Block and Garschina (1996), Block and Posner (2008), Davidson (2008), Davidson and Block (2011), Hanke (2008), Hazlitt (1979), Hollenback (2013, 2014), Hoppe (1994), Hoppe et al. (1998), Howden (2013), Huerta de Soto (1995, 1998, 2006, 2010, 2018), Hülsmann (1996, 2000, 2002; 2003; 2008), Murphy (2010), Polleit (2010), Reisman (1996, 2009), Rothbard (1962 [1991]; 1963 [2008]; 1962 [2009]); 1962 [1991], and Salerno (2010a, b, 2011).

In any case, the use of the core-periphery concepts is vague enough to conclude that it is wiser to avoid them. The monetary influences between countries can be explained easily without recurring to such concepts, and no explanatory power is lost.

Moreover, the mistaken idea of the deterioration in the terms of trade derives from the core-periphery concepts themselves, because they explicitly present a hierarchical relation between core and periphery, and therefore a case of subordination. In reality, however, in the context of a free market, trade is performed to mutual advantage, otherwise it would not happen. There are no winners and losers; there are only winners.[41] There are no leaders[42] and followers, no hierarchies. Of course, if the government intervenes in the marketplace, then there is no free trade and commercial relations may not be to mutual benefit. But this could be blamed directly on such interventionism (Hayek 1974 [2008]), not on a so-called core-periphery dynamic or a "dependence theory".

But, is it true that there are countries whose economies affect those with smaller ones? Absolutely,[43] but the concepts of core and periphery are not precise enough to illustrate this relation and may lead to error. It is much better to describe countries and their relations by their own terms.

Terms of trade are irrelevant when it comes to the benefits of commerce. As long as both parties agree to a deal by mutual consent, they both profit, ex ante, necessarily. This applies both to those in the "core" and those in the "periphery". There is no reason why decreasing terms of trade may justify protectionism or subsidizing import substitution industries. This is so not only because these measures are inefficient in theory, but also due to the fact that free trade has already proven its wonders, for the last two hundred years (at least).

5.2.3 *The Case Study of Argentina*

The problems of the theory, presented in the previous section, can be illustrated with the case of Argentina.[44]

This country followed a specific economic model (defined as "agro-export") between 1880 and 1930, which was the basis for its subsequent progress. This allowed it to place itself in the first spots in the per capita GDP world ranking until the mid XXth century (Cortés Conde and Gallo 1972 [1986]).

Basically, the country specialized in the production and export of mainly agricultural products, while importing primarily manufactured and capital goods. Even so,

---

[41] At least ex ante, and, almost always, ex post as well.

[42] Of course, entrepreneurs typically initiate matters, but that is an entirely different issue. On entrepreneurship, see Kirzner (1973).

[43] According to an aphorism, when the U.S. sneezes, Canada catches a cold. But it is the same with relatively large Massachusetts, and small Rhode Island.

[44] For an economic history of Argentina see Rapoport (2005 [2013]).

this comparative advantage *was not self-evident*. The development of cattle raising precedes agriculture in Argentina and in fact, the Argentinian government hired "experts" in order to study the viability of incorporating the latter into its model. Nevertheless, opinions were not all positive. As Meir Zylberberg (2008, 38) explains:

> …The opinion of the sage German paleontologist Conrado Burmeister, which had been hired by the government. Mr. Burmeister declared in 1875 that Argentina's economy was essentially focused in livestock, and that any effort to transform it in agricultural would lead to the worst results.[45]

Of course, the "sage" was wrong. Comparative advantage is identified and refined through the market process, over time and by means of trial and error, in the context of entrepreneurial ventures.[46] It does not come about as a result of self-evident facts.

Changes in the terms of trade of agricultural products with respect to industrial products did frequently impact Argentina's economy, though. Lower terms of trade against farm goods entailed recurring balance of payments crises (Cortés Conde 2009). But this is neither necessarily an illustration nor corroboration of the claim that a comparative advantage pattern of development is the cause of these maladies.

Even Prebisch himself allows that although price variability is relevant, it is neither the only factor involved nor the *most important*. In fact, the causal factors that generate the business cycle in the core, and exacerbates it in the periphery, are monetary and financial in nature.[47] Price variability, in these cases, is intensified by specific institutional arrangements that promote the crisis. In particular, these are of a monetary nature:

> …Roberto Cortés Conde contends that…the recurring crisis in the agro-export period were created by monetary problems, and not as a result of disequilibrium in the balance of payments…it applies to the period the 'rational expectations' model, according to which, due to the increase in credit and money supply, the public bought gold as a consequence of the expectations of the devaluation of the currency, as a result of an increased money supply, which in turn lead to the draining of reserves and the depreciation of the peso. This is what created the failure of the gold standard in order to maintain convertibility in 1876, 1885 and 1890; even though since 1885 the monetary system was actually of dirty float. This means that, with the excess of money supply that was a characteristic of the second half of the 80's decade, there were lost, on the one hand, reserves as in the system of fixed exchange rate and, on the other hand, came about a depreciation of the currency, as in the flexible exchange rate. The problem appeared in those years because the money supply increased above the GDP. Avoiding the deterioration of its income, the government intervened by selling gold in the exchange market as to avoid currency depreciation. This, instead of strengthening the peso, promoted the public to buy foreign assets by using bank credit. Sovereign debt payments would not have affected greatly the balance of payments, but the true cause of the

[45] Translated from the original in Spanish by the first mentioned author of the present article.

[46] See the previous section on Ricardo and Taleb, in this chapter.

[47] See Hayek (1931, 1933 [1966]), Mises (1912 [1953]), Rothbard (1962 [2009]; 1963 [2000]; 1963 [2008]; 1983 [2008]); see also Chap. 4.

deep disequilibrium was such leak of deposits, when reserves were drained and the currency depreciated (Rapoport et al. 2007, 13–4).[48]

If the use of the core-periphery concepts, arguendo, is legitimate, then the cycle in the periphery countries could be explained by the Austrian theory, but as a subcycle of the cycle in the core countries. This is what happens in the case of Argentina.

As even Prebisch recognized, crises were not primarily due to changes in the terms of trade, but to monetary phenomena. That is, to the sort of problems identified by the Austrian business cycle theory (with a focus in the monetary factor).

5.2.4 Conclusion

As we have seen throughout this work, the Prebisch-Singer "theory of the deterioration in the terms of trade" is plainly wrong. Unsurprisingly, the policies derived from it, i.e. import substitution, subsidies and protectionism, led to a resounding failure that harmed the growth of those countries that implemented them. This also ensured their increasing and continued underdevelopment.[49] Particularly, in many Central and South American countries.

According to some scholars, the concepts of core and periphery, of which the theory of the deterioration in the terms of trade is built on, may make sense, to a small degree, in order to identify specific relations between countries. Obviously, these could still be used, but even in this view, it would be wise to make very strong clarifications beforehand.[50] Most importantly, if used, these must be focused on a specific relation at a particular space and time, and not presented as an unchanging category of specific countries or areas. For instance, in the XVIIIth century the US would have been classified as a periphery and the UK as a core because of the asymmetry in their productive and industrial structures. It would then would not be possible to explain how the US came to join the core in the XIXth and XXth centuries, when its industry surpassed that of the UK. The *relation* could be explained, *to some extent*, in that fashion, but not as a *quality* of the US or the UK per se. Commodities, industrial goods, services and technology are relatively more important at different times.

More importantly, if the core-periphery concepts are used, the specific relevant factors of the relation identified must be monetary and financial. However, this is not at all our position. As we see matters, this distinction confuses more than it clarifies.

Argentina, that was in the beginning of the last century an example of prosperity as a result of free trade, ended up decaying and facing one crisis after another due to

[48] Translated from the original in Spanish by the first mentioned author. On the gold standard in Argentina, see Salama (2000).

[49] See Gwartney et al. (1996), particularly on the free trade aspects of dirigisme.

[50] A possible analysis on this research line could be seen in Tejera et al. (2012).

protectionism and import substitutions policies derived especially from the theory analyzed in this work.

Bibliography

Ávila, Jorge. 2010. *Antídotos Contra el Riesgo Argentino*. Buenos Aires. Available at http://www.jorgeavilaopina.com/wp-content/Antdotos.pdf. Last visited April 25, 2018.

Bagus, Philipp. 2003. The Commons and the Tragedy of Banking. *Mises Daily*, November 12. Available at http://mises.org/story/1373. Last visited June 13, 2019.

Bagus, Philipp, David Howden, and Walter E. Block. 2013. Deposits, Loans and Banking: Clarifying the Debate. *American Journal of Economics and Sociology* 72 (3): 627–644. Available at https://onlinelibrary.wiley.com/doi/abs/10.1111/ajes.12023. Last visited June 13, 2019.

Ballardini, M., L. Verón, and A. Tejera. 2011. *Hacia un Posible Dialogo entre las Teorías del Ciclo de los Jóvenes Hayek y Prebisch*. Colombia (August): Primer Seminario de Economía Austríaca y Heterodoxa.

Ballardini, M., A. Tejera, and L. Verón. 2012. *Hacia un Posible Dialogo entre las Teorías del Ciclo de los Jóvenes Hayek y Prebisch*. Fundación Bases. Unpublished.

Barnett II, William, and Walter E. Block. 2008. Time Deposits, Dimensions and Fraud. *Journal of Business Ethics*. Available at https://link.springer.com/article/10.1007/s10551-008-9976-9. Last visited June 13, 2019.

———. 2009. Financial Intermediaries, the Intertemporal-Carry Trade, and Austrian Business Cycles; or; Crash and Carry: Can Fraudulent Time Deposits Lead to an Austrian Business Cycle? Yes. *Journal Etica e Politica/Ethics & Politics* XI (1): 455–469. Available at http://www2.units.it/~etica/2009_1/BARNETT_BLOCK.pdf. Last visited June 13, 2019.

———. 2005. In Defense of Fiduciary Media—A Comment; or, What's Wrong with "Clown" or Play Money? *Quarterly Journal of Austrian Economics* 8 (2): 55–69. Available at http://mises.org/journals/qjae/pdf/qjae8_2_4.pdf. Last visited June 13, 2019.

———. 2012. *Essays in Austrian Economics*. New York: Ishi Press.

Baxendale, Tony. 2010. Free Banking, the Balance Sheet and Contract Law Approach. *The Cobden Centre*, March 15. Available at http://www.cobdencentre.org/2010/03/free-banking-the-balance-sheet-and-contract-law-approach/. Last visited June 13, 2019.

Block, Walter, and Bryan Caplan. 2008. Walter E. Block Versus Bryan Caplan on Fractional Reserve Banking. *Lew Rockwell*, November 1. Available at http://www.lewrockwell.com/block/block110.html. Last visited June 13, 2019.

Block, Walter, and Kenneth M. Garschina. 1996. Hayek, Business Cycles and Fractional Reserve Banking: Continuing the De-Homogenization Process. *Review of Austrian Economics* 9(1), 1995: 77–94. Available at http://www.mises.org/journals/rae/pdf/rae9_1_3.pdf. Last visited June 13, 2019.

Block, Walter Versus Eric Posner. 2008. Posner vs. Block on Fractional Reserve Banking. *Lew Rockwell*, November 29. Available at http://www.lewrockwell.com/block/block114.html. Last visited June 13, 2019.

Block, Walter E., Lucas M. Engelhardt, and Jeffrey M. Herbener. 2018. Is the Virus of International Macroeconomic Interventionism Infectious? An ABCT Analysis. *Quarterly Journal of Austrian Economics* 21 (4): 339–374. Available at https://mises-media.s3.amazonaws.com/Is%20the%20Virus%20of%20International%20Macroeconomic%20Interventionism%20Infectious.pdf. Last visited June 13, 2019.

Boettke, Peter, and Christopher Coyne. 2005. Methodological Individualism, Spontaneous Order and the Research Program of the Workshop in Political Theory and Policy Analysis. *Journal of Economic Behavior and Organization* 57: 145–158.

Böhm von Bawerk, E. 1888 [1930]. *The Positive Theory of Capital*. New York: G.E. Stechert & Co.
Calvo, Guillermo A. 1998. Capital Flows and Capital-Market Crises: The Simple Economics of Sudden Stops. *Journal of Applied Economics*, Universidad del CEMA 1(November):35–54.
Cardoso, F.H., and E. Faletto. 1969. *Dependencia y Desarrollo en América Latina*. México: Siglo XXI.
Cortés Conde, R. 2009. The Political Economy of Argentina in the Twentieth Century. In *Cambridge Latin American Studies*. New York: Cambridge University Press.
Cortés Conde, R., and E. Gallo. 1972 [1986]. *La República Conservadora*. Buenos Aires: Hyspamérica Ediciones Argentina S.A.
Davidson, Laura. 2008. Fractional Reserve Banking Is Indeed Fraudulent. *Lew Rockwell*, November 17. Available at http://www.lewrockwell.com/orig9/davidson-l1.html. Last visited June 13, 2019.
Davidson, Laura, and Walter E. Block. 2011. The Case Against Fiduciary Media: Ethics Is The Key. *The Journal of Business Ethics* 98 (3): 505–511. Available at http://www.springerlink.com/content/j76323752648720g/. Last visited June 13, 2019.
Edwards, Sebastian. 2004. Financial Openness, Sudden Stops, and Current-Account Reversals. *American Economic Review* 94 (2): 59–64.
Etchebarne, Agustín. 2008. Los Términos de Intercambio y el Cambio Tecnológico. *Revista de Instituciones, Ideas y Mercados* 48 (May): 159–195.
Friedman, Milton. 1982. Focus on Milton Friedman. *Focus*, No. 1, July. An address by Dr. Milton Friedman to the Annual General Meeting of the Fraser Institute on March 23, 1982 in Vancouver, BC. Available at https://www.fraserinstitute.org/sites/default/files/focus-on-milton-friedman.pdf. Last visited April 12, 2019.
Garrison, Roger W. 2001. *Time and Money: The Macroeconomics of Capital Structure*. London: Routledge.
Gordon, Scott. 1993. *History and Philosophy of Social Science*. London: Routledge.
Gwartney, James, Robert W. Lawson, and Walter E. Block. 1996. *Economic Freedom of the World, 1975–1995*. Vancouver: The Fraser Institute.
Hanke, Steve. 2008. Banking Crises: Plus Ça Change…. *Globe Asia*, November, pp. 168–169. Available at https://www.cato.org/publications/commentary/banking-crises-plus-c-change. Last visited June 13, 2019.
Hayek, Friedrich A. 1931. *Prices and Production*. London: Routledge.
———. 1933 [1966]. *Monetary Theory and The Trade Cycle*. The Ludwig Von Mises Institute: Auburn.
———. 1944. *The Road To Serfdom*. Chicago: The University of Chicago Press.
———. 1948. The Use of Knowledge in Society. In *Individualism and Economic Order*. Chicago: University of Chicago Press.
———. 1968 [2002]. Competition as a Discovery Procedure. Institut für Weltwirtschaft, Kiel University, N° 56 Kieler Vorträge series. Trans. From German Der Wettbewerb als Entdeckungsverfahren, by Marcellus S. Snow. In *The Quarterly Journal of Austrian Economics* 5(3): 9–23.
———. 1974 [2008]. "The Pretense of Knowledge". Friedrich A. Hayek's Nobel Prize Lecture, Nobel Prize in Economics. Stockholm, Sweden. In *A Free Market Monetary System and The Pretense of Knowledge*. Auburn: Ludwig Von Mises Institute.
———. 1982 [1998]. *Law, Legislation and Liberty Vol. 1 Rules and Order, Vol. 2 The Mirage of Social Justice, Vol. 3 The Political Order of a Free People*. Great Britain: Routledge.
Hazlitt, Henry. 1979. Gold Versus Fractional Reserves Part 1. *The Freeman*, May. https://mises.org/library/gold-versus-fractional-reserves
Hoffmann, A., and G. Schnabl 2011. National Monetary Policy, International Economic Instability and Feeback Effects – An Overinvestment View. Working Papers on Global Financial Markets, No. 19, Graduiertenkolleg Konstitutionelle Grundlagen globalisierter Finanzmärkte – Stabilität und Wandel, Jena und Halle (Saale).

Hollenback, Frank. 2013. Insuring Deposits, Ensuring Insolvency. *Mises Daily*, July 24. Available at http://mises.org/daily/6487/Insuring-Deposits-Ensuring-Insolvency. Last visited June 13, 2019.

———. 2014. The Fraud in Fractional Reserve Banking. *Mises Canada Daily*, November 26. Available at http://us2.campaign-archive2.com/?u=7e6cc2f6072b7ebfaa847047f&id=189c14aa12&e=53fc31c1bb. Last visited June 13, 2019.

Hoppe, Hans-Hermann. 1992. On Praxeology and the Praxeological Foundation of Epistemology and Ethics. In *The Meaning of Ludwig von Mises*, ed. J. Herbener. Boston: Dordrecht.

———. 1994. How Is Fiat Money Possible? Or, The Devolution of Money and Credit. *Review of Austrian Economics* 7 (2): 49–74.

———. 1995. *Economic Science and the Austrian Method*. Auburn: The Ludwig Von Mises Institute. Available at https://mises.org/library/economic-science-and-austrian-method. Last visited September 16, 2019.

Hoppe, Hans-Hermann, with Guido Hülsmann and Walter E. Block. 1998. Against Fiduciary Media. *Quarterly Journal of Austrian Economics* 1 (1): 19–50. Available at http://www.mises.org/journals/qjae/pdf/qjae1_1_2.pdf. Last visited June 13, 2019.

Howden, David. 2013. A Simple Math Question for Bankers. *Mises Canada Daily*, December 28. Available at http://mises.us2.list-manage1.com/track/click?u=7e6cc2f6072b7ebfaa847047f&id=b10182ff5e&e=cb339c58df; http://www.economicpolicyjournal.com/2013/12/the-best-critique-i-have-ever-read.html?utm_source=feedburner&utm_medium=email&utm_campaign=Feed%3A+economicpolicyjournal%2FKpwH+%28EconomicPolicyJournal.com%29. Last visited June 13, 2019.

Huerta de Soto, Jesús. 1995. A Critical Analysis of Central Banks and Fractional-Reserve Free Banking from the Austrian Perspective. *Review of Austrian Economics* 8 (2): 25–38.

———. 1998. A Critical Note on Fractional-Reserve Free Banking. *The Quarterly Journal of Austrian Economics* 1 (4): 25–49.

———. 2006. *Money, Bank Credit and Economic Cycles*. Auburn: Ludwig von Mises Institute.

———. 2010. Economic Recessions, Banking Reform, and the Future of Capitalism. *Mises Daily*, November 1. Available at http://mises.org/daily/4817. Last visited June 13, 2019.

———. 2018. What Free-Banking Advocates Get Wrong. *Mises Wire*, February 26. Available at https://mises.org/wire/what-free-banking-advocates-get-wrong. Last visited June 13, 2019.

Hülsmann, Jorg Guido. 1996. Free Banking and the Free Bankers. *Review of Austrian Economics* 9 (1): 3–53. Available at http://www.mises.org/journals/rae/pdf/rae9_1_1.pdf. Last visited June 13, 2019.

———. 2000. Banks Cannot Create Money. *The Independent Review: A Journal of Political Economy* 5 (1): 101–110. Available at http://www.independent.org/pdf/tir/tir_05_1_hulsman.pdf. Last visited June 13, 2019.

———. 2002. Free Banking Fractional Reserves: Reply to Pascal Salin. *Review of Austrian Economics* 1 (3) Available at http://www.mises.org/journals/qjae/pdf/qjae1_3_8.pdf. Last visited June 13, 2019.

———. 2003. Has Fractional-Reserve Banking Really Passed the Market Test? *Independent Review* 7 (3): 399–422. Available at http://www.independent.org/publications/tir/article.asp?a=90. Last visited June 13, 2019.

———. 2008. *The Ethics of Money Production*. Auburn: Ludwig von Mises Institute.

———. 2009. How to Use Methodological Individualism. *Mises Daily*, July 27. Available at https://mises.org/library/how-use-methodological-individualism. Last visited September 16, 2019.

Infantino, Lorenzo. 1998. *Individualism in Modern Thought from Adam Smith to Hayek*. London: Routledge.

Keynes, John M. 1936 [2013]. *The General Theory of Employment, Interest and Money. Vol. VII of the Collected Writings of John Maynard Keynes*. Cambridge: Cambridge University Press.

Kirzner, Israel M. 1973. *Competition and Entrepreneurship*. Chicago: University of Chicago Press.

Krugman, Paul. 1998. Ricardo's Difficult Idea: Why Intellectuals Can't Understand Comparative Advantage. In *Freedom and Trade: The Economics and Politics of International Trade*, ed. G. Cook, vol. 2, 22–36. New York: Routledge.

Krugman, Paul, Maurice Obstfeld, and Marc J. Melitz. 2012. *International Economics: Theory & Policy*. 9th cd. Boston: Pearson.

Menger, Carl. 1871 [2007]. *Principles of Economics*. Auburn: The Ludwig Von Mises Institute.

Mises, Ludwig Von. 1912 [1953]. *The Theory of Money and Credit*. New Haven: Yale University Press.

———. 1949 [1998]. *Human Action – A Treatise on Economics*. The Scholar's edition. Auburn: Ludwig Von Mises Institute.

———. 1962. *The Ultimate Foundation of Economic Science*. New York: Van Nostrand.

Murphy, Robert P. 2010. The Fractional-Reserve Banking Question. *Mises Daily*, June 14. Available at http://mises.org/daily/4499. Last visited June 13, 2019.

Ocampo, José A. 2001. Raúl Prebisch y la Agenda del Desarrollo en los Albores del Siglo XXI. *Revista de la CEPAL* 2001 (75): 25–40.

Ocampo, Emilio. 2015. *Entrampados en la Farsa: El Populismo y la Decadencia Argentina*. Buenos Aires: Claridad.

Ocampo, Jose A., and María A. Parra. 2003. Los términos de intercambio de los productos básicos en el siglo XX. *Revista de la CEPAL* 79. Abril.

Polleit, Thorsten. 2010. The Faults of Fractional-Reserve Banking. *Mises Daily*, December 23. Available at http://mises.org/daily/4880. Last visited June 13, 2019.

Prebisch, Raul. 1921 [1991]. *Planes para estabilizar el poder adquisitivo de la moneda*. Investigaciones de seminario, Buenos Aires, Universidad de Buenos Aires. Reproducido en *Raúl Prebisch. Obras 1919–1948*, vol. I, Cap. 24. Buenos Aires: Fundación Raúl Prebisch.

———. 1930 [1991]. El estado económico. *Revista Económica* 3 (1) Buenos Aires. Reproducido en *Raúl Prebisch. Obras 1919-1948*, vol. I, Cap. 48. Buenos Aires: Fundación Raúl Prebisch.

———. 1932a [1991]. La acción de emergencia en el problema monetario. *Revista económica* 5 (2) Buenos Aires. Reproducido en *Raúl Prebisch. Obras 1919-1948*, vol. II, Cap. 55. Buenos Aires: Fundación Raúl Prebisch.

———. 1932b [1991]. Tendencias del Balance de Pagos. *Revista Económica* 5 (6) Buenos Aires. Reproducido en *Raúl Prebisch. Obras 1919-1948*, vol. II, Cap. 56. Buenos Aires: Fundación Raúl Prebisch.

———. 1944 [1991]. *La moneda y los ciclos económicos en la argentina*. Impreso por Rotaprint Argentina. Reproducido en *Raúl Prebisch. Obras 1919–1948*, vol. III, Cap. 108 al 116. Buenos Aires: Fundación Raúl Prebisch.

Rapoport, M. 2005 [2013]. *Historia Económica, Política y Social de la Argentina (1880-2003)*. Buenos Aires: Emecé.

Rapoport, M., A. Musacchio, and F. Medici. 2007. *Ciclos Económicos, Sector Externo y Sistema Monetario en la Argentina (Versión preliminar). Simposio N° 27, Experiencias históricas de política económica en América: historias comparadas e inserción internacional*. Instituto de Investigaciones de Historia Económica y Social, Universidad de Buenos Aires.

Reinhart, Carmen, and Guillermo Calvo. 2000. When Capital Inflows Come to a Sudden Stop: Consequences and Policy Options. In *Reforming the International Monetary and Financial System*, ed. Peter Kenen and Alexandre Swoboda, 175–201. Washington, DC: International Monetary Fund.

Reisman, George. 1996. *Capitalism*, 954–963. Ottawa: Jameson Books.

———. 2009. A Pro-Free-Market Program for Economic Recovery. *Mises Daily*, November 20. Available at http://mises.org/daily/3870. Last visited June 13, 2019.

Ricardo, David. 1817. *On the Principles of Political Economy and Taxation*, 3rd ed. London: John Murray. 1821. Available at http://www.econlib.org/library/Ricardo/ricP.html. Last visited August 15, 2018.

Rothbard, Murray N. 1983 [2008]. *The Mistery of Banking*. The Ludwig Von Mises Institute: Auburn.

———. 1988. The Myth of Free Banking in Scotland. *Review of Austrian Economics*. Available at http://mises.org/journals/rae/pdf/RAE2_1_15.pdf. Last visited June 13, 2019.

———.1962 [1991]. The Case for a 100 Percent Gold Dollar. In *Search of a Monetary Constitution*, ed. Leland B. Yeager, 94–136. Cambridge, MA: Harvard University Press and Auburn: Ludwig von Mises Institute. See also "The Logic of Action One", pp. 364–384. Available at http://mises.org/story/1829; http://mises.org/rothbard/100percent.pdf. Last visited June 13, 2019

———. 1962 [2009]. *Man, Economy and State*, Scholar's Edition, 2nd ed. Auburn: Ludwig Von Mises Institute.

———. 1963 [2000]. *America's Great Depression*. The Ludwig Von Mises Institute: Auburn.

———. 1963 [2008]. *What Has Government Done with Our Money*. The Ludwig Von Mises Institute: Auburn.

Salama, E. 2000. *La Argentina y el Abandono del Patrón Oro*. Documento de Trabajo N°28. Departamento de Economía, Facultad de Ciencias Económicas, Universidad Nacional de La Plata. Noviembre.

Salerno, Joseph T. 2010a. *Money, Sound and Unsound*. Auburn: Ludwig von Mises Institute.

———. 2010b. White Contra Mises on Fiduciary Media. *Mises Daily*, May 14. Available at http://mises.org/daily/4389. Last visited June 13, 2019.

———. 2011. Dr. Joseph Salerno Explains Everything You Ever Wanted to Know About Money (But Were Afraid to Ask). *The Daily Bell*, July 3. Available at http://www.thedailybell.com/2602/Anthony-Wile-Dr-Joseph-Salerno-Explains-Everything-You-Ever-Wanted-to-Know-About-Money-But-Were-Afraid-to-Ask. Last visited June 13, 2019.

Schiff, Peter. 2006. Gold's Rise Is No Conundrum. *321Gold*, January 27. Available at http://www.321gold.com/editorials/schiff/schiff012706.html. Last visited May 5, 2019.

Selgin, George A. 1988. Praxeology and Understanding: An Analysis of the Controversy in Austrian Economics. *Review of Austrian Economics* 2: 19–58.

Smith, Adam. 1776 [1904]. *An Inquiry into the Nature and Causes of the Wealth of Nations*, 5th ed. London: Methuen & Co., Ltd. Available at http://www.econlib.org/library/Smith/smWN.html. Last visited August 15, 2018..

Stigler, George J. 1966. *The Theory of Price*, 3rd ed. New York: Macmillan.

Stolper, Wolfgang F., and Paul A. Samuelson. 1941. Protection and Real Wages. *The Review of Economic Studies* 9 (1): 58–73.

Taleb, Nassim N. 2012. *Antifragile: Things That Gain from Disorder*. New York: Random House.

Tejera, A., L. Verón, and A. Futerman. 2012. *El Ciclo Económico Periférico: Algunas Definiciones*. XLVII Reunión Anual AAEP (November). http://www.aaep.org.ar/anales/works/works2012/Tejera.pdf. Last visited April 25, 2018.

Thornton, Mark. 2000. "Review of Black 47 and Beyond: The Great Irish Famine in History, Economy, and Memory, by Cormac O Gráda". Book Review. *The Quarterly Journal of Austrian Economics* 3 (2): 89–93.

———. 2008. What Caused the Irish Potato Famine? *The Free Market*, April 1998, 16(4). Available at https://mises.org/library/what-caused-irish-potato-famine. Last visited August 15, 2018.

Toye, John F.J., and Richard Toye. 2003. The Origins and Interpretation of the Prebisch-Singer Thesis. *History of Political Economy* 35 (3): 437–467.

White, Lawrence. 1977. *The Methodology of the Austrian School Economists*. New York: Center for Libertarian Studies. Available at https://mises.org/library/methodology-austrian-school-economists-0. Last visited September 16, 2019.

Woods, Thomas E., Jr. 2009. *Meltdown: A Free-Market Look at Why the Stock Market Collapsed, the Economy Tanked, and Government Bailouts Will Make Things Worse*. Washington D.C.: Regnery Publishing.

Zylberberg, Meir. 2008. *Las Raíces Totalitarias del Fracaso Argentino*. Buenos Aires: Ediciones Cooperativa.

Chapter 6
Political Philosophy

I define anarchist society as one where there is no legal possibility for coercive aggression against the person or property of any individual. Anarchists oppose the State because it has its very being in such aggression, namely, the expropriation of private property through taxation, the coercive exclusion of other providers of defense service from its territory, and all of the other depredations and coercions that are built upon these twin foci of invasions of individual rights.

Murray Rothbard (2016)

Abstract This chapter is divided in two sections, both dealing with political philosophy from a libertarian perspective. In section 1, we maintain that statism cannot logically be defended in theory, while anarchism can be. We attempt to buttress both of these claims in this essay. Our main contention is that the statists' defense of the state is based not on sound theory nor practical evidence, but on a belief structured as an *a priori* truth. We attempt to show why this is wrong.

What are the specifics? We deny that there are any "market failures" which require statism to overcome and ameliorate. We maintain that taxation is indeed a violation of private property rights and cannot be justified either deontologically or pragmatically. The theory that regards tax payments as club dues is unwarranted. Without taxes, there can be no such thing as government.

As an alternative, there would be, of course, institutions that provide typical public sector services, such as armies, courts, police, but this, too, would be anarchy, of the anarcho-capitalist variety. Moreover, there is presently a state of anarchism between the some 200 nations of the world, in the absence of any over-riding world government. But this situation of anarchy between countries is vastly prefer-

---

This section of the present chapter is based on our paper Futerman, Alan G., and Block, Walter E. 2019. "The Fallacy of *A Priori* Statism." *Stetson Law Review*, Vol. 49, pp. 73-91. Available at https://www2.stetson.edu/law-review/wp-content/uploads/2020/01/3.-49.1-FutermanBlock.pdf (last visited May 8, 2021).

A. G. Futerman, W. E. Block, *The Austro-Libertarian Point of View*,
https://doi.org/10.1007/978-981-16-4691-1_6

able to an all-encompassing world government. Even an inveterate statist would pause before calling for an end to this anarchistic situation.

Also, secession is justified as an implication of free association. If a person is forced to associate with others against his will, this constitutes a rights violation. However, we take secession to its logical end point: to the individual level. That means, at least potentially, seven billion plus nations, one for each of us. That, in turn, would be equivalent to anarchism. Statists assume that it is inconceivable that a government should not exist. Hopefully, the present essay will enable them to look at the issue via a different perspective.

In Section 2, we try to respond to several criticisms of the Anarcho-Capitalist position. We do so by analyzing Professor Robert T. Miller's (Abstract, Stetson Law Rev 49: 93, 2019) critique of our perspective. This author offers two main criticisms of our views (Futerman and Block, Stetson Law Rev 49: 73, 2019). He first charges that our "doctrines implausibly assume that the transaction costs of allocating goods and services by means of the market will virtually always be lower than those of allocating goods and services by means of government regulation" (Miller, *supra* note 303). And second, "[W]hen extreme libertarians make strong normative claims . . . they are implicitly adopting some moral system or other . . . " (*Id.*). However, "when these suppressed premises are stated in full, they either become implausible or they no longer support the very strong conclusions extreme libertarians assert"(*Id.*).

This section of the chapter is an attempt to defend our perspective against these criticisms offered by Miller. By so doing, we are responding to criticisms against Anarcho-Capitalism articulated by many others, too, and thus supplying a stronger foundation for this theory.

Keywords Libertarianism · Anarchism · Capitalism

JEL Classifications K10 · K11 · K20 · K30 · P48

6.1 The Fundamental Basis of Statism, and the Anarcho-Capitalist Alternative

6.1.1 Introduction

In this chapter, we attempt to undermine the intellectual case for statism and to defend anarchism. Part II addresses the fallacy of *a priori* statism, and Part III presents the case for free market anarchism. The burden of Part IV is to deal with objections. We conclude in Part V.

6.1.2 A Priori Statism

In the field of epistemology, the *a priori*, in Kant's view (Kant 1781), corresponds to that knowledge which is independent of experience[1] and, according to John Stuart Mill, *before* experience. According to the latter's philosophy:

> We cannot acquire any genuine knowledge *a priori*, then. Mill holds that knowledge can be obtained only by empirical observation, and by reasoning which takes place on the ground of such observations. This principle stands at the heart of his radical empiricism. Sense perceptions are the 'original data, or ultimate premises of our knowledge' (*System*, VII: 7)—knowledge of greater levels of complexity is arrived at solely by inferences from that original data. (Macleod 2016)

Statism may be defined as the doctrine holding the government as a solution to virtually every problem. This definition is ours and refers to the essence of this viewpoint. Observe that we do not say that Statism holds the government only as the solution to *social* problems, given that in some extreme views the State is also viewed as a super entity that transcends this world. Hegel is an example of this viewpoint:

> Hegel is clear about the supereminent role of the state that stands above all else in giving expression to the Spirit (*Geist*) of a society in a sort of earthly kingdom of God, the realization of God in the world. True religion complements and supports this realization and thus cannot properly have supremacy over or be opposed to the state. (Duquette 2019)

Statists place the government above the rights and welfare of the individual.[2] The state is understood as an end in itself, while individuals are seen merely as a means to its ends.[3]

It is obvious that for statists, the superiority of the government is to be taken *a priori*.[4] For the statist mentality, it is not relevant to analyse the *actual* performance of this institution, or to determine which are its legitimate functions (if any).[5] For them, the government is not only conceptualized independently of and/or before experience, but also *apart* from experience.[6] The state's multiple failures (under

---

[1] The *a priori* is knowledge that is absolutely "independent of all experience." *Id.* at 136, *quoted in* Bruce Russell, *A Priori Justification and Knowledge*, STAN. ENCYCLOPEDIA PHIL. (May 19, 2014), https://plato.stanford.edu/archives/sum2017/entries/apriori/.

[2] *See* Binswanger (2013).

[3] *Id.*

[4] *See* Grutzmacher v. Howard Cty., 851 F.3d 332, 333 (4th Cir. 2016) (explaining the statist belief in absolute power of government).

[5] For limited government libertarians, or "minarchists"—as opposed to "statists," who want a totalitarian organization, or widespread interventionism—the only legitimate function of government is to protect from violence those in its geographical area. To this end, the only proper institutions are *defensive* armies to quell attack from abroad, police to do so against domestic criminals, and courts to determine guilt or innocence. *See generally* ROBERT NOZICK, ANARCHY, STATE, AND UTOPIA 162 (1974) or AYN RAND, ATLAS SHRUGGED 1075 (50th Anniversary ed., Signet 1996) (1957).

[6] This is the idea we will try to defend in the present essay.

either complete socialism or modern interventionism) are almost completely ignored.[7]

Statists take the so-called public sector as a viable and functional tool to organize society independent of any further consideration.[8] If the state fails, then the failure is not the fault of *the* state.[9] The superiority of this organization in solving any conceivable problem is to be taken as a non-falsifiable theory, which is immunized in different ways. The most relevant example of the latter approach is when socialists of different variants claim that the utter failure of socialism's application throughout the world was "not real socialism."[10]

Often, the state intervenes in the economy, harms it (or destroys it), and later the market is blamed.[11] Von Mises explained:

> Anti-capitalistic policies sabotage the operation of the capitalist system of the market economy. The failure of interventionism does not demonstrate the necessity of adopting socialism. It merely exposes the futility of interventionism. All those evils which the self-styled 'progressives' interpret as evidence of the failure of capitalism are the outcome of their allegedly beneficial interference with the market. Only the ignorant, wrongly identifying interventionism and capitalism, believe that the remedy for these evils is socialism.[12]

Cause and effect are constantly ignored. The reason for this misapprehension is that the state is understood as *the* solution (Kozinski 1991). So if the solution did not appear, then it is not the theory that went wrong, but something else. The truth is that this view is not a theory at all. It is only faith and, to be more specific: faith in the state. Why faith? Faith is defined as:

> Faith, inner attitude, conviction, or trust relating human beings to a supreme God or ultimate salvation. In religious traditions stressing divine grace, it is the inner certainty or attitude of love granted by God himself. In Christian theology, faith is the divinely inspired

---

[7] But not *totally* ignored. Interventionists such as Joseph Stiglitz, Paul Samuelson, and Paul Krugman will readily concede that no government is perfect. See PAUL SAMUELSON, ECONOMICS: AN INTRODUCTORY ANALYSIS 12 (1948), Krugman (2014), Stiglitz (2008). However, the very strong presumption of these writers is that on the rare occasions when the state does err, these errors almost always result from doing too little, not too much, and in the latter case, the solution is not to pull back, but to improve efficiency in intervention.

[8] Interventionists such as Paul Samuelson consider that the state must get involved in instances where the market apparently fails. *See* SAMUELSON, *supra* note 210, at 40–41.

[9] See Marshall and Cole (2017).

[10] See Niemietz (2017). Further, Noam Chomsky once described the idea "*that the society created by Lenin and Trotsky and moulded* [sic] *further by Stalin . . . has some relation to socialism*" as a "*fantasy*". Owen Jones recently wrote that "*A socialist society . . . doesn't exist yet, but one day it must.*" Stephen Resnick, a professor of—oddly enough—economics, said: "*We can't concede the end of communism. Communism hasn't been tried on a society-wide basis.*" *Id.*

[11] LUDWIG VON MISES, HUMAN ACTION—A TREATISE ON ECONOMICS 312 (The Ludwig von Mises Institute 1998) (1940) [hereinafter VON MISES, HUMAN ACTION]; LUDWIG VON MISES, SOCIALISM: AN ECONOMIC AND SOCIOLOGICAL ANALYSIS 527 (J. Kahane trans., Yale Univ. Press 1951) (1922), https://mises-media.s3.amazonaws.com/Socialism%20An%20Economic%20and%20Sociological%20Analysis_3.pdf [hereinafter VON MISES, SOCIALISM].

[12] VON MISES, Socialism, *supra* note 214, at 532.

> human response to God's historical revelation through Jesus Christ and, consequently, is of crucial significance. [13]

Naturally, in the sense that we use the term here, the faith placed in God in religion is directed by statists to thc Statc. And this is compatible with the most extreme versions of statism, as shown above regarding Hegel's conception of the State.[14]

As a new logical fallacy, to support the state always and irrespective of the context as a solution to every problem, we can name it the fallacy of *a priori* statism.

For statists, the concepts of "solution" and "state" go with each other. Since the State is conceptualized as an all-powerful agent, its action (defined or not) is understood as the solution to every problem. Therefore, when problems are not solved *through* the state, then *more* government intervention is logically required. The syllogism goes like this:

> The state is the solution to every problem (major premise).
> There is a problem that needs to be solved (minor premise).
> The state should intervene in order to solve it (conclusion).

However, if interventionism results in chaos, the major premise is never changed. Instead, the resulting chaos solidifies the unfalsifiable nature of statism because neither the government's alleged success nor failure harms the theory. For statists, the state is always and necessarily the solution.

How do the views of those who advocate liberty stack up in contrast to the socialist statists? There are, essentially, two schools of thought on this matter, and we offer both.

First, there are those who do not hold libertarianism as *the* solution to every problem. The main idea, here, is that individuals *must* be free to solve their own problems. It does not assume that the *solution* to these difficulties is always and ever the free enterprise system (it is not oriented toward magic), but only that freedom is a necessary (but not sufficient) condition in order to find a solution. In other words, libertarianism is based on the *condition* to find solutions: not the solution *itself* (von Hayek 1974).

Statists often resort to the "Nirvana Fallacy," by comparing the market as it is (including interventions all throughout) with an ideal State. Harold Demsetz explains on a related matter:

> The view that now pervades much public policy economics implicitly presents the relevant choice as between an ideal norm and an existing 'imperfect' institutional arrangement. This *nirvana* approach differs considerably from a *comparative institution* approach in which the relevant choice is between alternative real institutional arrangements. In practice, those who adopt the nirvana viewpoint seek to discover discrepancies between the ideal and the real and if discrepancies are found, they deduce that the real is inefficient (Demsetz 1969).

---

[13] *Faith*, ENCYCLOPAEDIA BRITANNICA, https://www.britannica.com/topic/faith (last updated Jun. 16, 2017).

[14] "Everything in the State, nothing against the State, nothing outside the State"; is Benito Mussolini's perspective on this matter. Quoted in Rifkind (2012).

This fallacy[15] derives from the statists major premise that the state is the solution for everything. This stark contrast between libertarianism's conditions-based and Statism's solution-based approach demonstrates the difference between a sound political theory and utopia or magic (and this is to say a lot: statism often turns into a dystopia).

Taken as a super-entity with anthropomorphic characteristics, the State is often seen as an acting agent (Manwaring 1938). The "organic theory of the state" is a theory that:

> ...pictures the politico-economic state as a living organism, a large-scale manifestation of the same basic biological laws as those studied to-day by means of the microscope and test-tube. Thus pictured, political, economic and social institutions become literally organs of the body-politic or functions of the economic order, in much the same way that the heart is an organ performing a necessary function in the human body.[16]

This theory, therefore, is a logical conclusion of the Statist approach. Here, the State is the *real* entity; it is comprised of individuals who are to it what the organs of the body are to the person: necessary, but subservient.[17]

Nevertheless, since the State is not a super-entity, but an institution run by individuals, some people must necessarily direct its functions. In this respect, these individuals are the ones that define themselves as the "voice" of society, or the "voice" of the party, and rule the State (and its citizens).[18]

Given that interventionism fails, but the *idea* of interventionism persists, only the incumbents are blamed for statism's disastrous consequences. Mao, Stalin, or Pol Pot are, for statists, heretics who do not represent the ideas they claim to stand for.[19] Thus, given that the State does not work by itself, but through specific individuals, and these are the ones blamed for its failures, statism is immunized from being refuted—politicians may be censured, but not the institution of which they are agents. In this respect, politicians are both necessary to apply the theory (guiding the state) and defend it (by being held responsible for the state's failures). But the idea of the State remains unharmed.

There is also a second perspective within the libertarian community. Under this perspective, all market transactions are at least beneficial *ex ante* and, usually, *ex post* also. In the *ex ante* sense, this is apodictic, logically undeniable.[20] It is not

[15] *See also* Stearns (1994) (explaining how "through the 'nirvana fallacy,' scholars erroneously compare real-world institutions with some abstract or ideal institution, even if the institution has never existed or . . . has been proven impossible to devise").

[16] *Id.*

[17] *Id. See also* McCloskey (1963) (explaining that critics of the organic theory "argue that if the state is an organism, it is therefore both ontologically higher and more valuable than its parts").

[18] *See* McCloskey, *supra* note 224, at 311 (analogizing the state to an organism that can develop its ideas through select individuals with power).

[19] *See* Niemietz, *supra* note 213.

[20] von Mises, Human Action, *supra* note 214, at 648.

falsifiable[21]—a quality that (is/makes it) the be-all and end-all about scientific propositions for the followers of Karl Popper. In saying this, are these libertarians not admitting that they are partaking in something similar to the socialists' claims of infallibility? This fact cannot be denied. Not only are there strong parallels between the two stances—they are indistinguishable.

We just got finished lambasting the views of our friends on the left for this stand of theirs; are we not now embracing the very same philosophical principle? Yes and no. The "yes" part consists of the fact that this perspective, too, is making a claim "independent of experience" or "before experience." It is thus also an *a priori* claim. Not, of course, that socialism necessarily leads to beneficial effects, but, rather, that only laissez faire capitalism is the condition to achieve this end.[22]

In support of the apriorism viewpoint of the left,[23] there is nothing wrong with this modality, per se. What distinguishes Austrian economics from the mainstream in political economy is that the former does indeed embrace this methodology.[24]

---

[21] It is sometimes claimed that psychoanalysis or Freudianism, too, is an *a priori* system. It is, to the extent that all critics are dismissed as having mental diseases. If so, then it would be impossible to logically refute this system of psychology; thus, it, too, would be held on an *a priori* basis, as a tautology. *Id.* at 35. For the avid Freudian, to deny this viewpoint, or denigrate, is to engage in irrationality.

[22] See Murray (2011).

[23] Even though statists never present themselves in this way, they nevertheless implicitly resort to this methodology. See Murray N. Rothbard, *In Defense of "Extreme Apriorism"* (1957), *reprinted in* Economic Controversies 103, 107 (2011), https://mises.org/sites/default/files/Economic%20Controversies_2.pdf.

[24] See Hans-Hermann Hoppe, *Austrian Rationalism in the Age of the Decline of Positivism, in* The Economics and Ethics of Private Property 347, 348 (2d. ed.1993), https://mises-media.s3.amazonaws.com/Economics%20and%20Ethics%20of%20Private%20Property%20Studies%20in%20Political%20Economy%20and%20Philosophy_3.pdf; Hans-Hermann Hoppe, Economic Science and the Austrian Method 8–9 (1995), https://mises.org/sites/default/files/Economic%20Science%20and%20the%20Austrian%20Method_3.pdf; Ludwig von Mises, Theory and History: An Interpretation of Social and Economic Evolution 104 (Ludwig von Mises Institute 2007) (1957), https://mises-media.s3.amazonaws.com/Theory%20and%20History%20An%20Interpretation%20of%20Social%20and%20Economic%20Evolution_1.pdf; von Mises, Human Action, *supra* note 214, at 32; Murray N. Rothbard, *Lange, Mises and Praxeology: The Retreat from Marxism* (1971), *reprinted in* Economic Controversies 801, 806 (Ludwig von Mises Institute 2011), https://mises.org/sites/default/files/Economic%20Controversies_2.pdf; Murray N. Rothbard, *Praxeology: The Methodology of Austrian Economics* (1976), *reprinted in* Economic Controversies 59, 59 (Ludwig von Mises Institute 2011), https://mises.org/sites/default/files/Economic%20Controversies_2.pdf; Murray N. Rothbard, *Praxeology as the Method of the Social Sciences* (1973), *reprinted in* Economic Controversies 29, 33 (Ludwig von Mises Institute 2011), https://mises.org/sites/default/files/Economic%20Controversies_2.pdf; Rothbard, *Praxeology, Value Judgments, and Public Policy*, *supra* note 229, at 92; Rothbard, *In Defense of "Extreme Apriorism," supra* note 230, at 107; Murray N. Rothbard, Man, Economy, and State with Power and Market 649 (2d ed. 2009), https://mises.org/sites/default/files/Man,%20Economy,%20and%20State,%20with%20Power%20and%20Market_2.pdf; George A. Selgin, Praxeology and Understanding: An Analysis of the Controversy in Austrian Economics 15 (Ludwig von Mises Institute 1990) (1988), https://mises-media.s3.amazonaws.com/Praxeology%20and%20Understanding%20An%20

Why, then, do we reject the *a priori* stance of the statists? Even more basic, how are libertarian apriorists different from their socialist *counterparts*? There are several reasons.

First, just because an argument seems logical does not mean it is correct. Consider the following syllogism:

Major premise: 8 is larger than 9.
Minor premise: 7 is larger than 8.
Conclusion: 7 is larger than 9.

As a classical syllogism, this accords with the formal laws of logic, just like some *a priori* arguments do; and yet—each and every line of it is false. Similarly, the claims of the statists, who argue in an *a priori* manner and fulfil some of the requirements of logic, may still very properly be rejected.

Second, empirical evidence indicates a gradual phenomenon. Yes, there is no pure laissez faire capitalist society on the face of the earth, but some are closer than others (James Gwartney et al. 1996). And, the closer a society is to pure laissez faire capitalism, the closer they are to conquering poverty.[25] That is, the more economically free a country is, the greater is not only its per capita income, but also its growth rate.[26] This empirical proof is something the statists surely cannot even come close to matching. To the degree that capitalism applied, growth and development followed, whereas to the degree that statism applied, destruction and poverty ensued.[27] This is what renders statist principles not only independent of experience, but apart from and *against* it.

Third, when markets seem to fail, libertarians are able to specify in great and exhaustive detail exactly *why*: [28] it is almost *always* due to *lack* of free enterprise and private property rights, not *because* of them.[29] The statists may offer the non-falsifiable claim that had Venezuela, Cuba, the U.S.S.R., the People's Republic of

Analysis%20of%20the%20Controversy%20in%20Austrian%20Economics_3.pdf; Batemarco (1985); Block (1999); Fox (1992); Hans-Hermann Hoppe, *On Praxeology and the Praxeological Foundation of Epistemology and Ethics*, *in* THE MEANING OF LUDWIG VON MISES 134, 151 (Jeffrey M. Herbener ed., 1992); Hülsmann (1999); Mario J. Rizzo, *Praxeology and Econometrics: A Critique of Positivist Economics*, *in* NEW DIRECTIONS IN AUSTRIAN ECONOMICS 40, 49 (Louis M. Spadaro ed., Institute for Humane Studies 1978), https://mises-media.s3.amazonaws.com/New%20Directions%20in%20Austrian%20Economics_2.pdf; Murray N. Rothbard, *Praxeology and the Method of Economics* (1973), *reprinted in* 18 AUSTRIAN ECONOMICS: A READER 55, 76–79 (Richard M. Ebeling ed., 1991); Wiśniewski (2014); Block (1973, 1980); Hoppe (1989); Thorsten Polleit, *Mises's Apriorism Against Relativism in Economics*, MISES INSTITUTE (Apr. 25, 2008), https://mises.org/library/misess-apriorism-against-relativism-economics; Thorsten Polleit, *True Knowledge from A Priori Theory*, MISES INSTITUTE (Jun. 8, 2011), https://mises.org/library/true-knowledge-priori-theory.

[25] *Id.* at 91.

[26] *Id.* at 89.

[27] *Id.*

[28] Francis M. Bator, *The Anatomy of Market Failure* (1958), *reprinted in* THE THEORY OF MARKET FAILURE: A CRITICAL EXAMINATION 35, 48 (Tyler Cowen ed., 1988).

[29] VON MISES, SOCIALISM, *supra* note 214, at 362.

China, or D.P.R.K. had better leaders, their economies would not have been the basket cases they turned out to be. But statists never offer, nor *can* they offer, a coherent reason for justifying that better government leadership is more effective at fixing failing economies than free enterprise.[30] In very sharp contrast indeed, defenders of free enterprise can and do bear this burden. For example, break-up of the family? Due to government welfare programs.[31] Teenaged unemployment? The minimum wage law is responsible.[32] The business cycle? The result of central banking and monetary policy.[33] Highway fatalities? They emanate from road socialism.[34] Poor housing? Rent control, [35] zoning, and building codes.[36] Chief executive officer

---

[30] *Id.* at 184. *See also* ROTHBARD, MAN, ECONOMY, AND STATE POWER, *supra* note 231, at 1306–08 (explaining free market in terms of human morality).

[31] See CHARLES MURRAY, LOSING GROUND: AMERICAN SOCIAL POLICY FROM 1950–1980, at 124 (1984).

[32] See Shapiro (1990) ("Most studies conclude that teenagers fare the worst from minimum wage increases."). See also Chap. 3.

[33] MURRAY N. ROTHBARD, THE MYSTERY OF BANKING 186 (2d ed. 2008), https://mises-media.s3.amazonaws.com/Mystery%20of%20Banking_2.pdf (for instance, using the Bank of England as an example of "how the Central Bank . . . had generated and perpetuated . . . inflations and contractions, and how it had borne the primary responsibility for unsound money and for booms and busts").

[34] See WALTER E. BLOCK, THE PRIVATIZATION OF ROADS AND HIGHWAYS: HUMAN AND ECONOMIC FACTORS 170 (2009), https://mises-media.s3.amazonaws.com/The%20Privatization%20of%20Roads%20and%20Highways_2.pdf (arguing that "competition between private highway owners would reduce the motor vehicle death rate").

[35] See CHARLES W. BAIRD, RENT CONTROL: THE PERENNIAL FOLLY 54–55 (1980); R. W. GRANT, RENT CONTROL AND THE WAR AGAINST THE POOR: IDEOLOGY, THE POOR AND THE ROLE OF POLITICAL FORCE # (1989); Block et al. (1998); Block (2002); Milton Friedman & George J. Stigler, *Roofs or Ceilings?: The Current Housing Problem* (1946), *reprinted in* RENT CONTROL: MYTHS AND REALITIES 87, 102 (Walter Block & Edgar Olsen eds., 1981), http://www.walterblock.com/wp-content/uploads/publications/RentControlMythsRealities.pdf; Grampp (1950); Friedrich A. Hayek, *The Repercussions of Rent Restrictions* (1930), *reprinted in* RENT CONTROL: MYTHS AND REALITIES 169, 175 (Walter Block & Edgar Olsen eds., 1981), http://www.walterblock.com/wp-content/uploads/publications/RentControlMythsRealities.pdf; Gary Galles, *Rent Control Makes for Good Politics and Bad Economics*, MISES (Apr. 10, 2017), https://mises.org/blog/rent-control-makes-good-politics-and-bad-economics.

[36] See MICHAEL GOLDBERG ET AL., ZONING: ITS COSTS AND RELEVANCE FOR THE 1980S, at 40–41 (Walter Block ed., 1980), https://www.fraserinstitute.org/sites/default/files/zoning-costs-and-relevance-for-the-1980s.pdf; BERNARD H. SIEGAN, LAND USE WITHOUT ZONING 95–96 (1972); Walter E. Block, *Private Urban Planning and Free Enterprise*, *in* CITIES AND PRIVATE PLANNING: PROPERTY RIGHTS, ENTREPRENEURSHIP AND TRANSACTION COSTS 93, 96–97 (David Emanuel Andersson & Stefano Moroni eds., 2014); Siegan (1970).

salaries out of control? Laws[37] against corporate raiding.[38] This list could go on and on. And on. And the statists have nothing, nothing at all, to match it.

However, a critic may object to this alternative libertarian position. He might do so on the ground that we are ultimately resorting to empirical claims (in favour of markets) in order to reject *a priori* statements (by statists). If so, we would thereby be refuting a foundation of the free market system exclusively on an *a priori* basis. This is so because we are not confronting our *a priori* proposition with that of statists, since if we do, and in the absence of any further considerations (such as empirical evidence that supports our contention), how are we to claim our position is better than the other? The answer is that statism is wrong on the theoretical level too.[39] The difficulty (or, more specifically, impossibility) of economic calculation in a socialist system makes it *logically impossible* to claim that the state is the solution to any problem, let alone every problem.[40]

On the other hand, we rely upon the general praxeological axiom (or principle) that every human action is an attempt to pass from a less to a more satisfactory state of affairs.[41] Therefore, our claim that market transactions are beneficial in the *ex ante* sense can be properly defined and defended. Thus, the solid theoretical foundation of the market system is what explains its success in empirical cases. Conversely, the utter empirical failure of statism always contradicts its fundamental claim, therefore requiring ways to immunize the theory without ever changing its original contention.

---

[37] See Murray N. Rothbard, *Rethinking The '80s* (1992), *reprinted in* Making Economic Sense 103, 104 (2d ed. 2006), https://mises-media.s3.amazonaws.com/Making%20Economic%20Sense_3.pdf; Murray N. Rothbard, *Michael R. Milken vs. The Power Elite* (1989), *reprinted in* Making Economic Sense 181, 182 (2d ed. 2006), https://mises-media.s3.amazonaws.com/Making%20Economic%20Sense_3.pdf; Llewellyn Rockwell, *Michael R. Milken: Political Prisoner?*, *in* The Economics of Liberty 70, 104 (Llewellyn H. Rockwell ed., 1990), https://mises-media.s3.amazonaws.com/The%20Economics%20of%20Liberty_2.pdf; Norman Barry, *The Logic and Morality of Takeovers: Do Corporate Takeovers Deserve Their Reviled Status?*, FEE (July 1, 2000), https://fee.org/articles/the-logic-and-morality-of-takeovers/.

[38] A corporate raider is defined as:

> A person or business that attempts to take control of a corporation, against its wishes, by buying its stock and replacing its management, often for the purpose of selling off its assets.

Corporate Raider, Black's Law Dictionary (11th ed. 2019).

[39] See von Mises, Socialism, *supra* note 214, at 211; Ayn Rand, *War and Peace*, 1 Objectivist Newsletter 44, 44 (1962).

[40] See von Mises, Socialism, *supra* note 214, at 135–36.

[41] See Ludwig von Mises, Human Action, *supra* note 214, at 13. This axiom is that from which economic laws are ultimately derived in the Austrian tradition. See also Chap. 1.

6.1.3 Anarchism

Murray Rothbard defines the non-aggression principle ("NAP"), the essence of the libertarian philosophy, in the following way:

> [t]he fundamental axiom of libertarian theory is that no one may threaten or commit violence ("aggress") against another man's person or property. Violence may be employed only against the man who commits such violence; that is, only defensively against the aggressive violence of another. In short, no violence may be employed against a non-aggressor. Here is the fundamental rule from which can be deduced the entire corpus of libertarian theory. [42]

Once one accepts the NAP, the anarcho-capitalist position readily, and logically, follows. This foundational building block of libertarianism maintains that it is illicit, and thus should be illegal, to threaten or initiate violence against innocent targets.[43] This philosophical perspective does not oppose violence per se. Pacifism is not a requirement; physically forceful self-defence is certainly a valid response to criminality.[44] Boxing and sadomasochism, too, are legitimate, since both parties have agreed to take part in these activities.[45] This is an inviolate aspect of libertarianism: those who violate the NAP are outlaws and should be subject to proper punishment.[46]

---

[42] Murray N. Rothbard, *War, Peace, and the State*, *in* The Myth of National Defense: Essays on the Theory and History of Security 65, 66 (Hans-Hermann Hoppe ed., 2003), https://mises-media.s3.amazonaws.com/Myth%20of%20National%20Defense%2C%20The%20Essays%20on%20the%20Theory%20and%20History%20of%20Security%20Production_3.pdf. *See also* Murray N. Rothbard, The Ethics of Liberty 51–52 (New York Univ. Press 1998) (1982), https://mises-media.s3.amazonaws.com/The%20Ethics%20of%20Liberty_0.pdf.

[43] *See* Rothbard, *War, Peace, and the State*, *supra* note 250, at 66.

[44] See Rothbard, The Ethics of Liberty, *supra* note 250, at 77.

[45] See Laurence M. Vance, *The Simplicity of Libertarianism*, Future of Freedom, June 2015, at 15, 19, https://www.fff.org/explore-freedom/article/the-simplicity-of-libertarianism/.

[46] On libertarian punishment theory, see Robert Nozick, Philosophical Explanations 363–73 (1981), http://skepdic.ru/wp-content/uploads/2013/05/Nozick.pdf; Rothbard, The Ethics of Liberty, *supra* note 250, at 88; William Barnett II, Walter E. Block & Gene Callahan, *The Paradox of Coase as a Defender of Free Markets*, 1 N.Y.U. J. L. & Liberty 1075, 1090 (2005); Walter E. Block, *Austrian Law and Economics: The Contributions of Adolf Reinach and Murray Rothbard on Law, Economics, and Praxeology*, 7 Q. J. Austrian Econ. 69, 75 (2004); Walter E. Block, *Berman on Blackmail: Taking Motives Fervently*, 3 Fla. St. U. Bus. Rev. 57, 70 (2003); Walter E. Block, *Libertarian Punishment Theory: Working for, and Donating to, the State*, 1 Libr. Papers, art. no. 17, at 1, (2009); Walter E. Block, *Libertarianism vs. Objectivism; A Response to Peter Schwartz*, 26 Reason Papers 39, 50–51 (2003); Walter E. Block, *Market Inalienability Once Again: Reply to Radin*, 22 T. Jefferson L. Rev. 37, 38 (1999); Walter E. Block, *Radical Libertarianism: Applying Libertarian Principles to Dealing with the Unjust Government, Part II*, 28 Reason Papers 85, 129 (2006); Walter E. Block, *Reply to Frank van Dun's "Natural Law and the Jurisprudence of Freedom,"* 18 J. Libr. Stud. 65, 70 (2004); Walter E. Block, *Toward a Libertarian Theory of Guilt & Punishment for the Crime of Statism*, in Property, Freedom and Society: Essays in Honor of Hans-Hermann Hoppe 137, 141 (Jörg Guido Hülsmann & Stephan Kinsella eds., 2009), https://mises-media.s3.amazonaws.com/Property%2C%20Freedom%2C%20and%20Society%20Essays%20in%20Honor%20of%20Hans-Hermann%20

How, and in what way, is the State necessarily a violator of this precept? This comes about in several ways. First, all governments levy taxes on the inhabitants of their territory. Were any private individual to levy taxes against someone else, it would be pellucidly clear that this would constitute theft. Yes, the golf or tennis club is justified in imposing club dues on its members; but this is because they have *agreed* to be so assessed. But the same does not at all apply to citizens of a country.[47]

A second argument on behalf of statism is that government is needed to overcome "market failure."[48] There are three main forms of this contention: Externalities, public goods and monopoly.[49]

First, consider externalities.[50] It is alleged, in the case of spillover benefits, that the market will provide an insufficient amount.[51] For example, it is maintained that private parties will only educate themselves if they can benefit from such activities (Friedman 1961). But education has social benefits, too, that are disregarded by market participants. For example, people who engage in schooling will be better voters, less likely to engage in criminal activity, or less likely to have need for public assistance.[52] But this positive externalities argument is subject to a fatal flaw. The

Hoppe_2.pdf; Anthony Gregory & Walter E. Block, *On Immigration: Reply to Hoppe*, 21 J. LIBR. STUD. 25, 37 (2007), https://mises-media.s3.amazonaws.com/21_3_2.pdf; N. Stephan Kinsella, *Punishment and Proportionality: The Estoppel Approach*, 12 J. LIBR. STUD. 51, 52 (1996), https://mises-media.s3.amazonaws.com/12_1_3_0.pdf; Herbert Morris, *Persons and Punishment*, 52 THE MONIST 475, 476 (1968); Charles B. Olson, *Law in Anarchy*, 12 LIBR. F., Nov.–Dec. 1979, at 1, 4, http://rothbard.altervista.org/articles/libertarian-forum/lf-12-6.pdf; Roy Whitehead & Walter E. Block, *Taking the Assets of the Criminal to Compensate Victims of Violence: A Legal and Philosophical Approach*, 5 J.L. SOC'Y 229, 243 (2003); Walter E. Block, *The Non-Aggression Axiom of Libertarianism*, LEWROCKWELL (February 17, 2003), http://archive.lewrockwell.com/block/block26.html; Marko Marjanovic, *Least, Sufficient Force: Libertarian Theory of Defense*, VOLUNTARYIST READER (Jan. 7, 2013), https://voluntaryistreader.wordpress.com/2013/01/07/least-sufficient-force-libertarian-theory-of-defense/.

[47] For a rejection of this argument when applied to the United States, see Lysander Spooner, 6 NO TREASON: THE CONSTITUTION OF NO AUTHORITY 12–17 (1870), http://lf-oll.s3.amazonaws.com/titles/2194/Spooner_1485_Bk.pdf.

[48] See THE THEORY OF MARKET FAILURE: A CRITICAL EXAMINATION (Tyler Cowen ed., 1988).

[49] There are numerous others, but these are the most cited in the economics literature.

[50] *See generally* Bryan Caplan, *Externalities*, LIBR. ECON. & LIBERTY, http://www.econlib.org/library/Enc/Externalities.html (last visited July 5, 2019).

[51] See Walter E. Block, *National Defense and the Theory of Externalities, Public Goods, and Clubs*, *in* THE MYTH OF NATIONAL DEFENSE: ESSAYS ON THE THEORY AND HISTORY OF SECURITY PRODUCTION 301, 305 (Hans-Hermann Hoppe ed., 2003), https://mises-media.s3.amazonaws.com/Myth%20of%20National%20Defense%2C%20The%20Essays%20on%20the%20Theory%20and%20History%20of%20Security%20Production_3.pdf.

[52] See Murray N. Rothbard, *Airport Congestion: A Case of Market Failure?*, *in* MAKING ECONOMIC SENSE 192, 192–93 (2d ed. 2006), https://mises-media.s3.amazonaws.com/Making%20Economic%20Sense_3.pdf; BRIAN SIMPSON, MARKETS DON'T FAIL! 85 (2005); Walter E. Block, *Was Milton Friedman a Socialist? Yes*, 1 MEST J., Jan. 2013, at 11, 14, http://mest.meste.org/MEST_1_2013/_02.pdf; Jack High & Jerome Ellig, *The Private Supply of Education: Some Historical Evidence*, *in* THE THEORY OF MARKET FAILURE: A CRITICAL EXAMINATION 361, 361 (Tyler Cowen ed., 1988); Gil Guillory, *What Are You Calling Failure?*, MISES (May 5, 2005), http://

reductio ad absurdum[53] is as follows: *A* smiles at *B*, or cleans himself so that he will not engage in any olfactory insult, or whistles a merry tune in the presence of others. He then bills *B* for these "benefits." *B* retorts, indignantly, that he has not contracted for any such "services" and thus refuses to pay *A* for "providing" them. But this is precisely to what the positive externalities argument amounts.[54]

Then, too, there is the case of negative externalities, such as smoke pollution. Statists maintain that in the free society, people will be allowed to pollute the air and waterways, and that only government can protect these amenities.[55] But the historical record demonstrates that states have undermined, not supported, private property rights.[56] The point is that this sort of pollution constitutes an invasion of smoke particles, and governments have not treated this activity in that manner. Rather, governments have supported and allowed such rights violations.[57]

Second, public goods. Here, it is maintained there are some goods and services, preeminently lighthouses[58] and national defense[59], which either the market cannot

---

www.mises.org/story/1806; D. W. MacKenzie, *The Market Failure Myth*, MISES (Aug. 26, 2002), https://mises.org/library/market-failure-myth; Christopher Westley, *The Myth of Market Failure*, MISES (Jun. 14, 2002), https://mises.org/library/myth-market-failure.

[53] Defined as:

> a mode of argumentation that seeks to establish a contention by deriving an absurdity from its denial, thus arguing that a thesis must be accepted because its rejection would be untenable. It is a style of reasoning that has been employed throughout the history of mathematics and philosophy from classical antiquity onwards.

Nicholas Rescher, *Reductio ad Absurdum*, INTERNET ENCYCLOPEDIA OF PHIL., http://www.iep.utm.edu/reductio/ (last visited July 5, 2019).

[54] For a refutation of this statist defense, see Walter E. Block, *Public Goods and Externalities: The Case of Roads*, 7 J. LIBR. STUD. 1 (1983), https://mises-media.s3.amazonaws.com/7_1_1_0.pdf.

[55] See ROTHBARD, MAN, ECONOMY, AND STATE, *supra* note 234, at 181–82.

[56] *E.g.*, Kelo v. City of New London, 545 U.S. 469, 501 (2005) (O'Connor, J., dissenting) ("It holds that the sovereign may take private property currently put to ordinary private use, and give it over for new, ordinary private use, so long as the new use is predicted to generate some secondary benefit for the public—such as increased tax revenue, more jobs, maybe even esthetic pleasure.").

[57] See ROTHBARD, THE ETHICS OF LIBERTY, *supra* note 250, at 56.

[58] For a refutation of this argument as it concerns lighthouses, see William Barnett II & Walter E. Block, *Coase and Bertrand on Lighthouses*, 140 PUB. CHOICE 1, 11–12 (2009), http://www.walterblock.com/wp-content/uploads/2009/06/Coase-and-Bertrand-on-Lighthouses.pdf; William Barnett II & Walter E. Block, *Coase and Van Zandt on Lighthouses*, 35 PUB. FIN. REV. 710, 729 (2007), http://journals.sagepub.com/doi/abs/10.1177/1091142107302182; Ronald H. Coase, *The Lighthouse in Economics*, 17 J. L. & ECON. 357, 359 (1974).

[59] For a refutation of this argument as it concerns national defense, see ANTHONY DE JASAY, SOCIAL CONTRACT, FREE RIDE: A STUDY OF THE PUBLIC GOODS PROBLEM 166 (1989), https://oll.libertyfund.org/titles/jasay-social-contract-free-ride-a-study-of-the-public-goods-problem; Murray N. Rothbard, *The Fallacy of the "Public Sector"* (1961), *reprinted in* ECONOMIC CONTROVERSIES 419, 426 (2011), https://mises-media.s3.amazonaws.com/Economic%20Controversies_2.pdf; DAVID SCHMIDTZ, THE LIMITS OF GOVERNMENT: AN ESSAY ON THE PUBLIC GOODS ARGUMENT # (1991); Walter E. Block, *National Defense and the Theory of Externalities, Public Goods, and Clubs*, *supra* note 259, at 317; Hans-Hermann Hoppe, *Fallacies of the Public Goods Theory and the Production of Security*, 9 J. LIBR. STUD. 27, 28 (1989), http://www.mises.org/journals/jls/9_1/9_1_2.pdf; Jeffrey Hummel, *National Goods vs. Public Goods: Defense, Disarmament and*

provide at all or, at best, would be in grave short supply. This argument is predicated upon excludability and rivalrousness. In this respect, Rothbard explained:

> A and B often benefit, it is held, if they can force C into doing something. . . . [A]ny argument proclaiming the right and goodness of, say, three neighbors, who yearn to form a string quartet, forcing a fourth neighbor at bayonet point to learn and play the viola, is hardly deserving of sober comment.[60]

Another argument regarding public goods relates to inequality. Supporters of government attempt to justify such takings on the grounds that they will do "good" with the proceeds.[61] But would Mr. Jones be justified in seizing Mr. Smith's car on the ground that he would then turn over this automobile to Mr. Green, who is poor? Hardly.[62]

Third, is monopoly. There is no dispute concerning governmental imposed monopoly, such as the U.S. Post Office, or the special grant of monopoly privilege given by the United Kingdom government to the British East Asian Company. That is a failure, alright, but it is hardly a market failure. Rather, it constitutes a government failure.

In contrast, what is under debate is sheer large size, garnered by satisfying customers to a greater extent than competitors, buying factors of production more cheaply, and innovating. Also in play is the concentration ratio: what percentage of an industry is accounted for by one or a few firms. For example, IBM had no particular government grant of privilege, but, it was very successful, profitable, and, according to at least some calculations, comprised 100% of the computer market for a time.

One difficulty is that the definition of an "industry" is highly contentious and arbitrary. The plaintiffs in an anti-trust suit want to define the industry as narrowly as possible, so as to boost the concentration ratio. For example, dry breakfast cereal. The defendants wish for a wide definition so as to reduce this ratio. For example, all

---

Free Riders, 4 REV. AUSTRIAN ECON. 88, 93–94 (1990), http://www.mises.org/journals/rae/pdf/rae4_1_4.pdf; E. C. Pasour, Jr., *The Free Rider as a Basis for Government Intervention*, 5 J. LIBR. STUD. 453, 463 (1981), http://www.mises.org/journals/jls/5_4/5_4_6.pdf; Larry Sechrest, *Privateering and National Defense: Naval Warfare for Private Profit* (1999), *reprinted in* THE MYTH OF NATIONAL DEFENSE: ESSAYS ON THE THEORY AND HISTORY OF SECURITY PRODUCTION 239, 239–40 (Hans-Hermann Hoppe ed., 2003), https://mises-media.s3.amazonaws.com/Myth%20of%20National%20Defense%2C%20The%20Essays%20on%20the%20Theory%20and%20History%20of%20Security%20Production_3.pdf; Larry Sechrest, *Privately Funded and Built U.S. Warships in the Quasi-War of 1797–1801*, 12 INDEP. REV. 101 (2007); Larry Sechrest, *Public Goods and Private Solutions in Maritime History*, 7 Q. J. AUSTRIAN ECON. 3, 3 (2004), https://mises-media.s3.amazonaws.com/qjae7_2_1.pdf.

[60] *See* Rothbard, *The Fallacy of the "Public Sector," supra* note 268, at 178.

[61] *See, e.g.*, Hawaii Housing Authority v. Midkiff, 467 U.S. 229, 242–43 (1984) (reasoning that the State's attempt "to reduce the perceived social and economic evils of a land oligopoly" was "a classic exercise of a State's police powers").

[62] Murray N. Rothbard, *Freedom, Inequality, Primitivism and the Division of Labor*, MODERN AGE, Summer 1971, at 226, 237 (explaining that the primitive community was unhappy because of the perception that personal success was the result of exploitation of others).

cereals, better yet, all breakfast foodstuffs, even better, all food. Another problem with this market failure is the so-called "dead weight loss." Large firms with few competitors in the "industry" are accused of cutting back on quantity in order to artificially boost price, and thus creating a gap between the value people place on this lessened quantity and the marginal costs of supplying it. But this is to engage in interpersonal comparisons of utility, something highly problematic in technical economics. For example, Muhammad Ali could well be accused of being a "monopolist." He wishes to engage, say, in only six fights per year, and the all-knowing, omni-benevolent government calculates that he really "should" be engaging in nine pugilistic encounters annually. He is "cheating" the public of three boxing matches per year. We all value those additional fights more than it costs the champion boxer. To say the least, this way of looking at the world is mighty peculiar.[63]

Let us now consider secession, another basic building block of libertarianism. [64] It is clear that if people are not allowed to separate—or secede—from each other,

[63] For an extended refutation of the claim that large sized firms, with few or no competitors constitutes the market failure of monopoly, see DOMINICK T. ARMENTANO, THE MYTHS OF ANTITRUST (New Rochelle, N.Y.: Arlington House, 1972); DOMINICK T. ARMENTANO, ANTITRUST AND MONOPOLY: ANATOMY OF A POLICY FAILURE (New York: Wiley, 1982); DOMINICK T. ARMENTANO, ANTITRUST: THE CASE FOR REPEAL (Revised 2nd ed., Auburn AL: Mises Institute, 1999); DON ARMSTRONG, COMPETITION VS. MONOPOLY (Vancouver: The Fraser Institute, 1982); Walter E. Block, *Austrian Monopoly Theory – a Critique*, 1 J. OF LIBERTARIAN S. 271–279 (1977); WALTER E. BLOCK, AMENDING THE COMBINES INVESTIGATION ACT (Vancouver: The Fraser Institute, 1982); Walter E. Block, *Total Repeal of Anti-trust Legislation: A Critique of Bork, Brozen and Posner*, 8 REV. OF AUSTRIAN ECON. 35–70 (1994); Donald J. Boudreaux, Thomas J. DiLorenzo, *The Protectionist Roots of Antitrust*, 6 REV. OF AUSTRIAN ECON. 81–96 (1992); Thomas J. DiLorenzo, *The Myth of Natural Monopoly*, 9 REV. OF AUSTRIAN ECON. 43–58 (1996); Jack High High, *Bork's Paradox: Static vs Dynamic Efficiency in Antitrust Analysis*, 3 CONTEMPORARY POL. ISSUES 21–34 (1984–1985); Fred McChesney, *Antitrust and Regulation: Chicago's Contradictory Views*, 10 CATO JOURNAL (1991); ROTHBARD, MAN, ECONOMY, AND STATE, *supra* note 234; William F. Shugart II, *Don't Revise the Clayton Act, Scrap It!*, 6 CATO JOURNAL 925 (1987); Fred L. Smith, Jr., *Why not Abolish Antitrust?*, REGULATION 23 (Jan-Feb, 1983). On monopsony, a "monopoly" for buyers: Walter E. Block and William Barnett II, *Monopsony Theory*, 7(1/2) AMERICAN REVIEW OF POLITICAL ECONOMY 67–109 (June/December, 2009).

[64] *See* LUDWIG VON MISES, NATION, STATE, AND ECONOMY: CONTRIBUTIONS TO THE POLITICS AND HISTORY OF OUR TIME 60 (Leland B. Yaeger trans., N.Y. Univ. Press 1983) (1919), https://mises-media.s3.amazonaws.com/Nation%2C%20State%2C%20and%20Economy_3.pdf. *E.g.*, Ian Bremmer, *Not Just Catalonia: 3 More Places with Dreams of Independence*, TIME (Oct. 2, 2017), https://time.com/4963163/catalan-kurds-referendum-independence/ (reporting Biafra, Flanders, Donetsk, and Luhansk separatist movements); Clyde H. Farnsworth, *Quebec, by Razor-Thin Margin, Votes "No" on Leaving Canada*, N.Y. TIMES, Oct. 31, 1995, at A1 (reporting Quebec's referendum campaign to leave Canada); Parisa Hafezi & Tulay Karadeniz, *Khamenei Says Iran, Turkey Must Act Against Kurish Secession: TV*, REUTERS (Oct. 4, 2017, 3:38 PM), https://www.reuters.com/article/us-mideast-crisis-iran-turkey/khamenei-says-iran-turkey-must-act-against-kurdish-secession-tv-idUSKBN1C91YW (reporting that Iran's "Supreme Leader" said "Iran and Turkey should prevent Iraq's Kurdistan region from declaring independence"); Raphael Minder, *A Year After Catalonia Secession Vote, New Unrest and Still No Resolution*, N.Y. TIMES (Oct. 1, 2018), https://nyti.ms/2OqHn9P (reporting Catalonia's independence referendum).

then the law of free association is undermined.[65] But this law is also one of the basic building blocks of the libertarian philosophy.[66] Thus, the very concept of the State, for this reason as well, runs contrary to human freedom.[67] It cannot be denied that some governments do allow for peaceful secession. For example, the Constitution of the Principality of Lichtenstein provides:

> Individual communes have the right to secede from the State. A decision to initiate the secession procedure shall be taken by a majority of the citizens residing there who are entitled to vote. Secession shall be regulated by a law or, as the case may be, a treaty. In the latter event, a second ballot shall be held in the commune after the negotiations have been completed.[68]

However, while this is necessary for full liberty to be attained, it is not sufficient. For the law of free association mandates that not only may large entities within one country secede from each other, but that this right applies all the way down to the individual level. Let us consider an example: If the people of Quebec vote to secede from Canada, should this be allowed? Of course. But suppose, then, that Montrealers wish to separate from that province; would it be unjust to prevent that decision?[69] Certainly it would, otherwise people would be compelled to associate with other Quebecers against their will. But this is only the beginning of the story, for the same principle applies to the Mont-Royal district in that city, to a single block in that neighbourhood, right down to the *individual* level. The ideal situation from the point of view of the freedom philosophy is seven (plus) billion countries, one for each person. Then, we would all be sovereign.

The argument employed by the statists is that if we ever attained such a situation, Smith and Jones might get into an altercation, and we would need a government to quell all such disturbances.[70] But this argument is subject to a powerful *reductio ad*

[65] The slave wishes not to associate with his master. Slavery is the preeminent example of the violation of the right of free association. *See* Kenneth L. Karst, *The Freedom of Intimate Association*, 89 Yale L.J. 624, 638 (1980).

[66] See Thomas Kleven, *Why International Law Favors Emigration over Immigration*, 33 U. Miami Inter-Am. L. Rev. 69, 80 (2002) ("The starting point for a libertarian analysis is people's freedom to choose with whom to associate.").

[67] *See* Rivka Weill, *Secession and the Prevalence of Both Militant Democracy and Eternity Clauses*, 40 Cardozo L. Rev. 905, 941 (2018) ("For example, the Bulgarian Constitution of 1991 grants freedom of association, but organizations' activities 'shall not be contrary to the country's sovereignty and national integrity, or the unity of the nation.'") (quoting Bulgaria's Constitution of 1991 with Amendments through 2015, Constitute art. 44 § 2 (2018)).

[68] Constitution of the Principality of Liechtenstein, Sept. 15, 2003, LR 101, art. 4, § 2, http://hrlibrary.umn.edu/research/liechtenstein-constitution.pdf.

[69] Whether to rejoin Canada, or to set up a small country of their own, a city-state as it were, it matters not which. *But see* Lea Brilmayer, *Secession and Self-Determination: A Territorial Interpretation*, 16 Yale J. Int'l L. 177, 181 (1991) ("Proponents of secession therefore face a very slippery slope in formulating a right to secede that does not open the door to complete anarchy.").

[70] *Contra* Jarret B. Wollstein, *Arguments Against Anarchy*, Mises (Feb. 9, 2010), https://mises.org/library/arguments-against-anarchy ("The belief that government is necessary to insure social order is a pure superstition . . . .").

absurdum. For at present, Albania and Argentina, Brazil and Burundi, China and Chile are all in a state of anarchy with one another.[71] Indeed, *all* nations are now in this situation with every other one. If a national government is needed to keep Smith and Jones apart from each other, then it follows ineluctably that a world government is required to do so for groups of people—that is, countries.[72] But there are few who would espouse such a state of affairs, given that when the leadership went into the wrong hands, there would be no earthly alternatives to it. If the World Government were run on a democratic basis, then India and China, between them, if they could ever agree on anything, would pretty much run the entire planet. And these are far from the Western type democracies or republican governments that the moderate statist theorists (of the social democrat variety) often have in mind.[73]

6.1.4 Response to Common Criticisms

Critics of libertarianism often say that its system is as utopian as pure socialism.[74] In this sense, they pretend to be refuting the validity of libertarianism both as a viable philosophy and as a conceptual framework to judge reality as it is. In this respect, Paul Krugman claims that:

> "…when it comes to substance, libertarians are living in a fantasy world. Often that's quite literally true: Paul Ryan thinks that we're living in an Ayn Rand novel. More to the point, however, the libertarian vision of the society we actually have bears little resemblance to reality.

[71] Anarchism means that there is no political jurisdiction authoritatively placed above two lower powers. Albania and Argentina, Brazil and Burundi, China and Chile, and every other nation on the face of the earth, are in a state of anarchism with each other, given that there is no government placed above them in existence, such as a World Government. If there were the latter, then this statement in the text would be false. Also, multilateral organisms and international organizations (such as the UN), are not a World Government. See also Oleg I. Titunov, *The International Legal Personality of States: Problems and Solutions*, 37 St. Louis U. L.J. 323, 330 (1993).

[72] *Id.*

[73] *See* Leland M. Goodrich, *The Amount of World Organization Necessary and Possible*, 55 Yale L. J. 950, 961 (1946). Moreover, international bodies, such as the United Nations, should not be regarded as the World Government we have in mind here, since although its member countries theoretically *commit* to following certain standards, they often do not follow these standards. *Id.* at 952. For example, the members of the U.N. commit to respecting "human rights," but who are the members of the U.N. Commission on Human Rights? Egregious violators of rights, such as Saudi Arabia and Cuba. *See* Kenneth Anderson, *Squaring the Circle? Reconciling Sovereignty and Global Governance Through Global Government Networks*, 118 Harv. L. Rev. 1255, 1277 n.38 (2005) (reviewing Anne-Marie Slaughter, A New World Order (2004)) (explaining that human rights abusers have the greatest incentive to join the U.N. Commission on Human Rights). More importantly, no one is *forcing* Saudi Arabia to respect individual rights, so the U.N. is not a "government" that forces its members to act in a certain way. *See* Goodrich, *supra*, at 951–92 (explaining that the U.N. is "a voluntary association of sovereign states").

[74] *See* Duncan Whitmore, *Is Libertarianism Utopian?*, Mises (July 7, 2018), https://mises.org/wire/libertarianism-utopian (analyzing whether libertarianism is unachievable).

> "...In other words, libertarianism is a crusade against problems we don't have, or at least not to the extent the libertarians want to imagine."[75]

Here, we argue that statism is in fact the philosophy which omits both reality (because it constantly fails)[76] and theory (because it has long been refuted).[77] But how do we answer the same criticism being directed to libertarianism?

Let us explain our position with an analogy. Liberty is the essential *condition* required by any human being (Mill 1859).[78] As such, he must be free to think, act, and pursue values through his actions in order to survive. The fundamental condition for his existence is to be free of coercion. As such, liberty is not a solution by itself to man's survival requirements, but it is the *necessary* condition for it. Hence, we can draw a parallel between oxygen and liberty. If oxygen is progressively taken away from man, he will function and live as long as he can breathe. But the less oxygen, the less he will be able to function properly. Liberty, and libertarianism as the philosophy that identifies liberty's role in a social context, works the same way. This is why the criticism that "libertarianism is not practiced anywhere" is wrong.[79] *It is practiced everywhere and anywhere human beings are free to act and cooperate to the extent that coercion does not appear.*[80] It exists whenever any peaceful voluntary cooperation among men takes place.[81]

This is why the mixed economy, and even socialist countries, can function for a limited time.[82] The parts that function are the ones where liberty still exists, i.e. the

---

[75] Paul Krugman, Opinion, *Libertarian Fantasies*, N.Y. Times (Aug. 9, 2014, 9:09 AM), https://krugman.blogs.nytimes.com/2014/08/09/libertarian-fantasies/. See also Paul Krugman, Opinion, *Phosphorus and Freedom*, N.Y. Times (Aug. 10, 2014), https://nyti.ms/1oAAn6o.

[76] Gwartney, *supra* note 232, at vii. *E.g.*, Michael Debow, *The Politics of Good Intentions*, 14 Nw. J. Int'l L. & Bus. 471, 471–72 (1994) (reviewing Dwight R. Lee & Richard B. McKenzie, Failure and Progress: The Bright Side of the Dismal Science (1993) (providing the Soviet bloc as the most extreme form of statism that is "universally regarded as a complete failure").

[77] *E.g.*, John B. Judis, *Anti-Statism in America*, New Republic (Nov. 11, 2009), https://newrepublic.com/article/71077/anti-statism-america (explaining that Americans' skepticism about statism can be traced back to at least 1955).

[78] John Stuart Mill, On Liberty 53 (Batoche Books. Ltd. 2001) (1859), https://socialsciences.mcmaster.ca/econ/ugcm/3ll3/mill/liberty.pdf.

[79] *See, e.g.*, Michael Lind, *The Question Libertarians Just Can't Answer*, Salon (June 4, 2013, 8:17 PM UTC), https://www.salon.com/2013/06/04/the_question_libertarians_just_cant_answer/ (questioning why "not a single country in the world in the early twenty-first century is organized along libertarian lines").

[80] *See, e.g.*, David Boaz, *A History of Libertarianism*, Libertarianism (Jan. 15, 1997), https://www.libertarianism.org/publications/essays/history-libertarianism (explaining "the history of the movement for liberty, from Chinese philosopher Lao Tzu through the 20th century").

[81] Of course, there are millions, billions, maybe even trillions of voluntary transactions that take place throughout the world every day. See Gwartney, *supra* note 232, at 37.

[82] Paradoxically, corruption and illegality, e.g., black markets, allows statist economies to function far better than would otherwise be the case. *See* Chris Matthews, *When Corruption is Good for the Economy*, Fortune (Aug. 7, 2014), http://fortune.com/2014/08/07/corruption-economic-benefits/; *Corruption and Development: Not What You Think?*, Chris Blattman (Nov. 5, 2012), https://chrisblattman.com/2012/11/05/corruption-and-development-not-what-you-think/. Also,

oxygen which allows individuals to function. But the lack of oxygen will create negative results eventually: this is statism. So, it is not that libertarianism does not work nor cannot exist, quite the opposite. Since civilization is a fact, and there would be no civilization without liberty, libertarianism had always existed and still exists, to the extent that individuals are free. It had and it has to exist, as long as human beings want to survive. The fact that there are no perfect libertarian societies does not mean that the philosophy is not true because, as long as it applies, it enhances welfare for all. In contrast, if and as long as statism prevails, society degrades. Liberty is the oxygen that allows individuals, even in statist societies, to still live as human beings to the extent they are allowed. To equate statism with libertarianism because neither exists in full is to equate remedy and illness.

Another relevant point often made as a criticism of our view is this: How would Anarcho-Capitalism be implemented? In response, let us briefly discuss some often ignored realities of our social world. First, most social institutions are not designed nor centrally planned, but evolved (Hayek 1982) through a long, extended process of trial and error, learning and change. It is a dynamic process, and not a set of rules written in stone.

As such, Hayek explained:

> To understand our civilisation, one must appreciate that the extended order resulted not from human design or intention but spontaneously: it arose from unintentionally conforming to certain traditional and largely moral practices, many of which men tend to dislike, whose significance they usually fail to understand, whose validity they cannot prove, and which have nonetheless fairly rapidly spread by means of an evolutionary selection – the comparative increase of population and wealth – of those groups that happened to follow them. The unwitting, reluctant, even painful adoption of these practices kept these groups together, increased their access to valuable information of all sorts, and enabled them to be 'fruitful, and multiply, and replenish the earth, and subdue it' (Genesis 1:28). This process is perhaps the least appreciated facet of human evolution. (Hayek 1988)

Similarly, Douglass North maintained:

> The transmission that is put in place by past generations is described by them as the artifactual structure. This artifactual structure is more than the embodied learning of past generations transmitted as culture into the belief structure of present generations. It is also embodied in the institutional structure inherited from past generations. Hayek and some other authors who have built models derived from evolutionary theory have used the term collective learning to characterize this process. While the formal rules a society puts in place will surely reflect this heritage, it is the informal constraints embodied in norms of behavior, conventions and self imposed codes of conduct that is the most important 'carrier' of the artifactual structure. While the formal rules can be changed overnight (by a revolution for example) the informal constraints change much more slowly and play a critical role in the evolution of polities. 'Local learning' is derived from the specific environment (both physical and intellectual) of a society and as changes occur in that environment they are

countries where relatively free market prices are a rarity internally, such as the former U.S.S.R., can still avail themselves of terms of trade and interest rates in the rest of the world. *See* VON MISES, SOCIALISM, *supra* note 214, at 586.

gradually assimilated into the socio-cultural linguistic inheritance and embodied in the artifactual structure.[83]

Again, Hayek even related this process with human nature as such:

Man does not know most of the rules on which he acts; and even what we call his intelligence is largely a system of rules which operate on him but which he does not know. In animal societies and in a great measure in primitive human society, the structure of social life is determined by rules of action which manifest themselves only in their being obeyed. It is only when individual intellects begin to differ sufficiently (or individual minds become more complex) that it becomes necessary to express the rules in communicable form so that they can be taught by example and deviant behavior can be corrected and differences of view expressed about what is to be decided. Though man never existed without laws which he obeyed, he did exist for millennia without laws which he knew in the sense that he was able to articulate them.(Hayek 1964) (Hayek 1964)

Hence, most human institutions, patterns of behavior, customs and rules of social conduct are followed because they are incentive-compatible with a larger, extended order of social cooperation. Increasing cooperation, in turn, expands this social order and enhances cooperation and institutional refinement.

As Austrian economics makes clear, it is the subjective evaluation of individuals which gives rise to the social phenomenon as such. Institutions exist primarily in the human mind as a set of expected and actual behavior patterns, and not as written rules. Moreover, these institutions respond to the expectation that others will follow them too. Articulation of some of these institutions in a fully conceptual and written form is what makes increasing social cooperation easier, but they are not primary. For instance, Constitutions consist mainly in rules of the social game, in an articulate, written form. But they are useless if people do not *behave* according to what is written there, *as well as if* there is no social institution that enforces it. Enforcement and compliance are both relevant.

For instance, take property rights. As Harold Demsetz explained:

In the world of Robinson Crusoe property rights play no role. Property rights are an instrument of society and derive their significance from the fact that they help a man form those expectations which he can reasonably hold in his dealings with others. These expectations find expression in the laws, customs, and mores of a society. An owner of property rights possesses the consent of fellowmen to allow him to act in particular ways. An owner expects the community to prevent others from interfering with his actions, provided that these actions are not prohibited in the specifications of his rights. (Demsetz 1967)

In a similar light, James M. Buchanan explains that these institutions of social cooperation are followed because people find it in their self-interest to do so. According to Buchanan:

That is to say, the individual does not enter into social contract for the purpose of imposing constraints on himself; he could always accomplish this by more effective means. He enters into agreements with others to secure the benefits of behavioral limitation on their part. The

[83] Douglass C. North, *The Historical Evolution of Polities* 4, ECONOMIC HISTORY 9411007 (University Library of Munich, Germany, Revised 14 Dec. 1994), https://econwpa.ub.uni-muenchen.de/econ-wp/eh/papers/9411/9411007.pdf

> individual will find his own adherence to law unprofitable except insofar as this is directly related to others' behavior. This constraint on his own liberty is the cost side of the contract. Rationality precepts, strictly interpreted, suggest efforts toward maximizing 'law-abiding' by others and toward minimizing 'law-abiding' by the party in question. Law is simply a reciprocal relationship among parties, an embodiment of contract.[84]

And this very same incentive structure explains law-abiding behavior promoted by different social institutions, from simple rules of courtesy to respect for a constitutional order. Again, Buchanan explicates:

> Law-abiding on the part of an individual is the cost that he pays as a part of the overall legal-social contract between himself and others in the community, treated as a unit. In a private, personal utility sense, any limits on individual behavior are 'bads.' But rational persons accept such limits in exchange or trade for the 'goods' which law-abiding on the part of others represents. This behavior on the part of others creates 'goods' because of the predictable order, security, or stability that it generates in the individual's choice set. To the extent that other persons respect the limits laid down in law or rules, and to the extent that these are known by everyone, the individual can make his own private decisions in a reasonably predictable and stable social environment. This feature is applicable for many rules that might be called 'laws,' whether these be simple rules of the road, such as right-hand driving, or complex arrangements, such as those required among different owners of condominium units.[85]

As a summary on institutions, Douglass North observed:

> Institutions are the humanly devised constraints that structure political, economic, and social interaction. They consist of both informal constraints (sanctions, taboos, customs, traditions, and codes of conduct), and formal rules (constitutions, laws, property rights). Throughout history, institutions have been devised by human beings to create order and reduce uncertainty in exchange. Together with the standard constraints of economics they define the choice set and therefore determine transaction and production costs and hence the profitability and feasibility of engaging in economic activity. They evolve incrementally, connecting the past with the present and the future; history in consequence is largely a story of institutional evolution in which the historical performance of economies can only be understood as a part of a sequential story. Institutions provide the incentive structure of an economy; as that structure evolves, it shapes the direction of economic change towards growth, stagnation, or decline. (North 1991)

So, as we can see, institutions evolve. That includes, of course, the government and its functions. There is no law written in stone that says that the functions of government cannot be privatized. Privatization processes throughout history and throughout different societies have taken place, *as well as nationalizations*. Schools, roads, energy, you name it. They have been (and are) under the control of government or private enterprise at different times and places. To a great degree this depends on the philosophical ideas that prevail at that moment.

The same thing happened with the structure of government itself. Republics and democracies were seen as impossible, utopian ideals only two and a half centuries

[84] JAMES M. BUCHANAN, THE LIMITS OF LIBERTY: BETWEEN ANARCHY AND LEVIATHAN 98 (Indianapolis: Liberty Fund, 1999–2000).

[85] JAMES M. BUCHANAN, THE LIMITS OF LIBERTY: BETWEEN ANARCHY AND LEVIATHAN 101 (Indianapolis: Liberty Fund, 1999–2000).

ago. But they are now the most common form of government, at least in the West. What seems crazy today may be the normal one hundred years from now.

In this respect, Anarcho-Capitalism is an institutional arrangement based on privatizing government functions. Nothing more, nothing less. As such, its mode of supplying currently government services in the free market entails a specific incentive structure of its own. In very much the same way that government roads can be privatized, so police, military and courts can be as well.

There are many ways to do so, and we have mentioned some of the literature that specifies it. But the main point is that there is no reason to believe that, in principle, it cannot be done. In theory, it surely looks like a better institutional arrangement.

What is required, though, is that these alternatives be shown to the public, and be progressively implemented. Surely, every privatization process will be complex and with ups and downs as its application moves forward. But it can nevertheless be done. The key, though, is that the conditions for a private property society are that the social institutions of the market be respected by most participants. That is, it is required for most members of society to respect the rules of civilized social cooperation. However, a "new man" (as in the ideals of radical communists) is not a requisite. This is a system that is intended for human beings as they are, with an incentive structure more compatible with enhancing that side of them that tends to cooperation and exchange.

True enough, certain conditions would have to apply, such as a large development of the insurance industry, as well as a bottom-up process of demanding change. But this is not dissimilar to other social changes. They respond from bottom-up demands, and top down applications of those demands. And these sometimes feedback in a virtuous loop.

In this respect, the education on the values and principles of the free society is a fundamental requirement. This is the only way for a true libertarian society to emerge: with individuals who want to be free, in the full meaning of the term. And the prevailing philosophical ideas must be libertarian for a large proportion of the population to move forward in this direction.

In the view of Ludwig Von Mises:

> The propensity of our contemporaries to demand authoritarian prohibition as soon as something does not please them, and their readiness to submit to such prohibitions even when what is prohibited is quite agreeable to them shows how deeply ingrained the spirit of servility still remains within them. It will require many long years of self-education until the subject can turn himself into the citizen. A free man must be able to endure it when his fellow men act and live otherwise than he considers proper. He must free himself from the habit, just as soon as something does not please him, of calling for the police.[86]

It is not that the ideal of Anarcho-Capitalism cannot be applied, but that, as any other system, has requirements that must be fulfilled for it to be implemented. The main requirement (apart from widespread agreement[87] with libertarian ideas) is for

[86] LUDWIG VON MISES, LIBERALISM: IN THE CLASSICAL TRADITION 32–33 (Indianapolis: Liberty Fund, 2005) (1927).

[87] A significant minority might well suffice, if these people were amongst the leaders of the society.

the mechanism of the market and social cooperation to be sufficiently settled and respected by many if not most individuals so that it can be progressively extended to government functions. But, as with any other institutional development, it must evolve with human action itself, and not as the result of a centralized design. Otherwise, it will break. That is, perhaps, the challenge of our times. But for society to move towards this system, the key is to demand more degrees of freedom now. And, at the very least, to make these alternatives known.

As the market expands, and patterns of behavior adapt to increasing liberty, members of society will at least know there is an alternative. The future, though, will be up to them.

6.1.5 Conclusion

As we have tried to show throughout this work, statism is based on a proposition that is presented *a priori*. For statists, the government is the solution to every problem, and neither experience *nor* theory are relevant in order to disprove this claim.

Despite the fact that statists do not recognize their fundamental approach as *a priori*, nevertheless we have shown that it is so. Given that it is mistaken, both in theory and practice, we named it the fallacy of *a priori* statism.

On the other hand, we have explained why the market can be theoretically defended on an *a priori* basis, thereby refuting the possible criticism that *a priori* defences of the market economy resort to the same fallacy as statists.

A critic may claim that our treatment of "statism" is excessively broad and does not strictly correspond to any particular political philosopher or economist. In our defence, we offer this model only as a generalization—we think an accurate one—of the implicit premise behind statism: the state is, essentially, the only viable institution to guide society. Thus, we need not focus on any particular thinker. Rather we choose to analyse the statist approach as if it were an integrated and consistent view and take it to its logical conclusion. We thereby present its fundamental premise identified as an *a priori* proposition: "the state is the solution to every problem."

Again, we do not maintain that a mixed-economy advocate (who may sometimes favour markets) or a socialist (who could also be an anarchist, or a cooperativist) *necessarily* regards the state as such. But when it comes to choosing whether markets or states are more suitable, those who choose the latter accept the implicit premise described above—the state is always the solution.

Finally, although minarchism does not support full statism (given that it defends a state that only focuses on protecting individual rights through police, army, and courts of justice), we defended the claim that the market is a suitable replacement for these minimal state functions.

6.2 Critique of Anarcho-Capitalism: A Reply to Objections[88]

We are extremely grateful to Professor Robert T. Miller for his criticism of Futerman and Block (2019). We are strong proponents of Mill, who brilliantly articulated a defence for allowing, nay, encouraging, all sides of an argument to be heard. As such, he said:

> He who knows only his own side of the case, knows little of that. His reasons may be good, and no one may have been able to refute them. But if he is equally unable to refute the reasons on the opposite side; if he does not so much as know what they are, he has no ground for preferring either opinion. The rational position for him would be suspension of judgment, and unless he contents himself with that, he is either led by authority, or adopts, like the generality of the world, the side to which he feels most inclination. Nor is it enough that he should hear the arguments of adversaries from his own teachers, presented as they state them, and accompanied by what they offer as refutations. That is not the way to do justice to the arguments, or bring them into real contact with his own mind. He must be able to hear them from persons who actually believe them; who defend them in earnest, and do their very utmost for them. He must know them in their most plausible and persuasive form; he must feel the whole force of the difficulty which the true view of the subject has to encounter and dispose of; else he will never really possess himself of the portion of truth which meets and removes that difficulty.[89]

Professor Miller[90] is indeed a scholar who, a la Mill, "actually believe[s]" that radical libertarianism is misbegotten, defends his attack on anarcho-capitalism "in earnest," and does his "very utmost" for the doctrine of (limited) statism.[91] Thus, he can help move us that proverbial one-millionth of an inch closer to Truth, with a capital T.

Miller starts off in his abstract by launching an intellectual cannon shot over the bows of the good ship Futerman and Block (2019) ("FB"). There were two cannons launched. First, "In reality, the market has a transaction-cost advantage in some situations, and the government has such an advantage in other situations; economic efficiency requires that both mechanisms be used, each in those situations where it is cheaper."[92] Second, "libertarians make strong normative claims (e.g., that it is morally wrong for the government to take a person's property without his consent by means of taxation)" which is based upon "some moral system or other . . . ."[93] But

---

[88] This section of the present chapter is based on our paper Block, Walter E., and Futerman, Alan G. 2020. "Rejoinder to Miller on Anarcho-capitalism." *Quinnipiac Health Law Journal*, Vol. 24, No. 1, pp. 1–27. Available at https://heinonline.org/HOL/LandingPage?handle=hein.journals/qhlj24&div=5&id=&page (last visited May 8, 2021).

[89] *See* John Stuart Mill, On Liberty 36 (AHM Publ'g 1947) (1859). *See* John Stuart Mill, On Liberty 35–36 (Batoche Books 2001) (1859).

[90] Not to be confused with John Stuart Mill, despite the similarity of their last names, and, also, we aver, their political economic philosophies; that is, both ultimately embrace (to different degrees) statism.

[91] *See* Mill, *supra* note 308, at 35–36.

[92] Miller, *supra* note 303.

[93] *See id.*

"[w]hen these suppressed premises are stated in full, they either become implausible or they no longer support the very strong conclusions extreme libertarians assert."[94]

Our reply to the former first criticism is several fold. There are costs other than those involving transactions. All costs are subjective, as this concept consists of foregone opportunities, or alternative costs.[95] Strictly speaking they cannot be compared interpersonally.[96] So it is difficult to see how "in some situations" the market is preferred on this basis, and in other "situations" it is not. It cannot be denied that when costs are objectified, e.g., how many dollars does it cost government and the private sector to remove a ton of garbage, or deliver a pound of mail, these comparisons are not unreasonable. However, typically, the public sector comes out a long way second best on such matters.[97] As well, Miller also engages in moralizing: more efficiency is to be preferred to less. Yes, more efficiency is to be preferred to less, but only if the enterprise under consideration is a licit one. No good man would wish the Nazi concentration camps to have been run more efficiently.[98] So, efficiency is not an argument by itself. As to the second charge, this will be examined in the remainder of this essay.

It is difficult to see, as Miller contends, "That . . . a classical liberal state is more likely than the alternatives—including anarchy, even of the capitalist variety—to help people live good human lives, and that is pretty much all the normative justification such a state needs."[99] Why? This is due to the fact that the system of government favoured by this author engages in taxation.[100] This is a compulsory levy; and

---

[94] *Id.*

[95] *See* Don Lloyd, *Opportunity Cost, Comprehensive Definition?*, Mises Wire (Apr. 12, 2004), https://mises.org/wire/opportunity-cost-comprehensive-definition. See also Chapter 1, *supra.*

[96] *See id.*

[97] For further comparisons on mail, see Douglas K. Adie, Monopoly Mail: Privatizing The United States Postal Service (1989) (discussing operational and innovation failures at the United States Postal Service); Wilton D. Alston, *What Would Happen if the Post Office Had Competition?*, Lew Rockwell (June 6, 2007), https://www.lewrockwell.com/2007/06/wilton-alston/the-postal-monopoly; Peter G. Klein, *Economic Value and the Post Office*, Mises Institute (Dec. 31, 2017), https://mises.org/power-market/economic-value-and-post-office; Thomas G. Moore, *The Federal Postal Monopoly: History, Rationale, and Future*, *in* Free the Mail: Ending the Postal Monopoly 61–72 (ed. Peter J. Ferrara ed., CATO Institute 1990); George Priest, *The History of the Postal Monopoly in the United States*, 18 J. L. & Econ. 33 (1975); Llewellyn H. Rockwell Jr., *Can the Market Deliver Letters?*, Mises Inst. (Dec. 17, 2002), https://mises.org/es/library/can-market-deliver-letters. For further discussion of the issue in the context of sanitation, see E. S. Savas, *Refuse Collection: A Critical Review of the Evidence*, 6 J. Urban Aff. 1 (1979); Lawrence H. White, *Privatization of Municipally-Provided Services*, 2 J. Libertarian Stud. 187 (1978). It is also difficult to uncover empirical studies where the reverse is true. Miller offers no examples of these "other situations" in which "the market has a . . . cost advantage."

[98] *See* Miller *supra note* 303, at 93, 94.

[99] *Id.* Henceforth, all references to Miller unless otherwise indicated, will refer to this one essay of his.

[100] *See id.* at 105–06.

for libertarianism there is no difference in principle between compulsory taxes and plain robbery. The only difference is the institutional arrangement involved.[101]

Schumpeter, for instance, states:

> The theory which construes taxes on the analogy of club dues or of the purchase of the services of, say, a doctor only proves how far removed this part of the social science is from scientific habits of mind.[102]

And we cannot say that Schumpeter was a libertarian of the Rothbardian persuasion.[103] Yet, he recognized this fact.

Let us see, for instance, what Spooner opines:

> "It is true that the theory of our Constitution is, that all taxes are paid voluntarily; that our government is a mutual insurance company, voluntarily entered into by the people with each other; that each man makes a free and purely voluntary contract with all others who are parties to the Constitution, to pay so much money for so much protection, the same as he does with any other insurance company; and that he is just as free not to be protected, and not to pay tax, as he is to pay a tax, and be protected.
>
> "But this theory of our government is wholly different from the practical fact. The fact is that the government, like a highwayman, says to a man: "Your money, or your life." And many, if not most, taxes are paid under the compulsion of that threat.
>
> "The government does not, indeed, waylay a man in a lonely place, spring upon him from the roadside, and, holding a pistol to his head, proceed to rifle his pockets. But the robbery is none the less a robbery on that account; and it is far more dastardly and shameful.
>
> The highwayman takes solely upon himself the responsibility, danger, and crime of his own act. He does not pretend that he has any rightful claim to your money, or that he intends to use it for your own benefit. He does not pretend to be anything but a robber. He has not acquired impudence enough to profess to be merely a "protector," and that he takes men's money against their will, merely to enable him to "protect" those infatuated travellers, who feel perfectly able to protect themselves, or do not appreciate his particular system of protection. He is too sensible a man to make such professions as these.[104]

Let us consider Miller's next sally:

> Futerman and Block think that there are no market failures—none, ever. But when it comes to making good on this extraordinarily strong claim, their arguments seem manifestly unequal to such a monumental task. Take the standard example involving pollution: when one person pollutes, he may generate costs, spread over a great many other people, that in the aggregate exceed the benefits that the polluter captures by polluting. If so, such pollution is thus inefficient and ought not occur.[105]

---

[101] See David Gordon, *Yes, Taxation is Theft*, MISES WIRE (Nov. 15, 2019), https://mises.org/wire/yes-taxation-theft.

[102] JOSEPH A. SCHUMPETER, CAPITALISM, SOCIALISM AND DEMOCRACY 198 n.11 (Harper 1942).

[103] *See* Murray N. Rothbard, *Breaking Out of the Walrasian Box: The Cases of Schumpeter and Hansen*, 1 REV. OF AUSTRIAN ECON. 97, 99–100 (1987).

[104] LYSANDER SPOONER, TREASON: THE CONSTITUTION OF NO AUTHORITY AND A LETTER TO THOMAS F. BAYARD 17 (Pine Tree Press 1965) (1870).

[105] Miller, *supra* note 303, at 94.

But pollution is not a *market* failure. Rather, it is an instance of trespass.[106] Someone placcs smoke or dust particles onto the physical property, or into the lungs, of other people, without the latter's permission.[107] If that is not a violation of private property rights, then nothing is. Miller seems to be confusing the *origin* of the phenomenon (trespassing) with what is the *system* that can help solve it (the market, in our view, or the government, in his).[108]

The market, that is, the rights respecting system, cannot be responsible for a rights violation.[109] Rather, this is a *government* failure, insofar as the state takes it upon itself to maintain a monopoly position on law and order, and fails to do so.[110] Miller might as well say that murder, rape, kidnapping and theft are also *market* failures. However, that could not be further from the truth. None of these activities are remotely connected with the market or free enterprise.[111] Laissez faire capitalism necessarily involves the voluntary consent of each of the parties to the commercial interaction;[112] or, in the felicitous phrase of Nozick, "capitalist acts between consenting adults."[113]

Miller would not agree. He misconstrues our defence against this charge of his that pollution constitutes a market failure.[114] He writes:

> "How do Futerman and Block respond to the pollution example? They say that 'this sort of pollution constitutes an invasion of smoke particles,' which is true of some, though not all, forms of pollution, and 'governments have not treated this activity in that manner.' Their point, I assume, is that at common law what we call pollution was treated as a so-called nuisance, not a trespass, which latter involves a physical invasion of another's land. The difference matters because courts routinely enjoin trespasses but enjoin nuisances only in a more limited set of cases. For this reason, Futerman and Block conclude, governments 'have supported and allowed such rights violations,' presumably referring to those nuisance cases in which courts have not issued injunctions.
>
> Regardless of how true this all is, it amounts to saying that the government, under the common law and before the era of environmental regulation, did a very imperfect job of

---

106 See Walter E. Block, *Environmentalism and Economic Freedom: The Case for Private Property Rights*, 17 J. Bus. Ethics 1887, 1895 (1998); Thomas DiLorenzo, *Does Capitalism Cause Pollution?*, 38 Contemporary Issues Series (Washington University: Center for the Study of American Business, 1990); Morton H. Horwitz, The Transformation of American Law: 1780–1860 (Harvard Univ. Press 1977); Peter Lewin, *Pollution Externalities: Social Cost and Strict Liability*, 2 Cato J. 205 (1982); Murray N. Rothbard, *Law, Property Rights, and Air Pollution*, 2 Cato J. 55 (1982), *reprinted in* Economics and the Environment: A Reconciliation 233–279279 (Walter E. Block ed., Fraser Inst. 1990).

107 *See* Block, *supra* note 325, at 1889–90.

108 *See* Miller, *supra* note 303, at 103.

109 *See* Block, *supra* note 325, at 1888–92.

110 *See Id.* at 1889.; see also Ryan McMaken, *Property, Ownership, and Monopoly Police Forces*, Mises Wire (Aug. 15, 2014), https://mises.org/wire/property-ownership-and-monopoly-police-forces.

111 *See* Murray N. Rothbard, *What is the Free Market?*, Mises Inst. (Nov. 4, 2019), https://mises.org/library/what-free-market.

112 *Id.*

113 Robert Nozick, Anarchy, State, And Utopia 163 (1974).

114 *See* Miller, *supra* note 303, at 95.

> stopping inefficient pollution. But even if this is true, it is completely irrelevant. Futerman and Block were supposed to show that there was no market failure, that is, that the market would stop all inefficient pollution. To show that the government has stopped some inefficient pollution, but not all, obviously does nothing to show that the market would stop it all.[115]

This is problematic. Return to our argument that rape, murder, theft, kidnapping, are not *market* failures either. This is the case *not* because "the government has stopped some [of these crimes], but not all,"[116] the words Miller is attempting to put into the mouths of FB. Instead, pollution cannot count as a market failure because in an archaic system such as ours, governments, not markets, are assigned the task of stopping crimes of these sorts.[117] Nor it is the case that "government has stopped some inefficient pollution, but not all . . . ."[118] Rather, the state simply does not see pollution as the instance of crime that it is. In the 1919 case of *Holman v. Athens Empire Laundry Company*,[119] the Supreme Court of Georgia declared:

> The pollution of the air, so far as reasonably necessary to the enjoyment of life and indispensable to the progress of society, is not actionable.[120]

Not actionable? This means that pollution is not even a *failure* in the view of this Court, let alone a *market* failure.

Also highly problematic is this statement of Miller's:

> As anarchists, Futerman and Block think we ought not have any courts . . . .[121]

The position of anarcho-capitalists such as FB, is, rather, we ought not to have *government* courts; but we should indeed have private ones. [122]

---

[115] *Id.*

[116] Miller, *supra* note 303, at 96.

[117] *See* Block, *supra* note 325, at 1887; *see also* Ryan McMaken, *Property, Ownership, and Monopoly Police Forces*, Mises Wire (Aug. 15, 2014), https://mises.org/wire/property-ownership-and-monopoly-police-forces.

[118] Miller, *supra* note 303, at 96.

[119] Holman v. Athens Empire Laundry Co., 100 S.E. 207 (Ga. 2019).

[120] *See* Rothbard, *supra* note 325 (citing *Holman* 100 S.E).

[121] Miller, *supra* note 303, at 95 n.18.

[122] There is also a wealth of literature on this matter which appears to have escaped Miller's attention. *See generally Holman* 100 S.E., at 207; Bruce L. Benson, The Enterprise of Law: Justice Without the State (1990); Bruce L. Benson, *Justice Without Government: The Merchant Courts of Medieval Europe and Their Modern Counterparts*, *in* The Voluntary City: Choice, Community and Civil Society 127 (David T. Beito, Peter Gordon & Alexander Tabarrok, eds. 2009); Bruce L. Benson, *The Enterprise of Customary Law*, Mises Inst. (July 14, 2018), https://mises.org/library/enterprise-customary-law; Harold J. Berman and Felix J. Dasser, *The 'New' Law Merchant and the 'Old': Sources, Content and Legitimacy*, *in* Lex Mercatoria and Arbitration: A Discussion of the Law Merchant 21 (Thomas E. Carbonneau, ed., Juris Publ'g rev. ed. 1998) (1990); David Friedman, *Private Creation and Enforcement of Law – A Historical Case*, 8 J. Legal. Stud. 399 (1979); David Friedman, The Machinery of Freedom: Guide to Radical Capitalism (2d ed., 1989); Hans-Hermann Hoppe, Democracy – The god that failed: The Economics and Politics of Monarchy, Democracy, natural Order (2001);

Nor can we see our way clear to agreeing with Miller in this statement of his:

> [A]rguments showing the existence of market failures have been made and accepted by the likes of Friedrich Hayek, Ronald Coase, Milton Friedman, and Richard Epstein, none of whom can plausibly be called a statist.[123]

First, this is an argument from authority, a logical fallacy. Second, there is large, detailed and extensive literature on the non-existence of market failures,[124] none of which has been satisfactorily responded to by any of these four authorities. Yes, Miller is correct in maintaining that these prestigious economists and legal scholars all share the opinion that market failures exist, but since they do not so much as acknowledge, let alone attempt to refute, claims to the contrary that we mention, they are violating the John Stuart Mill insight.

Third, while to be sure none of these four are "a priori statists," this is not Miller's claim. Rather, he denies they are even plain old ordinary statists, that is, scholars who see a legitimate role for the government. But all four of them have been subjected to withering criticisms for their support of statism in this sense,[125] a group of

---

Daniel Popeo, *Privatizing the Judiciary*, FEE (Aug. 1, 1988), https://fee.org/articles/privatizing-the-judiciary/; David Osterfeld, *Anarchism and the Public Goods Issue: Law, Courts and the Police*, 9 J. LIBERTARIAN STUD. 47 (1989); Joseph R. Peden, *Property Rights in Celtic Irish Law*, 1 J. LIBERTARIAN STUD. 81 (1977); MURRAY N. ROTHBARD, FOR A NEW LIBERTY (Ludwig von Mises Instit. 2d ed. 2006) (1973) [hereinafter ROTHBARD, FOR A NEW LIBERTY]; Murray N. Rothbard, *Free Market, Police, Courts, and Law*, REASON, Mar. 1973, at 5; MURRAY N. ROTHBARD, THE ETHICS OF LIBERTY (1982) [hereinafter ROTHBARD, THE ETHICS OF LIBERTY]; Murray N. Rothbard, *On Denationalizing the Courts*, 2 ROTHBARD-ROCKWELL REPORT [pp. 304–306] (1991); Edward Stringham, *Justice Without Government*, 14 J. LIBERTARIAN STUD. 53 (1998–99); MORRIS TANNEHILL & LINDA TANNEHILL, THE MARKET FOR LIBERTY (Fox & Wilkes 3d ed. 1993) (1970); Morris Tannehill & Linda Tannehill, *Arbitration of Disputes*, MISES INST. (July 1, 2001), https://mises.org/library/arbitration-disputes; ADAM THIERER, JUDGEMENT DAY: THE CASE FOR ALTERNATIVE DISPUTE RESOLUTION (1992); WILLIAM C. WOOLRIDGE, UNCLE SAME THE MONOPOLY MAN (1970); Adam Young, *Arbitration on Trial*, MISES INST. (July 17, 2002), https://mises.org/library/arbitration-trial.

[123] Miller, *supra* note 303, at 94–95.

[124] See Walter E. Block, *All Government is Excessive: A Rejoinder to Dwight Lee's 'In Defense of Excessive Government,'* 16 J. LIBERTARIAN STUD. 35 (2002); *see also* THE THEORY OF MARKET FAILURE: A CRITICAL EXAMINATION (Tyler Cowen ed., 1988); Thomas DiLorenzo, *A Note on the Canard of 'Asymmetric Information' as a Source of Market Failure*, 14 Q. J. AUSTRIAN ECON. 249 (2011); THE MYTH OF NATIONAL DEFENSE: ESSAYS ON THE THEORY AND HISTORY OF SECURITY PRODUCTION (Hans-Hermann Hope ed., Ludwig von Mises Inst. 2003); D. W. MacKenzie, *The Market Failure Myth*, MISES INSTITUTE (Aug. 26, 2002, 12:00 AM), https://mises.org/library/market-failure-myth; Murray N. Rothbard, *Airport Congestion: A Case of Market Failure?*, 3 THE FREE MARKET 3 (1985); BRIAN SIMPSON, MARKETS DON'T FAIL (2005); Christopher Westley, *The Myth of Market Failure*, MISES INSTITUTE (June 14, 2002, 12:00 AM), https://mises.org/library/myth-market-failure; Thomas E. Woods Jr., *Krugman Failure, Not Market Failure*, LEW ROCKWELL (June 19, 2009), https://www.lewrockwell.com/2009/06/thomas-woods/krugman-failure-not-market-failure/; Thomas E. Woods Jr., *Response to the 'Market Failure' Drones*, MISES INSTITUTE (June 10, 2009, 12:00 AM), https://mises.org/library/response-market-failure-drones.

[125] It is exceedingly rare for any of them to even acknowledge it, let alone respond to it.

literature about which Miller seems unaware. For example, see criticisms on this ground of Hayek and Friedman,[126] Coase,[127] and Epstein.[128]

---

[126] *See generally* Walter E. Block, *Hayek's Road to Serfdom*, 12 J. LIBERTARIAN STUD. 339 (1996); Hans-Hermann Hoppe, *Why Mises (and Not Hayek)?*, MISES INST. (Oct. 4, 2011, 1:00 PM), https://mises.org/library/why-mises-and-not-hayek; Walter E. Block, *The Gold Standard: A Critique of Friedman, Mundell, Hayek, Greenspan*, 25 MANAGERIAL FIN. 15 (1999) [hereinafter Block, *The Gold Standard*]; Walter E. Block, *Fanatical, Not Reasonable: A Short Correspondence Between Walter E. Block and Milton Friedman* , 20 J. LIBERTARIAN STUD. 61 (2006) [hereinafter Block, *Fanatical, Not Reasonable*]; Ronald Hamowy, *Hayek's Concept of Freedom: A Critique*, 1 NEW INDIVIDUALIST REV. 28 (1961) (reviewing Friedrich Hayek, The Constitution of Liberty (1960)); ROTHBARD, *supra* note 343; Murray N. Rothbard, *48 Non-Libertarian Positions Held By Friedrich Hayek*, ECON. POL'Y J. (Jan. 2, 2014), https://www.economicpolicyjournal.com/2014/01/48-non-libertarian-positions-held-by.html.

[127] *See generally* William Barnett II & Walter E. Block, *Coase and Van Zandt on Lighthouses*, 35 PUB. FIN. REV. 710 (2007) [hereinafter Barnett & Block, *Coase and Van Zandt*]; William Barnett II & Walter E. Block, *Coase and Bertrand on Lighthouses*, 140 PUB. CHOICE 1 (2009) [hereinafter Barnett & Block, *Coase and Bertrand*]; Walter E. Block, *Coase and Demsetz on Private Property Rights*, 1 J. LIBERTARIAN STUD. 111 (1977) [hereinafter Block, *Coase and Demsetz on Private Property Rights*]; Walter E. Block, *Ethics, Efficiency, Coasean Property Rights and Psychic Income: A Reply to Demsetz*, 8 REV. AUSTRIAN ECON. 61 (1995); Walter E. Block, *O.J.'s Defense: A Reductio Ad Absurdum of the Economics of Ronald Coase and Richard Posner*, 3 EUR. J. L. & ECON. 265 (1996); Walter E. Block, *Private Property Rights, Erroneous Interpretations, Morality and Economics: Reply to Demsetz*, 3 Q. J. AUSTRIAN ECON. 63 (2000) [hereinafter Block, *Private Property Rights*]; Walter E. Block, *Private Property Rights, Economic Freedom, and Professor Coase: A Critique of Friedman, McCloskey, Medema and Zorn*, 26 HARV. J. L. & PUB. POL'Y 923 (2003); Walter E. Block, *Coase and Kelo: Ominous Parallels and Reply to Lott on Rothbard on Coase*, 27 WHITTER L. REV. 997 (2006); Walter E. Block, *A Response to Brooks' Support of Demsetz on the Coase Theorem*, 2 DIALOGUE (2010); Walter E. Block, *Rejoinder to Brooks on Coase and Demsetz*, 13 Q. J. AUSTRIAN ECON. 56 (2010); Walter E. Block, *Rejoinder to Boettke on Coasean Economics and Communism*, 5 ROMANIAN ECON. & BUS. REV. 9 (2010); Walter E. Block, William Barnett II & Gene Callahan, *The Paradox of Coase as a Defender of Free Markets*, 1 N.Y.U. J. L. & LIBERTY 1075 (2005); Roy E. Cordato, *Knowledge Problems and the Problem of Social Cost*, 14 J. HIST. ECON. THOUGHT 209 (1992); ROY E. CARDATO, WELFARE ECONOMICS AND EXTERNALITIES IN AN OPEN ENDED UNIVERSE: A MODERN AUSTRIAN PERSPECTIVE (Kluwer, 1992); Roy E. Cordato, *Market-Based Environmentalism and the Free Market: They're Not the Same*, 1 INDEP. REV. 371 (1997); Roy E. Cordato, *Time Passage and the Economics of Coming to the Nuisance: Reassessing the Coasean Perspective*, 20 CAMPBELL L. REV. 273 (1998); Roy E. Cordato, *Chasing Phantoms in a Hollow Defense of Coase*, 13 REV. AUSTRIAN ECON. 193 (2000); Thomas DiLorenzo, *When Did Ronald Coase Become the Ayatollah of Economic Theory?*, LEW ROCKWELL (January 2, 2014), https://www.lewrockwell.com/2014/01/thomas-dilorenzo/the-beltarian-cult/; Glenn Fox, *The Real Coase Theorems*, 27 CATO J. 373 (2007); Hans-Hermann Hoppe, *The Ethics and Economics of Private Property*, LEW ROCKWELL (October 11, 2004), https://www.lewrockwell.com/2004/10/hans-hermann-hoppe/the-ethics-and-economics-of-private-property/; Michael Krauss, *Tort Law, Moral Accountability, and Efficiency: Reflections on the Current Crisis*, 2 J. MKTS & MORTALITY 114 (1999); Elisabeth Krecke, *Law and the Market Order: An Austrian Critique of the Economic Analysis of Law*, 7 J. ECONOMISTES & ETUDES HUMANES 19 (1996); Lewin, *supra* note 325; Rothbard, *supra* note 325; Edward Stringham & Mark D. White, *Economic Analysis of Tort Law: Austrian and Kantian Perspectives*, *in* LAW AND ECONOMICS: ALTERNATIVE APPROACHES TO LEGAL AND REGULATORY ISSUES 374 (Margaret Oppenheimer & Nicholas Mercuro eds., 2004); Timothy D. Terrell, *Property Rights and Externality: The Ethics of the Austrian School*, 2 J. MKTS. & MORTALITY (1999).

[128] *See generally* Walter E. Block & David Gordon, *Blackmail, Extortion and Free Speech: A Reply to Posner, Epstein, Nozick and Lindgren*, 19 LOY. L.A. L. REV. 37 (1985); Walter E. Block, *Toward*

Next, consider our man Schmatz. Miller utilizes him to wax eloquent about public goods. He opines:

> National defense is a standard example. If someone undertakes to build and maintain a navy to keep foreign enemies far from our shores, everyone living in the protected area benefits from this, whether he contracts with the person supplying the navy or not. Hence, imagine some entrepreneur undertakes to sell naval protection services and starts soliciting people to buy his product. Say the price he offers is $100 per year, and Schmatz would happily pay $200 per year for the service. If naval protection services were like most goods, Schmatz and the entrepreneur would strike a deal and Schmatz would pay. But because of the nature of naval protection services, Schmatz may refuse to pay anything in the hopes that enough other people will sign up, for if they do, Schmatz will benefit from the entrepreneur's navy without paying a penny for it. In other words, Schmatz may conclude that his best option is to try to freeride on the payments of others. Everyone, however, is in the same position as Schmatz, and if enough people adopt the freeriding strategy, the entrepreneur will be unable to cover his costs and will go out of business—and there will be no navy, even though it was a good worth producing.[129]

There is more wrong here than you can take a stick at. First, who says "everyone living in the protected area benefits from this?"[130] What about pacifists? What about enemy aliens? Surely, even Miller would have to concede these folks do not benefit; the very opposite is obviously the case. Second, posit that we all do gain from having a navy. A private enterprise navy owner can tell the enemy that he is not going to protect anyone living in Taxachusetts, where, say, a disproportionate number of pacifists live who refuse to pay him for protection, but if they lay one hand on Texas, where men are men, he will kick their butt. All of those non-pacifists occupying pacifist-majority areas can move out. Namely, non-payers can be excluded from the stipulated "benefits" of the navy. This threat alone might suffice to raise a military at sea.

Advocates of the public good – market failure –would object on the ground that the funds raised in this manner would be insufficient; however, they lack any objective criterion on the basis of which this objection could be made. Insurance companies would also be relevant in this regard in a free market. What is the optimal amount of statist spending on the navy? This is an impossible question to answer unambiguously, in the absence of a free market. Again, both values and costs are subjective, and the issue cannot be rationally settled in the absence of a price system operating freely regarding defence or security.

---

a Libertarian Theory of Inalienability: A Critique of Rothbard, Barnett, Gordon, Smith, Kinsella and Epstein, 17 J. LIBERTARIAN STUD. 39 (2003); Walter E. Block & Richard Epstein, *Block-Epstein Debate on Eminent Domain*, MISES INST. (May 14, 2004), https://mises.org/library/block-epstein-debate-eminent-domain; Walter E. Block & Richard Epstein, *Debate on Eminent Domain*, 1 N.Y.U. J. OF L. & LIBERTY 1144 (2005); Walter E. Block, *Epstein on Alienation: A Rejoinder*, 33 INT'L J. SOC. ECON. 241 (2006); Walter E. Block, *In Defense of the Free Market*, BARRON'S (Feb. 4, 2012) (reviewing RICHARD A. EPSTEIN, DESIGN FOR LIBERTY: PRIVATE PROPERTY, PUBLIC ADMINISTRATION, AND THE RULE OF LAW (2011)).

[129] Miller, *supra* note 303, 96–97.

[130] *See id.*

Third, there is an extensive literature attesting to the non-public good of military protection,[131] and Miller fails to engage with it. This is a very serious oversight.

Our author also fails to see the intellectual power of Rothbard's "string quartet" refutation of the public goods argument. He states as follows: "[T]he benefits of a public good are non-excludable; the benefits of joining a string quartet . . . are perfectly excludable."[132]

First of all, there is no example of a public good – military, police, fire protection, whatever – that has not at some time or other been supplied in the private sector.[133] Second, it is possible to employ a *reductio ad absurdum* here: the three members of the string quartet will gain more from the participation of the violist, than the latter will lose by being compelled into joining them in their moment's musicale. Miller is in no position to dissent from this claim, given his parallel assertions about the costs and benefits of the navy. In neither case is it possible to ascertain the value of these contrary to fact costs and benefits. If Miller can argue his conclusion in favour of the navy, Rothbard is entitled to take the same stance in terms of the string players.

Third, if we posit that "the benefits of a public good are non-excludable,"[134] we are thus entitled to conclude that there is no such thing as a public good that needs to be supplied by the state. Or that if this good does fulfill the public good's conditions, then it would be irrelevant. Why? Because another, more fundamental, problem with the public goods concept is its contradictory definition.[135] Goods can be defined as economic goods or free goods. The latter are not scarce,[136] while the

---

[131] *See generally* Walter E. Block, *National Defense and the Theory of Externalities, Public Goods and Clubs*, *in* The Myth of National Defense: Essays on the Theory and History of Security Production 301 (Hans-Hermann Hoppe ed., Mises Inst. 2003); Cowen, *supra* note 256; Anthony de Jasay, Social Contract, Free Ride: A Study of the Public Goods Problem (1989); Hans-Hermann Hoppe, *Fallacies of the Public Goods Theory and the Production of Security*, 9 J. Libertarian Stud. 27 (1989); Jeffrey Hummel, *National Goods versus. Public Goods: Defense, Disarmament and Free Riders*, 4 R. Austrian Econ. 88 (1990); E.C. Pasour, Jr., *The Free Rider as a Basis for Government Intervention*, 5 J. Libertarian Stud. 453 (1981); 2 Murray N. Rothbard, The Logic of Action: Applications and Criticism from the Austrian School (1997); David Schmidtz, The Limits of Government: An Essay on the Public Goods Argument (1991); Larry Sechrest, *Privateering and National Defense: Naval Warfare for Private Profit*, *in* The Myth of National Defense: Essays on the Theory and History of Security Production 239 (Hans-Hermann Hoppe ed., Mises Inst., 2003); Larry Sechrest, *Public Goods and Private Solutions in Maritime History*, 7 Q. J. Austrian Econ. 3 (2004); Larry Sechrest, *Private Provision of Public Goods: Theoretical Issues and Some Examples from Maritime History*, 2 ICFAI J. Pub. Fin. 45 (2004); Larry Sechrest, *Privately Funded and Built U.S. Warships in the Quasi-War of 1797-1801*, 12 Indep. Rev. 101 (2007).

[132] Miller, *supra* note 303, at 97 n.22.

[133] *See supra* note 350.

[134] Miller, *supra* note 303, at 97 n.22.

[135] *See* Alan G. Futerman, *Hacia una Teoría de los Bienes Públicos como Bienes Políticos y el Rol Estatal*, 11 Revista Procesos de Mercado [Spain] 217 (2014).

[136] Scarcity is a subjective, relational concept, regarding the available quantity of means to achieve a certain set of ends. See Chapter 1.

former are indeed scarce. Economic goods are scarce, hence valuable. Free goods are not scarce, hence their value, though it exists, is zero.[137] Here is the problem: free goods are the ultimate non-excludability and non-rivalrousness, the be-all and end-all of being a public good. In normal conditions on planet earth, oxygen is free and the fact that *A* breathes does not exclude *B* from breathing. As long as *A* does not forcefully close *B*'s mouth and nose (which would count as a rights violation), *B* can breathe freely too. On the other hand, economic goods are scarce, therefore valuable, and hence will tend to have a price on the market. As long as a good fulfills these conditions, the market will have an *incentive* in providing it. But real non-excludable, non-rivalrous goods, that is, public goods, are *necessarily* free goods. But what is the purpose of providing such free goods? These are already *free*. However, if public goods are not free goods, then they must be economic goods. Then, they would not be non-excludable and/or non-rivalrous, but rather scarce, and the market would have an incentive to provide them. They would have a market price, just like private security and private education.

Public goods are in fact *political* goods, that is, what politicians or society (responding to the prevailing culture or philosophical ideas) regard as *essential*. In reality, public goods are understood as a moral idea, not as a technical, scientific concept.[138] It is their ambiguous definition that allows them to grow and expand to encompass more goods and services in the economy. In fact, the definition of public goods is one of the reasons why the government expands. As an example, we can theoretically stretch the definition enough to include almost all "private" goods and only leave a small set for the market. Are we exaggerating? Here is what a leading public goods theorist, Paul Samuelson, had to say about this:

> Thus, consider what I have given in this paper as the definition of a public good, and what I might better have insisted upon as a definition in my first and subsequent papers: 'A public good is one that enters two or more persons' utility.' What are we left? Two poles and a continuum (sic) in between? No. *With a knife-edge pole of the private-good case and with all the rest of the world in the public-good domain by virtue of involving some 'consumption externality*.'[139] (emphasis added).

This being the case, what are we to make of this statement of Miller's?

> I am pointing out that the arguments they make are, at best, gestures at well-known arguments to which there are well-known responses. If these gestures do nothing to convince me—and I am one of the freest of free marketeers and an enthusiastic cheerleader for capitalism —then it is nearly certain that they will not convince anyone who does not already

---

[137] In terms of commercial trade, that is. Air and ocean water are at present free goods. No one buys or sells them. However, if they both disappeared, life would disappear.

[138] They are based on, in economics, the pernicious doctrine of "market failure." Included here, in addition to so-called "public goods" would be externalities, monopoly, inequality, asymmetric information, etc. However, an exploration of all these concepts would take us too far off topic.

[139] Paul Samuelson, *Pure Theory of Public Expenditure and Taxation*, *in* The Collected Scientific Papers of Paul A. Samuelson 502 (in *Public Economics: An Analysis of Public Production and Consumption and their Relations to the Private Sectors: Proceedings of a Conference held by the International Economic Association*, J. Margolis and H. Guitton, eds. London: Macmillan.) (Massachusetts Institute of Technology: M.I.T. Press 1969 [1991]).

> agree with Futerman and Block's anarcho-capitalism. That is why I said above that the essay is in the nature of a manifest. It rallies the troops, but it does not convert the unconvinced.[140]

The difficulty here is that Miller gauges the success of FB in terms of how well they can convert "the freest of free marketeers" to the position of anarcho-capitalism which makes no compromise with statism, in contrast to an "enthusiastic cheerleader for capitalism" who makes all sorts of accommodations with this problematic system. But why should that be the criterion of success? Posit that "the freest of free marketeers and [the] enthusiastic cheerleader[s] for capitalism"[141] are just obdurate in their beliefs, will not listen to reason, and are ignorant of the complete case in favour of full laissez-faire capitalism. Why should that count as an objection to FB? Miller offers us no answer to this challenge.

Miller next launches into an intensive discussion of transaction costs, in an attempt to demonstrate that there are indeed market failures. He declaims:

> [A]market failure occurs when there is a market transaction that produces net aggregate benefits and that will nevertheless not occur because the transaction costs involved in effecting the transaction exceed the net aggregate benefits produced. Now, market transactions always involve some transaction costs . . . . Sometimes these costs are low, sometimes high, but they are always positive. To assert that there are *no* market failures, ever, is equivalent to asserting that, for every potential market transaction producing aggregate net benefits, the transaction costs associated with that transaction are less than those aggregate net benefits. Since these costs and benefits depend on so many empirical factors . . . it seems obviously impossible to say, *a priori*, that the transaction costs associated with a transaction producing aggregate net benefits will *always* be less than such benefits. Nothing in the nature of things requires this happy result, and so if things turned out this way, it would be the most incredible good luck (emphasis in the original).[142]

There are grave problems with this analysis. First of all, this is not what is meant by "market failure" in the economic literature. In the literature, incidences of this phenomenon include monopoly, monopsony, public goods, both positive and negative externalities, asymmetric information, inequality, and the like. In other words, it is an idiosyncratic notion of Miller's that these sorts of costs constitute "market failure" in the view of anyone other than himself.

Second, if it were true, then not only would there be some market failures out there, but they would be all over the place. For example, let us argue by analogy: "a market failure occurs when there is a market transaction that produces net aggregate benefits and that will nevertheless not occur because the transaction costs [e.g., labor or capital] involved in effecting the transaction exceed the net aggregate benefits produced."[143] There must be millions, billions, zillions of such examples. Market failures would be legion. Only a Bernie Sanders would welcome such a result; certainly not a self-styled supporter of limited government such as Miller.

---

[140] Miller, *supra* note 303, at 98.

[141] *See id.*

[142] Miller, *supra* note 303, at 98–99.

[143] *Id.* at 98.

Miller confuses the concept of market failure with that of *loss*. For instance, if a company goes bankrupt, that is not a market failure, but an all-too-often outcome of the free market. In such a case, expenses exceeded income and the company disappears. But the market continues. In fact, if it were not for free enterprise, no costs could have been identified in the first place, since there would be no price system. That is, the market assures that capital is allocated to maximize consumer satisfaction. In the absence of a market, losses therefore extend indefinitely, and resources are wasted.

Third, there is a difficulty with "aggregate benefits." These are contrary to fact conditionals. No one knows them; no one *can* know any such thing. This is because these so-called benefits can only be attained through market transactions, and in this situation described by Miller, they simply do not occur.

Fourth, transactions costs is a concept most heavily tied to Ronald Coase.[144] At times, he was a bitter critic of the free enterprise system.[145] Presumably, if he could have used this notion to undercut the case for economic freedom at those times, he most certainly would have done so. But even he did not go off the cliff in this manner, as per Miller. Coase did not claim that transactions costs, any more than any other kinds of costs under the sun, constituted a market failure. As to Miller's calculations[146] as to the low probability of there being no market failures, we cannot go along with Queen Victoria who famously said "we are not amused." In sharp distinction, the authors of the present essay are very amused. Equating market failure with losses, or the probability of finding that costs are above income *ex-post* of an action, renders Miller's calculations fallacious.

Of course, there is a chance that commercial action will not achieve its end, i.e., instead it will incur losses. But that is not a market failure. That is why there is uncertainty, and no perfect knowledge.[147] If there were no probability of incurring losses, man would be omniscient, hence a perfect being. But, as Mises said, a perfect being does not act.[148] The key to a proper system is not whether it is perfect, but rather whether it can allow mistakes to be uncovered and corrected. That is why the market is based on profit *and* losses.[149] What Miller regards as a problem of the free enterprise system, and defines as market failure, is precisely the mechanism that allows the market to operate and correct the inevitable mistakes that people make in economic activity.

On the other hand, which is the system that does not allow for mistakes to be revealed and subsequently corrected? A centrally planned one. That is, one run by

---

[144] See Ronald Coase, *The Problem of Social Cost*, 3 J. L. & ECON. 1 (1960).

[145] *See* Barnett & Block, *Coase and Van Zandt*, *supra* note 346; Barnett & Block, *Coase and Bertrand*, *supra* note 346.

[146] Miller, *supra* note 303, at 100.

[147] As opposed to the perfect competition model of neoclassical economics, which is the basis of Miller's criticisms. He seems to be unaware that there is a systematic (Misesian-Austrian) refutation of that school of thought.

[148] LUDWIG VON MISES, HUMAN ACTION: A TREATISE ON ECONOMICS 65 (4th ed., 1949).

[149] LUDWIG VON MISES, PROFIT AND LOSS 8 (Ludwig von Mises Instit. 2008) (1952).

government. Miller makes much of the undoubted fact that there is a probability there will be business losses. But this is a point *for* the market, not against it. This is what guarantees there will be progress, innovation and growth. Given that men can err, a system where mistakes cannot be identified is not only a system that *will not* improve, but one that *cannot* improve and never will.[150]

Moreover, we can also perform some quantitative analysis on this regard. The economy works through the functioning of the price system. More specifically, prices are the signals that allow entrepreneurs to allocate capital in the productive endeavours that most satisfy consumer wants. However, it is not prices themselves that guide the economic process, but *relative* prices. An absolute price, alone, says virtually nothing. Following Ludwig Von Mises,[151] Rogelio Pontón[152] showed that given the enormous number of relative prices in a modern economy, there is no computation mechanism in existence that would be able to centrally plan for them all on a rational basis (Hayek 1945). This insight was later brightly developed by Osvaldo H. Schenone,[153] whose explanation we now present. If the total economy has *a, b, c, d, ... N* goods and services, then p_{ab} is the relative price of good *a* in terms of *b*, or how many units of *b* must be delivered for a unit of *a*.

Following Schenone, relative prices can be shown as a matrix:

$$
\begin{matrix}
p_{11} & p_{12} & p_{13} & p_{14} & p_{15} & \cdots & p_{1N} \\
p_{21} & p_{22} & p_{23} & p_{24} & p_{25} & \cdots & p_{2N} \\
p_{31} & p_{32} & p_{33} & p_{34} & p_{35} & \cdots & p_{3N} \\
\cdot & \cdot & \cdot & \cdot & \cdot & \cdot & \cdot \\
p_{N1} & p_{N2} & p_{N3} & p_{N4} & p_{N5} & \cdots & p_{NN}
\end{matrix}
$$

This means that there are N^2-N pertinent relative prices in the economy.[154] But, since we know p_{ab}, we must also know p_{ba}, so all relative prices on the opposite side of the main diagonal of the matrix are irrelevant. On each side of the main diagonal of the matrix there are N(N-1)/2 relative prices, and therefore the pertinent relative prices are: N^2-N-N(N-1)/2. This is the same as the following expression: (N^2-N)/2.

[150] *See* LUDWIG VON MISES, SOCIALISM: AN ECONOMIC AND SOCIOLOGICAL ANALYSIS (Yale Univ. Press 1962) (1922).

[151] *Id.*

[152] ROGELIO T. PONTÓN, ENSAYOS SOBRE LA TEORÍA Y LA REALIDAD ECONÓMICA [Argentina] 11, 107, (2014).

[153] Osvaldo H. Schenone, ¿Cuántos precios relativos hay? Comentarios a Rogelio Pontón, (Nov. 2014) (unpublished commentary) (on file with authors).

[154] This is so because if we say that there are NxN=N^2 relative prices, there are N relative prices that are equal to one (given that these are relative prices for the same item, hence trivial, i.e., p_{aa}, the price of *a* in terms of *a* is still *a*. Therefore, the numbers of the main diagonal in the matrix are equal to 1). *See* Osvaldo H. Schenone, *supra* note 373.

According to Pontón, the number of goods in the Soviet economy in 1985 was 25 million.[155] That is, following the expression above, $(N^2-N)/2$, total pertinent relative prices for that economy were 312.5 trillion. But these prices *constantly* change, as values change. Hence, we are talking here not of trillions of relative prices, but quadrillions, or septillions (depending on the time frame), or more. How can a central planner get all the relevant information needed to compute costs and gains from interventions? It is essentially impossible. Miller mentions that physicists estimate there are at most 10^{82} observable atoms in the universe.[156] Pertinent relative prices for a modern economy are above that number, by many, many times.

Moreover, claiming that a government can know in any given situation that its intervention is less "costly" than the market alternative, would imply that it can calculate all consequences from its action, including its impact on relative prices. But this, as we have shown, cannot be done.

The government, by interfering in the market, necessarily affects relative prices. Arguendo, a passive observer would just need to know $(N^2-N)/2-(N-1)(N-2)/2$, or $N-1$, since by observing this number of relative prices, he can infer all the others (if this could be done at all). However, the economy is not a frozen picture, but an organic, moving, *process*. Hence, it is not just that it observes the arbitrating process of the market, but the government also distorts it. Thus, even if it could calculate the isolated result of its intervention beforehand, the change in the entire structure of relative prices that its actions would carry would also make any previous calculation irrelevant. The government cannot know beforehand how every economic agent will react to its intervention and would then remain in its state of ignorance with respect to the consequences of its actions. No government intervention can therefore be rationally defended on the grounds that it was more efficient.

Let's continue with Miller's critique. His "most serious criticism of Futerman and Block's essay [concerns] its reliance on what they call the non-aggression principle (NAP)."[157] Miller states:

> "[T]hey understand the NAP as prohibiting violence or threats of violence against both the person and the property of the innocent. From this principle, Futerman and Block say, 'the anarcho-capitalist position readily, and logically, follows.'
>
> But from a single premise, usually *very* little follows. When an author claims that great things follow from modest assumptions, what is usually happening is that the author is smuggling all the important premises into the argument, letting them do much of the work, and then pretending they are not there when they would become inconvenient for his argument. In my view, that is what Futerman and Block are doing here. The way they do it is by not defining the key terms in the NAP—terms like initiate, property, innocent, and illicit. Until these are spelled out in detail, the meaning of the NAP is far from clear (emphasis in the original).[158]

[155] And observe that this number is very low compared to any modern economy.

[156] Mille, *supra* note 303, at 100.

[157] Miller, *supra* note 303, at 101.

[158] *Id.*

We plead guilty to these charges. "Smuggling" is a bit much, but we throw ourselves onto the mercy of the court. Our only excuse is that not every article can say everything that Miller requires to convince him of the viability of anarcho-capitalism. But, again, we maintain, were he to immerse himself into the vast literature on this subject,[159] perhaps even he might become convinced.

What are the specifics of this charge? He asks, "[S]uppose a man owns a parcel of land. Does he also own the rights to minerals under the land as well?"[160] We need not fully answer this question he raises about the ad coelum doctrine; he should have done his homework and perused the pertinent publications.[161] Suffice it to say that a man's property extends as far down into the ground as he has homesteaded.[162]

---

[159] A small part of it mentioned herein.

[160] Miller, *supra* note 303, at 102.

[161] *See, e.g.*, Walter E. Block, *Homesteading, Ad Coelum, Owning Views and Forestalling*, 3 THE SOCIAL SCIENCES 96 (2008); Walter E. Block, *A Collection of Essays on Libertarian Jurisprudence: Sunshine and Property Rights*, 58 ST. LOUIS UNI. L. J. 541 (2014); Walter E. Block & Matthew A. Block, *Roads, Bridges, Sunlight and Private Property Rights*, 7 J. ECONOMISTES & ETUDES HUMANES 351 (1996); Walter E. Block, *Roads, Bridges, Sunlight and Private Property: Reply to Gordon Tullock*, 8 J. ECONOMISTES & ETUDES HUMANES 315 (1998). *But see* Gordon Tullock, *Comment on 'Roads, Bridges, Sunlight and Private Property', by Walter E. Block and Matthew A. Block*, 7 J. ECONOMISTES & ETUDES HUMANES 589 (1996). This literature also offers a response to Miller's objection that the ad coelum question has not been answered in FB: "[W]hen a man owns some land, does he own the airspace above the land?"

[162] *See generally* Walter E. Block, *Earning Happiness Through Homesteading Unowned Land: A Comment on 'Buying Misery with Federal Land' by Richard Stroup*, 15 J. SOC. POL. & ECON. STUD. 237 (1990); Walter E. Block, *Homesteading City Streets; An Exercise in Managerial Theory*, 5 PLAN. & MKTS. 18 (2002); Walter E. Block, *On Reparations to Blacks for Slavery*, 3 HUM. RTS. REV. 53 (2002); Walter E. Block & Michael R. Edelstein, *Popsicle sticks and homesteading land for nature preserves*, 7 ROMANIAN ECON. & BUS. REV. 7 (2012); WALTER E. BLOCK & PETER LOTHIAN NELSON, WATER CAPITALISM: THE CASE FOR PRIVATIZING OCEANS, RIVERS, LAKES, AND ACQUIFERS (2015) [hereinafter BLOCK & NELSON, WATER CAPITALISM]; Walter E. Block & Guillermo Yeatts, *The Economics and Ethics of Land Reform: A Critique of the Pontifical Council for Justice and Peace's 'Toward a Better Distribution of Land: The Challenge of Agrarian Reform,'* 15 J. NAT. L. RES. & ENVTL. L.37 (1999–2000); Block & Epstein, *supra* note 347, *Debate on Eminent Domain…*; Per Bylund, Man and Matter: A Philosophical Inquiry into the Justification of Ownership in Land from the Basis of Self-Ownership (2005) (Master's Thesis, Lund University) (on file with authors); Per Bylund, *Man and Matter: How the Former Gains Ownership of the Latter*, 4 LIBERTARIAN PAPERS 1 (2012); HUGO GROTIUS, LAW OF WAR AND PEACE (A.C. Campbell trans. 1814) (1625); HANS-HERMANN HOPPE, THE ECONOMICS AND ETHICS OF PRIVATE PROPERTY: STUDIES IN POLITICAL ECONOMY AND PHILOSOPHY (2004); Hans-Hermann Hoppe, *Of Private, Common, and Public Property and the Rationale for Total Privatization*, 3 LIBERTARIAN PAPERS 1 (2011); N. Stephan Kinsella, *A Libertarian Theory of Contract: Title Transfer, Binding Promises, and Inalienability*, 17 J. LIBERTARIAN STUD. 11 (2003); N. Stephan Kinsella, *How We Come to Own Ourselves*, MISES INST. (Sept. 7, 2006), https://mises.org/library/how-we-come-own-ourselves; N. Stephan Kinsella, *What Libertarianism Is*, MISES INST. (Aug. 21, 2009), https://mises.org/library/what-libertarianism; N. Stephan Kinsella, *What Libertarianism Is*, *in* PROPERTY, FREEDOM AND SOCIETY: ESSAYS IN HONOR OF HANS-HERMANN HOPPE (Jörg Guido Hülsmann & Stephan Kinsella eds., 2009); N.Stephan Kinsella, *Homesteading, Abandonment, and Unowned Land in the Civil Law*, MISES INST.(May 22, 2009), https://mises.org/wire/homesteading-abandonment-and-unowned-land-civil-law; John Locke, *An Essay Concerning the True Origin, Extent and End of Civil Government*, *in* SOCIAL CONTRACT 17 (E. Barker ed., 1962); ELLEN FRANKEL PAUL,

Miller continues in this vein:

> Suppose the minerals under the land are liquid in form, such as oil, so that when a landowner drills a well and starts pumping oil, he is also reducing the amount of oil under his neighbor's parcel, for the oil flows from one place underground to another. Is he stealing his neighbor's oil? If so, and if the neighbor may enjoin him, how can he possibly remove just his own oil? If he is not stealing his neighbor's oil and the neighbor may not enjoin him, then the neighbor will have a strong incentive to dig his own oil well to grab as much of the oil as possible before it is all gone. The result, it is easy to show, is that people will dig an inefficiently large number of oil wells.[163]

Again, our answer is the same. It is a bit much to require of authors that in any one short article, they anticipate all objections that can be launched, particularly when these challenges have already been dealt with.[164]

Miller then launches Demsetz (1967) against us. That scholar makes much of the fact that "[T]he rules of property law will change when the old rules become inefficient."[165] But Demsetz has also had his comeuppance.[166] The criticism of Demsetz is much the same as that which obtains against Coase, since the former is a warm supporter of the latter.[167] In a nutshell, it is that Coasean-Demsetzian

PROPERTY RIGHTS AND EMINENT DOMAIN (Routledge 2008) (1987); SAMUEL PUFENDORF, Natural Law and the Law of Nations Oxford Univ. Press 1927) (1672); Murray N. Rothbard, *Confiscation and the Homestead Principle*, 1 LIBERTARIAN F. 11 (1969); ROTHBARD, FOR A NEW LIBERTY, *supra* note 341.; ROTHBARD, THE ETHICS OF LIBERTY, *supra* note 341; Michael S. Rozeff, *Original Appropriation and Its Critics*, LEW ROCKWELL (Sept. 1, 2005), https://www.lewrockwell.com/2005/09/michael-s-rozeff/original-appropriation-and-its-critics/; Carl Watner, *The Proprietary Theory of Justice in the Libertarian Tradition*, 6 J. LIBERTARIAN STUD. 289 (1982).

163 Miller, *supra* note 372, at 102.

164 For a discussion on ownership of liquids, underground or otherwise, see BLOCK & NELSON, WATER CAPITALISM, *supra* note 382.

165 Miller, *supra* note 303, at 104 (quoting Harold Demsetz, *Toward a Theory of Property Rights*, 57 AM. ECON. REV. 347, 350 (1967)).

166 *See, e.g.*, Block, *Coase and Demsetz on Private Property Rights*, *supra* note 346; Harold Demsetz, *Ethics and Efficiency in Property Rights Systems*, *in* TIME, UNCERTAINTY AND DISEQUILIBRIUM: EXPLORATION OF AUSTRIAN THEMES (Mario Rizzo, ed.) (Lexington Mass.: D.C. Heath and Co, 1979); Walter E. Block, *Ethics, Efficiency, Coasean Property Rights and Psychic Income: A Reply to Demsetz*, 8 REV. AUSTRIAN ECON. 61 (1995); Harold Demsetz, *Block's Erroneous Interpretations*, 10 REV. AUSTRIAN ECON. 101 (1997); Walter E. Block, *Private Property Rights, Erroneous Interpretations, Morality and Economics: Reply to Demsetz*, 3 Q. J. AUSTRIAN ECON. 63 (2000).

167 See Block's many criticisms of Coase. Ibid., plus:

Walter E. Block, *On Ronald Coase as political economist*, 43 RUTGERS LAW RECORD 117-132 (2015–2016); Barnett & Block, *Coase and Van Zandt*, *supra* note 346; Barnett & Block, *Coase and Bertrand*, *supra* note 346; Block, *Coase and Demsetz on Private Property Rights...*, *supra* note 346; Walter E. Block, *O.J.'s Defense...*, *supra* note 346; Walter E. Block, *Private Property Rights, Economic Freedom, and Professor Coase...*, *supra* note 346; Walter E. Block, *Coase and Kelo...*, *supra* note 346; Walter E. Block, *A Response to Brooks' Support of Demsetz...*, *supra* note 346; Walter E. Block, *Rejoinder to Brooks...*, *supra* note 346; Walter E. Block, *Rejoinder to Boettke...*, *supra* note 346; Walter E. Block, *Rejoinder to Bertrand on lighthouses*, 6 ROMANIAN ECON. AND B. REV. 49–67 (2011); Walter E. Block, "The Dangerous Fanatic Ronald Coase, RIP", *Economic Policy Journal*, (September 16, 2013), https://www.economicpolicyjournal.com/2013/09/walter-block-on-dangerous-fanatic.html; Walter E. Block, William Barnett II & Gene Callahan, *The Paradox of Coase...*, *supra* note 346.

economics is to settle disputes over property rights in favour of maximizing GDP in the future, not on the basis of justice, namely, property titles emanating from the past. To wit, suppose that Bill Gates, a rich man, can better utilize the property of Jones, a poor man and they are in dispute as to who is the proper owner. Then, according to this view, the good in question should be seized from Jones, who holds otherwise licit title to the house or car under dispute, and given to Gates. It is difficult to imagine a greater injustice. Nor will this really lead to a maximization of GDP, since if we extrapolate from this miscarriage of justice, property titles, the bedrock of a civilized order, will no longer be secure.

Here is the next arrow Miller aims at the backsides of FB:

> Now consider the doctrine of necessity in property law. Under this doctrine, a person is indeed permitted to enter on the land of another and make use of his things, even contrary to the expressed wishes of the landowner—*if doing so is necessary to save life or limb.* Thus, in the famous case of *Ploof v. Putnam*, Ploof and his family were sailing on Lake Champlain when a storm blew up. Finding themselves in danger of drowning, they attempted to tie up on a dock owned by Putnam, whose servant prevented them from doing so and ordered them away. Ploof's craft foundered and, although no one was killed, Ploof and his wife and children were injured. The court held that Putnam had acted wrongly because Ploof had a right to tie up his boat on Putnam's dock for as long as the danger persisted (though Ploof would be liable for any damage to the dock that might result from his boat being there). Now, this strikes me as an eminently sensible result, in accord with not only the ancient doctrines of the common law but also the principles of economic analysis, the best moral philosophy, and the better angels of our nature. But what are we to make of this under the NAP? If we read the NAP literally, Putnam was entirely within his rights to eject the Ploofs, even if this meant that all the Ploof children would surely be drowned. If we are to avoid this absurd result, then the NAP is grossly incomplete: the word property in the NAP must be understood in such a way as to accommodate the doctrine of necessity.[168]

The best refutation of the "doctrine of necessity" is to realize that, paradoxically, the Ploofs of the world, that is, really, all of us, will be better off, far better, under a regime of private property rights, strictly interpreted, than when they are breached. Jean Valjean of *Les Misérables* can steal a loaf of bread under this doctrine, since he is starving. But, if he is allowed to get away with any such thing, bread will tend to disappear from the shelves, and we will all go hungry. Yes, strictly enforced and defended private property rights are seemingly tough on the Ploofs and Valjeans of the world, but this institution is what keeps us all from starving. We calculate with 99.987% certainty that we are correct in this empirical analysis of ours.[169]

Rothbard's analysis of the "doctrine of necessity" is definitive:

> It may well be objected to our theory as follows: that a theory of property rights or even of self-ownership is derivable from the conditions by which man survives and flourishes in this world, and that therefore in this kind of extreme situation, where a man is faced with the choice of *either* saving himself *or* violating the property rights of the lifeboat owner (or, in the above example, of the 'homesteader' in the boat), it is then ridiculous to expect him to surrender his life on behalf of the abstract principle of property rights. Because of this kind of consideration, many libertarians who otherwise believe in property rights gravely weaken them on behalf of the 'contextualist' contention that, given a choice between his life and aggressing against someone else's property or even life, it is moral for him to com-

---

[168] Miller, *supra* note 303, at 104–05.

[169] Hey, if Miller can engage in such calculations, so can we. Who says we learn nothing from him?

> mit the aggression *and* that therefore in such a situation, these property rights cease to exist. The error here on the part of the 'contextualist' libertarians is to confuse the question of the *moral* course of action for the person in such a tragic situation with the totally separate question of whether or not his seizing of lifeboat or plank space by force constitutes an invasion of someone else's property right. For we are not, in constructing a theory of liberty and property, i.e., a 'political' ethic, concerned with all *personal* moral principles. We are not herewith concerned whether it is moral or immoral for someone to lie, to be a good person, to develop his faculties, or be kind or mean to his neighbors. We are concerned, in this sort of discussion, solely with such 'political ethical' questions as the proper role of violence, the sphere of rights, or the definitions of criminality and aggression. Whether or not it is moral or immoral for 'Smith'–the fellow excluded by the owner from the plank or the lifeboat–to force someone else out of the lifeboat, or whether he *should* die heroically instead, is not our concern, and not the proper concern of a theory of political ethics.[170]

The *context* in which Ploof acts certainly explains why he does it, but it does not render him free to do as he pleases without later compensating the owner of the property. Hence, even the "doctrine of necessity" does not completely abrogate property rights, but rather tries to identify the context of the violation and subsequent compensation on the part of the violator. This is the same as distinguishing between a murderer and a mere trespasser. Both are violations of rights, but they are not the same. That is why the law has categories.

The ethical conduct of Putnam is a separate issue. Political philosophy is different than private morality. Putnam can be immoral in the very same way an excessive gambler can be, and yet there should be nothing in the law that forces morality on either of them. A rich man can refuse sending money to the poor,[171] and the latter may die of hunger. But that does not imply the former must be forced to do so. Yet, it may also be a life and death situation. True enough, there is a relation between the proper principles to guide one's life and the proper principles to rule society, but these are essentially different: the former are private and individual, while the latter are public and systemic.[172] Just one exception in the law system may destroy it, while a breach of private morality may only harm those involved in the situation. If equality before the law is to be respected, no exceptions should be made.

Our debating partner next uses the word "illicit" as a stick with which to beat up on us.[173] Let us clarify matters. We are deontological libertarians in the mould of Rothbard.[174] Utilitarian calculations are not for us. "Illicit" means "should be against the law" and is only very indirectly related to morality. Miller asserts that "[E]ven Kant allowed that the right to property was not absolute,"[175] but this is yet another

---

[170] Rothbard, The Ethics of Liberty, *supra* note 341, at 152; *see also* Walter E. Block, *The Non-Aggression Axiom of Libertarianism*, Lew Rockwell (Feb. 17, 2003), https://www.lewrockwell.com/2003/02/walter-e-block/turning-their-coats-for-the-state/.

[171] And we do not say that is immoral per se.

[172] Libertarianism is only relevant to the latter. It is a theory that attempts to explain just law; it is totally silent on private morality

[173] Miller, *supra* note 303, at 106-07.

[174] *Cf.* Rothbard, The Ethics of Liberty, *supra* note 341 (a review of this work will show these authors' similarities to Rothbard); see also Rothbard, For a New Liberty, *supra* note 341.

[175] Miller, *supra* note 303, at 107.

argument from the same authority. Can the philosopher Kant never be wrong? Evidently not, for Miller.

The author ends on a positive note, and so shall we. As we said at the outset, we are extremely grateful to Professor Miller for writing his constructive criticism of FB. Although we do not agree with the condemnation, we acknowledge that he has given us a run for our money, and forced us to think more deeply about the issues he raises. We are delighted with his last sentence: "The world is certainly more interesting with a few anarcho-capitalists running loose in it."[176] We return the compliment: The world is certainly more interesting with lots of statists such as Miller running loose in it.

Bibliography

Batemarco, Robert. 1985, July. Positive Economics and Praxeology: The Clash of Prediction and Explanation. *Atlantic Economic Journal* 31.

Binswanger, Harry. 2013. Statism: Whether Fascist or Communist, It's the Deadly Opposite of Capitalism, *Forbes* (Nov. 13, 2013, 12:38 AM), https://www.forbes.com/sites/harrybinswanger/2013/11/13/statism/#1ca6f4ba5f5c.

Block, Walter E. 1973. A Comment on "The Extraordinary Claim of Praxeology" by Professor Gutiérrez. *Theory & Decision* 3: 377–378.

Block, Walter E. 1980. On Robert Nozick's "On Austrian Methodology." *Inquiry* 23: 397.

Block, Walter E. 1999. Austrian Theorizing: Recalling the Foundations. *Quarterly Journal of Austrian Economics*, 2: 21–24.

Block, Walter E. 2002 A Critique of the Legal and Philosophical Case for Rent Control. *Journal of Business Ethics* 40: 75.

Block, Walter E., et al. 1998. Rent Control: An Economic Abomination. International *Journal of Value-Based Management* 11: 253.

Christopher Macleod. 2016. *John Stuart Mill.* Stanford Encyclopedia Philosophy (Aug. 25, 2016). https://plato.stanford.edu/archives/spr2017/entries/mill/

David A. Duquette. 2019. *Hegel: Social and Political Thought.* Internet Encyclopedia Philosophy. https://www.iep.utm.edu/hegelsoc/ (Last visited July 5, 2019).

Demsetz, Harold. 1967. Toward a Theory of Property Rights. *The American Economic Review* 57 (2): 347.

Demsetz, Harold. 1969. Information and Efficiency: Another Viewpoint. *Journal of Law and Economics* 12 (1): 1.

Fox, Glenn. 1992. The Pricing of Environmental Goods: A Praxeological Critique of Contingent Valuation. *Cultural Dynamics* 5: 245–250.

Friedman, Milton. 1961. Capitalism and Freedom. *New Individualist Review* 1 (3): 10. http://lf-oll.s3.amazonaws.com/titles/2136/NewIndividualistReview_1360_Bk.pdf.

Friedrich A. Hayek. 1982. *Law, Legislation and Liberty.* London: Routledge, 1998.

———. 1988. The Fatal Conceit: The Errors of Socialism 6. In *The Collected Works of F.A Hayek*, ed. W. W. Bartley III. London: Routledge, 1992.

Friedrich von Hayek. 1974. Prize Lecture: The Pretence of Knowledge. *Nobel Prize* (Dec. 11, 1974). https://www.nobelprize.org/prizes/economic-sciences/1974/hayek/lecture/

Grampp, William D. 1950. Some Effects of Rent Control, *Southern Economic Journal* 16: 425.

Hayek, Friedrich A. 1945. The Use of Knowledge in Society. *American Economic Review* 35: 519.

[176] *Id.* at 108.

Hayek, Friedrich A. 1964. Kinds of Order in Society. *New Individualist Review* 3 (2): 461. https://oll.libertyfund.org/title/friedman-new-individualist-review.

Hoppe, Hans-Hermann. 1989. In Defense of Extreme Rationalism: Thoughts on Donald McCloskey's The Rhetoric of Economics. The Review of Austrian Economics 2: 179–186.

Hülsmann, Jörg Guido. 1999. Economic Science and Neoclassicism. *Quarterly Journal of Austrian Economics* 2: 3–4.

Immanuel Kant. 1781. *Critique of Pure Reason*, vol. 127, trans. Paul Guyer and Allen W. Wood. Cambridge University Press, 1998.

James Gwartney et al. 1996. *Economic Freedom of the World: 1975–1995 vii*. https://www.fraser-institute.org/sites/default/files/EconomicFreedomoftheWorld1975-1995.pdf

John Stuart Mill. 1859. *On Liberty*, 53. Batoche Books, 2001. https://socialsciences.mcmaster.ca/econ/ugcm/3ll3/mill/liberty.pdf

Kozinski, Alex. 1991. The Dark Lessons of Utopia. *University of Chicago Law Review* 58 (575): 577.

Krugman, Paul. 2014. Why Economics Failed, *N.Y. Times* (May 1, 2014), https://www.nytimes.com/2014/05/02/opinion/krugman-why-economics-failed.html.

Manwaring, W.H. 1938. Organic Theory of the State. *The Scientific Monthly* 47 (48): 48.

Marshall, Monty G., and Cole, Benjamin R. 2017. State Failure: The Problem of Complex Societal-Systems. In *States and Peoples in Conflict: Transformations of Conflict*, eds. Michael Stohl, Mark I. Lichbach and Peter Nils Grabosky, 184–185.

McCloskey, H. J. 1963. The State as an Organism, as a Person, and as an End in Itself. *Philosophical Review* 72: 306–307.

Murray N. Rothbard. 2016. *The Rothbard Reader*, 268–269, ed. Joseph T. Salerno and Matthew McCafrey. Auburn: Ludwig Von Mises Institute.

Niemietz, Kristian. 2017. But That Wasn't REAL Socialism! (Part 1: The USSR), *Institute of Economic Affairs* (Jul. 21, 2017), https://iea.org.uk/but-that-wasnt-real-socialism-part-1/.

North, Douglass C. 1991. Institutions. *The Journal of Economic Perspectives* 5 (1): 97.

Rifkind, David. 2012. 'Everything in the state, nothing against the state, nothing outside the state': Corporativist urbanism and Rationalist architecture in fascist Italy. *Planning Perspectives* 27: 51.

Rothbard, Murray N. 2011. Praxeology, Value Judgments, and Public Policy (1976). *Economic Controversies* 81: 95–97. https://mises.org/sites/default/files/Economic%20Controversies_2.pdf.

Shapiro, Daryl Marc. 1990. Will an Increased Minimum Wage Help the Homeless? University of Miami Law Review 45: 651–685.

Siegan, Bernard H. 1970 Non-Zoning in Houston. *The Journal of Law and Economics* 13: 71–120.

Stearns, Maxwell L. 1994. The Misguided Renaissance of Social Choice. *Yale Law Journal* 103: 1229–1230.

Stiglitz, Joseph E. 2008. *Government Failure vs. Market Failure: Principles of Regulation* 2 (Columbia University, Working Paper, 2008), https://doi.org/10.7916/D82F7V5C.

Wiśniewski, Jakub Bożydar. 2014. The Methodology of the Austrian School of Economics: The Present State of Knowledge. *Ekonomia – Wroclaw Economic Review* 27(1): 39.

Chapter 7
Law

The Constitution and the Supreme Court: The Judicial Road to Big Government

> *Classical liberalism regarded those laws best that afforded the least discretionary power to executive authorities, thus avoiding arbitrariness and abuse. The modern state seeks to expand its discretionary power—everything is to be left to the discretion of officials.*
>
> Ludwig Von Mises (2011).

Abstract We attempt to analyze the U.S. Constitution from a libertarian point of view. Also, to show how certain Supreme Court rulings and constitutional interpretations progressively allowed for excessive growth in government, particularly in the areas of denial and denigration of private property rights, intervention in trade, production, consumption, and individual freedoms. Hence, we analyze the complex and slow institutional path to increasing interventionism.

Keywords Constitution · Supreme Court · Liberty · Government

JEL Code K10

A. G. Futerman, W. E. Block, *The Austro-Libertarian Point of View*,
https://doi.org/10.1007/978-981-16-4691-1_7

7.1 Introduction[1]

The Constitution[2] is the written law that presumably orders the functions of government. It explicitly provides what the government may and may not do, as well as indicating what are the rights of the individual (which the government is mandated to protect). For instance, it is explicit that the President has no war making powers, and only Congress can declare war.

However, the Constitution has been interpreted repeatedly in different ways, thereby altering the (traditional) spirit of freedom[3] by which it was originally enacted[4] and paving the way for increasing intervention.[5] These interpretations were performed, primarily, by the various Supreme Courts.[6] This institution, in a series of fundamental findings, set jurisprudence on matters affecting the free market directly, and which would become the basis for subsequent interventionist policies by the federal and state governments.

In this work, we present those cases which we regard as the most important in order to better understand the current state of US jurisprudence in relation to government usurpation. As such, we posit that although laws are legislated by Congress, and policies are enacted by the executive, it is the Supreme Court that has almost the sole power of rendering those laws and policies *legitimate*, by *referring* to their Constitutional status. As such, it is in its power to set the tone for the future of the country, as well as the scope and scale of government. Hence, the Supreme Court is more important, perhaps the most important, of institutions in a republic, and the one which has the key to its future.[7,8]

---

[1] In writing this chapter, we are inspired by Andrew Napolitano's path-breaking work on the US Constitution. Although this chapter is mainly focused on the United States, hopefully it has wider implications.

[2] THE CONSTITUTION, *Justia*, https://law.justia.com/constitution/us/constitution-text-only.html (last visited Sep. 7, 2019); AMENDMENTS, *Justia*, Available at https://law.justia.com/constitution/us/amendments-text-only.html (last visited Sep. 7, 2019).

[3] Of course, apart from allowing slavery.

[4] At least according to the Conservative tradition.

[5] Much of which is predicated upon the existence of market failures. For a libertarian critique of this approach see Cowen (1988), DiLorenzo (2011), Hoppe (2003), Rothbard (1985), and Simpson (2005). For a critique of the public goods approach see Block (2003a), de Jasay (1989), Futerman (2014), Hoppe (1989a), Hummel (1990), Pasour Jr. (1981), Rothbard (1997), Schmidtz (1991), and Sechrest (2003, 2004a, b, 2007).

[6] Although lower federal and state courts of course did their part.

[7] Stalin once asked, "How many divisions does the Pope of Rome have?", see Higgs (2005). Of course, the same could be queried about the nine judges. They have no military might at their disposal either, apart from a few court police.

[8] In saying this we risk committing the fallacy of the diamonds – water paradox. Menger, Walras and Jevons in their marginal revolution taught the economics profession to look at matters from a marginal point of view. See on this Jevons (1871), Menger (1950), and Walras (1874). To buttress this point, we note that it is the president who nominates candidates for the judiciary, including the

7.2 The US Constitution

Let us take a basic minarchist libertarian perspective.[9] What is the fundamental principle of the Constitution? It is that governmental legitimacy stems from the consent of the governed. However, are there legitimate governments that operate in the absence of this consent? Yes, those that are based on the natural law tradition, because it recognizes inalienable rights,[10] whether the governed consent to them or not. In this branch of the libertarian philosophy, the *Natural Law Tradition* is the legal name for the Non-Aggression Principle (NAP).[11] We refer, here, to natural[12] rights. And these are the ones that the Constitution is said to defend.

Of course, all sorts of contradictions in the Constitution have been analyzed by libertarians.[13] Including, of course, where is the *consent*, if any, that the governed give, and to *whom*. Thomas Jefferson himself thought that each and every 19 years the Constitution must be rewritten by the new generation, to regain the consent of the governed.[14]

Supreme Court, and congressional approval is necessary for their appointments. It is difficult to overestimate the importance of the courts, but they are only one of the three branches of government.

[9] See on this: Nozick (1974). See also Long and Machan (2008), Machan (2002), and Machan et al. (2012).

[10] There is a debate about the subject of inalienability. Of course, involuntary servitude is beyond any debate, it is evil. But what about voluntary slavery? Can there be such a thing? In the view of Boldrin and Levine (2008) at 254: "Take the case of slavery. Why should people not be allowed to sign private contracts binding them to slavery? In fact economists have consistently argued against slavery – during the nineteenth century David Ricardo and John Stuart Mill engaged in a heated public debate with literary luminaries such as Charles Dickens, with the economists opposing slavery, and the literary giants arguing in favor." For more on this libertarian rejection of inalienablity see Andersson (2007), Block (1969, 1979, 1988, 1999, 2001a, 2002a, 2003b, 2004, 2005, 2006a, 2007a, b, 2009a, b), Frederick (2014), Kershnar (2003), Lester (2000), Mosquito (2015), ROBERT NOZICK, *supra* note 406, at 58, 283, 331; Steiner (1994), and Thomson (1994).

[11] The NAP means the following: [t]he fundamental axiom of libertarian theory is that no one may threaten or commit violence ('aggress') against another man's person or property. Violence may be employed only against the man who commits such violence; that is, only defensively against the aggressive violence of another. In short, no violence may be employed against a non-aggressor. Here is the fundamental rule from which can be deduced the entire corpus of libertarian theory. Rothbard (2003). See also Rothbard (1998).

[12] Also referred to as fundamental rights, or pre-political rights, which are euphemisms to refer to natural rights, but they are devoid of any religious connotation. Hence, they sound secular, since natural rights appear religious or mystical (due to the metaphysical meaning attached to the concept of the *natural*).

[13] Spooner (1966).

[14] As Thomas Jefferson claimed, "Every constitution then, and every law, naturally expires at the end of 19 years" In Jefferson (1958). Observe that if consent does not exist, it does not imply that the government will disappear, although this should be the logical conclusion. After all, the Boston Tea Party took place because of a 3% tax on Tea by British authorities, but much later (in 1794), Hamilton and Washington had to stop another rebellion arising also due to taxation (the "Whiskey Rebellion"). See *Whiskey Rebellion*, ENCYCLOPEDIA.COM, https://www.encyclopedia.com/history/united-states-and-canada/us-history/whiskey-rebellion (last visited Sept. 7, 2019).

Legislation abrogating rights, such as excessive taxation, is a clear-cut case of a government lacking the consent of the governed. When early Americans noted that King George III opposed just laws, and imposed taxation without representation, they saw no consent, no adherence to natural law. What was behind American Independence was the idea of living free from outside control.[15] If the king had approved of an American representative in Parliament, this would have taken some of the wind out of the sails of the revolution. But not all of it, of course.

The path to big government can be seen in several contradictions in the Constitution, mainly dealing with the superiority of the federal government at the expense of the states. For instance, Art. 1, Sect. 4 of the Constitution provides:

> The Times, Places and Manner of holding Elections for Senators and Representatives, shall be prescribed in each State by the Legislature thereof; *but the Congress may at any time by Law make or alter such Regulations*, except as to the Places of chusing Senators (emphasis added).

Slavery was also clearly opposed to individual rights,[16] but was Constitutional. For instance, in Art. 4, Sect. 2:

> No Person held to Service or Labour in one State, under the Laws thereof, escaping into another, shall, in Consequence of any Law or Regulation therein, be discharged from such Service or Labour, but shall be delivered up on Claim of the Party to whom such Service or Labour may be *due* (emphasis added).

This meant, for instance, that a slave who successfully escaped the South at the beginning of the XIXth Century could be legally persecuted in the North and returned to his owner in the South.

However, the Constitution also included great advances in the field of individual rights and was indeed a fundamental foundation stone in the positive development of the US. Life, liberty and the pursuit of happiness were also founding principles of the US, and the unprecedented growth and prosperity of the country did owe a huge part to that which the Declaration of Independence, Constitution and Bill of Rights got right.

Moreover, further developments in the amendments also followed this path. For instance, the Fourth Amendment protected private property and privacy:[17]

---

[15] See on secession, Von Mises (2002). At the same time, secession opens the gate to full self-governance or anarchy: Brilmayer (1991) ("Proponents of secession therefore face a very slippery slope in formulating a right to secede that does not open the door to complete anarchy."). See also Chap. 6.

[16] Of course, many of these problems were later fixed, through the 13th amendment.

[17] For the libertarian rejection of a per se right of privacy, as opposed to being free of unwarranted government invasions of privacy, see MURRAY N. ROTHBARD, *supra* note 408, THE ETHICS… at Ch. 16, who avers "But is there really such a right to privacy? How can there be? How can there be a right to prevent Smith by force from disseminating knowledge which he possesses? Surely there can be no such right. Smith owns his own body and therefore has the property right to own the knowledge he has inside his head, including his knowledge about Jones. And therefore he has the corollary right to print and disseminate that knowledge. In short, as in the case of the 'human right' to free speech, there is no such thing as a right to privacy except the right to protect one's property

> The right of the people to be secure in their persons, houses, papers, and effects, against unreasonable searches and seizures, shall not be violated, and no Warrants shall issue, but upon probable cause, supported by Oath or affirmation, and particularly describing the place to be searched, and the persons or things to be seized.

Also, the Fifth Amendment secured the right of every citizen to not being forced to incriminate itself:

> No person shall be held to answer for a capital, or otherwise infamous crime, unless on a presentment or indictment of a Grand Jury, except in cases arising in the land or naval forces, or in the Militia, when in actual service in time of War or public danger; nor shall any person be subject for the same offense to be twice put in jeopardy of life or limb; nor shall be compelled in any criminal case to be a witness against himself, nor be deprived of life, liberty, or property, without due process of law; nor shall private property be taken for public use, without just compensation.

Hence, the key to government's respect for individual rights is due process, including notice, hearing, impartiality, fairness, and the right of appeal. Moreover, substantive due process protects areas of human behavior and thought which are immune from any government action (for instance, see *Obergefell v. Hodges*[18]).

However, despite these protections, the path to big government, with some exceptions, has been a constant throughout American history. It is our purpose to show how that took place, and why contradictions in the Constitution and subsequent interpretations by the Supreme Court were the elements that made it possible.

7.3 Supreme Court Cases and the Progressive Erosion of Freedom

Let us begin at the beginning, with the founding of the US.[19] After the establishment of the federal government, the debate over a Constitution culminated in 1787. Then, based on the Articles of Confederation, the Constitution was written and later

---

from invasion. The only right 'to privacy' is the right to protect one's property from being invaded by someone else. In brief, no one has the right to burgle someone else's home, or to wiretap someone's phone lines. Wiretapping is properly a crime not because of some vague and woolly 'invasion of a 'right to privacy',' but because it is an invasion of the property right of the person being wiretapped." See also Block (2016a, 2017) and Block et al. (2006).

[18] *Obergefell v. Hodges*, 576 U.S. (2015), *Justia*, https://supreme.justia.com/cases/federal/us/576/14-556/ (last visited Sep. 8, 2019). The Supreme Court ruled here that same sex marriage is included in the right to marry, and as a fundamental right it is protected and guaranteed by the Due Process Clause and the Equal Protection Clause of the Fourteenth Amendment.

[19] The exact founding of the US is currently a controversial issue. For instance, we note that the New York Times dates this at 1619: *The 1619 Project*, THE NEW YORK TIMES, https://www.nytimes.com/interactive/2019/08/14/magazine/1619-america-slavery.html (last visited Sep. 9, 2019). Of course, this project comes with a specific political agenda. Most historians date this more than a century and a half later, in 1776.

approved. Let us now observe how its interpretation changed over time, and what that meant for government's growth.

Legislators are both able and entitled to create laws. But not any new enactment. The Constitution provides, at least in theory, a limit to what they can legislate. *Marbury v. Madison*,[20] the case that established the principle of *judicial review*, meant that, regarding laws that contradict the Constitution, these can be declared null and void.

This case took place when John Adams promoted the Judiciary Act of 1801 in order to gain further control in the appointment of judges; this occurred just before Jefferson took office. As such, one of the judges recently appointed, William Marbury, demanded that his commission be delivered, but the new Secretary of State James Madison denied it. Marbury petitioned the Supreme Court for a writ of mandamus to obtain the commission for himself. John Marshall recognized that Section 13 of the Judiciary Act of 1789 contradicted Article II, Section II[21] of the Constitution and ruled against Marbury. Unconstitutional laws, henceforth, were *not* valid laws.

We mention this case for several reasons. Primarily, because it shaped the history of the Supreme Court, the right to judicial review, i.e. the right and power of the judicial branch to pass judgement on the behavior of the other two branches and declare them void if they violated the Constitution.

However, the ruling of the Supreme Court may not have taken place. This is so because Marbury filed his complaint with the Supreme Court,[22] but that was not the *original* jurisdiction of this case. Justice Marshall used it anyway to increase the power of the Supreme Court, thus creating judicial review. What does this mean? It means that the three branches of government are equal, but each is superior to the other in the *essence* of what they do: The executive, with respect to the military; Congress, regarding legislation; and the Judiciary, insofar as determining what the

---

[20] *Marbury v. Madison*, 5 U.S. 1 Cranch 137 137 (1803), *Justia*, https://supreme.justia.com/cases/federal/us/5/137/ (last visited Aug. 28, 2019).

[21] "The President shall be Commander in Chief of the Army and Navy of the United States, and of the Militia of the several States, when called into the actual Service of the United States; he may require the Opinion, in writing, of the principal Officer in each of the executive Departments, upon any Subject relating to the Duties of their respective Offices, and he shall have Power to Grant Reprieves and Pardons for Offences against the United States, except in Cases of Impeachment. He shall have Power, by and with the Advice and Consent of the Senate, to make Treaties, provided two thirds of the Senators present concur; and he shall nominate, and by and with the Advice and Consent of the Senate, shall appoint Ambassadors, other public Ministers and Consuls, Judges of the supreme Court, and all other Officers of the United States, whose Appointments are not herein otherwise provided for, and which shall be established by Law: but the Congress may by Law vest the Appointment of such inferior Officers, as they think proper, in the President alone, in the Courts of Law, or in the Heads of Departments. The President shall have Power to fill up all Vacancies that may happen during the Recess of the Senate, by granting Commissions which shall expire at the End of their next Session."

[22] Paradoxically, it was Marshall himself who did not give Marbury his commission. But he did not have to recuse himself because he was at the Supreme Court (there is no court superior to the Supreme Court).

Constitution and law *mean*. Therefore, the Supreme Court can void governmental behavior it interprets as conflicting with the Constitution. Judicial review had previously existed on the State level, but it was new on the Federal level.[23] That was Marshall's contribution.

The *supremacy clause*, stating that the Constitution is superior to ordinary legislation, was later used to interpret subjects relating to property rights. In *Martin v. Hunter's Lessee*,[24] the Supreme Court ruled that the federal treaty stating that Lord Fairfax was the legitimate owner of a specific property, took precedence over the ruling of Virginia's Supreme Court, which previously awarded a part of this acreage to David Hunter. Thus, federal rulings were not only related to specific judicial subjects such as the appointment of judges, but also to private property rights. Although title to this land was not granted on the basis of homesteading in the Lockean tradition,[25] the key is that the Supreme Court did not take this approach only to settle the specific issue, but in addition demonstrated the superior status of the federal government (and the treaties it signs with other powers) *vis a vis* the States. Hence, property rights could not only be understood as a matter of ownership based on homesteading, but as a political ruling.

This determination also guaranteed a homogeneous treatment of law in every state. The issue was settled not only as an issue of *legitimate* property ownership, but also as an act of *judicial interpretation*. Whether David Hunter, Denny Martin, or others homesteaded the land, was not the only issue.

However, not every case was ruled according to strict constitutional construction. For instance, *Calder v. Bull*[26] set a precedent of respect for property rights and a person's use and disposal of his own possessions. In that case the estate of Norman Morrison was under dispute. Mr. Caleb Bull and his wife, who had a right to such inheritance since they were the stated beneficiaries, were denied this benefit by a court in Connecticut. There was a statute of limitations law[27] in that state that forbade appeals after the period of a year and a half from the ruling. Hence, when Caleb Bull appealed the decision after that permitted time period, his lawsuit was denied. Hence, he wanted the state to change the law, so that he could appeal. After

---

[23] It was not in the Constitution. In this respect, many institutional developments exist today as a tradition, but not as the result of any fundamental legislation. For instance, Texas has two Supreme Courts.

[24] *Martin v. Hunter's Lessee*, 14 U.S. 1 Wheat. 304 304 (1816), *Justia*, https://supreme.justia.com/cases/federal/us/14/304/ (last visited Aug. 28, 2019).

[25] On the application of homesteading principles to several areas, see Block (1990, 2002b, c), Block and Edelstein (2012), Block and Nelson (2015), Block and Yeatts (1999–2000), Block and Epstein (2005), Bylund (2005, 2012), Grotius (1814), Hoppe (1993, 2011), Kinsella (2003, 2009a, b), Locke (1948), Paul (1987), Pufendorf (1673), Rothbard (1969, 1973a); MURRAY N. ROTHBARD, *supra* note 408, THE ETHICS OF…; Watner (1982).

[26] *Calder v. Bull*, 3 U.S. 3 Dall. 386 386 (1798), *Justia*, https://supreme.justia.com/cases/federal/us/3/386/ (last visited Aug. 28, 2019).

[27] For a libertarian critique of such legislation see Alston and Block (2007), Block (1993, 2001b); Walter E. Block, *On Reparations to...*, *supra* note 422; Walter E. Block and Guillermo Yeatts, *The Economics and Ethics...*, *supra* note 422; Crepelle and Block (2017); Block (2016b).

Bull succeeded in this demand with the Connecticut legislators, Calder, who also wanted to inherit Morrison's estate, appealed to the Supreme Court. However, this constituted *ex post facto* law. The court held that Caleb Bull was not demanding *criminal* rights, but rather his legitimate right to inherit, and therefore Connecticut's new legislation was not *ex post facto* law.

In any legal system, prevailing issues preventing justice can indeed be interpreted correctly, in favor of respecting rights. On criminal matters, in contrast, there cannot be any valid *ex post facto* laws, at least in the view of most commentators.[28,29]

Property rights do not pertain only to material possessions. They also include other rights such as life (understood as self-ownership), which are also defended by the Constitution. This is what is regarded as the *habeas corpus*[30] right.

In this respect, certain interpretations of the law and the Constitution may also be incompatible with private property rights. As such, the establishment of the Federal Reserve System (1913) was only possible because of precedents concerning the creation of national banks, and the legitimacy afforded them based on judicial powers. *McCulloch v. Maryland*[31] is a case in point. After Maryland imposed taxes on the Second National Bank of the United States in 1818, and a state's appeal court stated that its existence was unconstitutional,[32] the Supreme Court under John Marshall reinterpreted the meaning of "necessary" in the context of Art. I, Section VIII[33] of the Constitution, to allow Congress to create banks. Not only is this an

---

[28] For an alternative view, see Walter E. Block, *Ex post…*, *supra* note 424.

[29] Crimes against humanity are an exception, such as with the Nuremburg Trials imposed on Nazi leaders.

[30] "Latin for 'that you have the body.' In the US system, federal courts can use the writ of habeas corpus to determine if a state's detention of a prisoner is valid. A writ of habeas corpus is used to bring a prisoner or other detainee (e.g. institutionalized mental patient) before the court to determine if the person's imprisonment or detention is lawful. A habeas petition proceeds as a civil action against the State agent (usually a warden) who holds the defendant in custody. It can also be used to examine any extradition processes used, the amount of bail, and the jurisdiction of the court" in *Habeas Corpus* (2017).

[31] *McCulloch v. Maryland*, 17 U.S. 4 Wheat. 316 316 (1819), *Justia*, https://supreme.justia.com/cases/federal/us/17/316/ (last visited Aug. 28, 2019).

[32] Since the constitution did not textually state that the government could create one.

[33]

> The Congress shall have Power To lay and collect Taxes, Duties, Imposts and Excises, to pay the Debts and provide for the common Defence and general Welfare of the United States; but all Duties, Imposts and Excises shall be uniform throughout the United States;

To borrow Money on the credit of the United States;

To regulate Commerce with foreign Nations, and among the several States, and with the Indian Tribes;

To establish an uniform Rule of Naturalization, and uniform Laws on the subject of Bankruptcies throughout the United States;

To coin Money, regulate the Value thereof, and of foreign Coin, and fix the Standard of Weights and Measures;

To provide for the Punishment of counterfeiting the Securities and current Coin of the United States;

example of how the hermeneutics[34] of law is relevant, but also of how important it is to consider what is *not* said in a specific document. If the Constitution would have had an amendment specifically dealing with the government's prohibition of creating banks, such precedence would not have taken place. And it would have been more difficult to establish the Fed (although, if government would have exerted enough pressure, it would have implemented a Constitutional amendment, such as with the Income Tax and the 16th Amendment). Also, this was another measure against States' rights.

The historical context is relevant. After the charter of the First National Bank expired in 1811, this was the second attempt to establish one. Maryland established a tax on the Second National Bank in 1818, but McCulloch, head of the branch in Baltimore, refused to pay it. After the state appeals court in Maryland ruled it unconstitutional, the Supreme Court under Marshall not only approved of the creation of the Bank, but also used this case to expand the power of the federal government. This was achieved by establishing a *connection* between government's power of taxing and spending, and that in the meantime it *can* have the money in a bank. Hence, the *non-sequitur*, the government can create banks.

To establish Post Offices and post Roads;

To promote the Progress of Science and useful Arts, by securing for limited Times to Authors and Inventors the exclusive Right to their respective Writings and Discoveries;

To constitute Tribunals inferior to the supreme Court;

To define and punish Piracies and Felonies committed on the high Seas, and Offences against the Law of Nations;

To declare War, grant Letters of Marque and Reprisal, and make Rules concerning Captures on Land and Water;

To raise and support Armies, but no Appropriation of Money to that Use shall be for a longer Term than two Years;

To provide and maintain a Navy;

To make Rules for the Government and Regulation of the land and naval Forces;

To provide for calling forth the Militia to execute the Laws of the Union, suppress Insurrections and repel Invasions;

To provide for organizing, arming, and disciplining, the Militia, and for governing such Part of them as may be employed in the Service of the United States, reserving to the States respectively, the Appointment of the Officers, and the Authority of training the Militia according to the discipline prescribed by Congress;

To exercise exclusive Legislation in all Cases whatsoever, over such District (not exceeding ten Miles square) as may, by Cession of Particular States, and the Acceptance of Congress, become the seat of the Government of the United States, and to exercise like Authority over all Places purchased by the Consent of the Legislature of the State in which the Same shall be, for the Erection of Forts, Magazines, Arsenals, dock-Yards, and other needful Buildings;—And

To make all Laws which shall be necessary and proper for carrying into Execution the foregoing Powers, and all other Powers vested by this Constitution in the Government of the United States, or in any Department or Officer thereof.

[34] Interpretation and its methodology. However, for a criticism of the movement which bears this name, especially in economics, see Gordon (1986), Hoppe (1989b), and Rothbard (1989, 1996).

Even though judges were conscious that this ruling implied a transgression of the limits established by the constitution, on *McCulloch v. Maryland*[35] we read:

> We admit, as all must admit, that the powers of the Government are limited, and that its limits are not to be transcended. *But* we think the sound construction of the Constitution must allow to the national legislature that discretion with respect to the means by which the powers it confers are to be carried into execution which will enable that body to perform the high duties assigned to it in the manner most beneficial to the people. Let the end be legitimate, let it be within the scope of the Constitution, and all means which are appropriate, which are plainly adapted to that end, which are not prohibited, but consist with the letter and spirit of the Constitution, are Constitutional (emphasis added).

Let us now look at the commerce clause and its fundamental consequences. In *Gibbons v. Ogden*[36] the Supreme Court ruled that the federal government's control over interstate commerce could not be challenged by States nor their laws (due to the interstate commerce clause). As such, interstate commerce could in fact thwart monopolies within States when they attempted to expand. It is important in this context to be clear on what a monopoly is. In the mainstream or neoclassical economic perspective, monopolies are firms that control prices (raise them above perfectly competitive levels) and quantities supplied (lower them compared to what would ensue under pure competition). This understanding has been subject to withering criticism from Austrian school economists. One problem arises in using perfect competition (homogeneous products, an indefinitely large number of sellers, no profits) as a criterion of success. Another is with their definition of industry. The narrower it is, the higher the concentration ratios. A third is that cost curves are subjective, based upon alternatives foregone, not objective, as the neoclassicals would have it. A fourth is that their analysis commits interpersonal comparisons of utility, in its analysis of "dead weight loss". In the Austrian view, in contrast, monopoly is necessarily due to government favors, subsidies, entry restrictions, not to market forces. Here, a free-market monopoly would be a veritable contradiction in terms.[37]

Concerning the interstate commerce clause, the right of Congress "to regulate" meant "to keep regular", but was improperly *interpreted* as "to regulate". Of course, these are not at all the same. This clause gives Congress plenary powers, to regulate commerce with foreign nations, and among the several states, etc. The latter meaning provides the federal government with an all-encompassing power; no state nor individual can override it.

Thus, in *Gibbons v. Ogden*[38] we read:

> We are now arrived at the inquiry -- What is this power?

[35] 17, U.S. 421.

[36] *Gibbons v. Ogden*, 22 U.S. 9 Wheat. 1 1 (1824), *Justia*, https://supreme.justia.com/cases/federal/us/22/1/ (last visited Aug. 28, 2019).

[37] For more on this, see DiLorenzo (1996), O'Driscoll Jr. (1982), McChesney (1991), and Pasour Jr. (1982).

[38] 22 U.S. 196–197.

> It is the power to regulate, that is, to prescribe the rule by which commerce is to be governed. This power, like all others vested in Congress, is complete in itself, may be exercised to its utmost extent, and acknowledges no limitations other than are prescribed in the Constitution. These are expressed in plain terms, and do not affect the questions which arise in this case, or which have been discussed at the bar. If, as has always been understood, the sovereignty of Congress, though limited to specified objects, is plenary as to those objects, the power over commerce with foreign nations, and among the several States, is vested in Congress as absolutely as it would be in a single government, having in its Constitution the same restrictions on the exercise of the power as are found in the Constitution of the United States. The wisdom and the discretion of Congress, their identity with the people, and the influence which their constituents possess at elections are, in this, as in many other instances, as that, for example, of declaring war, the sole restraints on which they have relied, to secure them from its abuse. They are the restraints on which the people must often they solely, in all representative governments.

> The power of Congress, then, comprehends navigation, within the limits of every State in the Union, so far as that navigation may be in any manner connected with 'commerce with foreign nations, or among the several States, or with the Indian tribes.' It may, of consequence, pass the jurisdictional line of New York and act upon the very waters to which the prohibition now under consideration applies.

Also, the Constitution's Supremacy Clause, that in theory protected the supremacy of the Constitution, was assumed to be in favor or against private property rights and free trade according to the *interpretation* it was given. Instead of protecting individual rights and defining their context of application, limiting the power of the state, and freeing the individual, it was used in the very opposite direction. An instance of this is *Champion v. Ames,*[39] where the Supreme Court emphasized that Congress had power over regulating commerce, particularly interstate commerce (in that case, lottery tickets).[40]

Can items be excluded from interstate commerce too (or, is this power included in the Commerce Clause)? Yes, the Supreme Court has so resolved.[41] And it has never been reversed either. Note that power to police is a state power. But, in reality, the federal government acts with police power by using the Commerce Clause.

On the other hand, the Supreme Court did rule against regulating production, such as in *Hammer v. Dagenhart.*[42] This case dealt with the interstate shipment of goods from mines or factories using child labor. Firms could not use children in the labor force, according to the Keating-Owen Act (1916). Thus, Congress used the Commerce Clause to prohibit this interstate shipment of goods. It was said that the

---

[39] *Lottery Case*, 188 U.S. 321 (1903), *Justia*, https://supreme.justia.com/cases/federal/us/188/321/ (last visited Aug. 28, 2019).

[40] For another relevant case where the Supreme Court again approved of Congressional power to regulate interstate commerce, this time through the Interstate Commerce Commission (ICC), concerning railroad rates (Shreveport Rate Cases) see *Houston E. & W. Tex. Ry. Co. v. United States*, 234 U.S. 342 (1914), *Justia*, https://supreme.justia.com/cases/federal/us/234/342/ (last visited Aug. 28, 2019).

[41] *Hammer v. Dagenhart*, 247 U.S. 251 (1918), *Justia*, https://supreme.justia.com/cases/federal/us/247/251/ (last visited Aug. 28, 2019).

[42] Ibid.

produce of such labor can stay in the state, but not go to other states. At *Hammer v. Dagenhart*, the Supreme Court ruled against it.

At the time (1918), the common understanding was that states have the power to police or regulate on the basis of health, safety, welfare and morality; so, the federal government *cannot* override them in these areas. But regulating the *movement* of goods does not give Congress the right to regulate the *conditions* of their production either (in fact, the tenth Amendment[43] gives that power to the states). Of course, avoiding child labor is indeed a good intention, but this means employed is plagued with unintended consequences. Child welfare was improved despite these efforts, not because of them. It is only a society that achieves enough wealth that makes child labor irrelevant what causes the latter to cease to exist, so free markets (that create such wealth) were and are the real cure for this terrible practice. Suppose these initiatives were employed during a historical epoch when their labor was needed for their very survival. Then, they would have been condemned to death. At present, in underdeveloped countries such laws and practices[44] banish children to prostitution or seeking food in garbage dumps.[45]

However, returning to the commerce clause and contrary to the false production-distribution dichotomy of John Stuart Mill,[46] both are but two faces on the same coin. Thus, recognizing Congress's power to regulate over commerce *implies* doing so with respect to production too. This can be illustrated with the case *National Labor Relations Board (NLRB) v. Jones & Laughlin Steel Corporation,*[47] where the National Labor Relations Act (1935) was thought to function as a way for Congress to regulate labor disputes. How so? By interpreting that relations between labor and management *affect* interstate commerce, and therefore are under the control of the federal government. Of course, this implied a way to strengthen unions, since the original idea was that this law would prevent companies from discriminating against unionized workers. It meant the legitimization of strikes, whether all workers agree or not.[48]

The NLRB issued regulations regarding labor practices which interfered with interstate commerce.[49] Hence, Congress can intervene according to this interpreta-

---

[43] "The powers not delegated to the United States by the Constitution, nor prohibited by it to the States, are reserved to the States respectively, or to the people."

[44] Boycotting products produced with child labor.

[45] See on this Block (2008a), DiLorenzo (2004), Kauffman (1992), McElroy (2001), Nardinelli (1990), Rojas (2010), Rose (1998), and Tucker (2008).

[46] Mill (1870).

[47] *National Labor Relations Board v. Jones & Laughlin Steel Corporation*, 83 F.2d 998 (fifth Cir. 1936), *Justia*, https://law.justia.com/cases/federal/appellate-courts/F2/83/998/1479028/ (last visited Aug. 28, 2019).

[48] For a libertarian analysis of labor strikes see Baird (1990, 2000, 2013), Block (2008b, 2010a), Evans and Block (2002), Heldman (1977), Heldman et al. (1981), Hutt (1973, 1989), Petro (1957), Reynolds (1984, 1987, 2009), Rothbard (1991a), Schmidt (1973), and Shea (2010).

[49] See *National Labor Relations Board v. Jones & Laughlin Steel Corporation*, 83 F.2d 998 (5th Cir. 1936), *Justia*, https://law.justia.com/cases/federal/appellate-courts/F2/83/998/1479028/ (last visited Aug. 28, 2019).

tion of the commerce clause. But the problem with this entire endeavor is that the NLRB is *not* Congress. More specifically, they promulgated rules regarding strikes. The dispute concerned whether private actions can be regarded as affecting all State activities or interstate commerce. One would have thought that twenty or thirty people going on strike cannot be allowed to affect a million workers, but this reasoning was rejected.[50] Moreover, the Supreme Court upheld it on the theory that other similar behavior from other groups of twenty or thirty people, if *aggregated* together, could influence interstate commerce, and that Congress understood this implicitly when creating the NLRB. Therefore, it was *assumed* that they gave NLRB the power to regulate interstate commerce.

However, at a different time, findings of the Supreme Court established that certain labor conditions were a private business, protected by the Fourteenth Amendment. For instance, in *Lochner v. New York* case,[51] the Court ruled against the Bakeshop Act of the state of New York (1895), that regulated baker's working hours. This case in New York dealt with baker Joseph Lochner, who employed labor that worked more hours than permitted. However, the government has no right to interfere in private, voluntary contracts at mutual benefit. The Supreme Court invalidated the standard set by New York, and applied a strict scrutiny test, where the right to work is a pre-political right, i.e. a natural right.

Justice Harlan argued that the onus of proof was on he who *opposes* the law, and not by its *proponents*. However, if one intends to legislate, it is assumed that one must do so on a *rational* basis, and therefore the citizen has the right to ask government officials for the justification of their acts, not the other way around. Of course, after the "Lochner era" ended, the right to engage in economic activity was implicitly no longer regarded as fundamental. Rehabilitating Lochner,[52] of course, would make it difficult for both the federal government and the states to regulate economic activity.

Consider *United States v. Carolene Products* Co.,[53] where the Supreme Court ruled in favor of a ban to commerce filled milk by Congress,[54] where a company doing just that (Carolene Products), was found not persuasive *enough* in its argument that there was *no* rational basis for the law. Here, Congress forbid the sale of filled milk in interstate commerce. But Congress decided to forbid it, despite absence of fraud. The Commerce Clause was used as the justification.

Observe that congressional regulation previously oversaw intranational exports from a state. But the question was, can Congress also regulate intranational imports into a state? The route can indeed be regulated by Congress, if the movement from

---

[50] Ibid.

[51] *Lochner v. New York*, 198 U.S. 45 (1905), *Justia*, https://supreme.justia.com/cases/federal/us/198/45/ (last visited Aug. 28, 2019).

[52] A very desirable goal, according to libertarian law.

[53] *United States v. Carolene Products Co.*, 304 U.S. 144 (1938), *Justia*, https://supreme.justia.com/cases/federal/us/304/144/ (last visited Aug. 28, 2019).

[54] This refers to milk or cream, which has been combined with fats, vegetable oils, and other such additives not produced from dairy cows.

one state has an *effect* on the entering movement to the other state. What qualifies as an effect? A "rational basis", the lowest test courts apply to congressional behavior (there must always be a rational basis for what Congress does). However, in reality, what is to be regarded as rational in this context ended up being arbitrary.[55]

The Court's legitimization of government intervention in business did not end with unions or trade. With United States v. Darby,[56] the Supreme Court upheld the 1938 Fair Labor Standards Act, by which Congress could regulate minimum wages and weekly hours, among others. The justification? Its impact, again, on interstate commerce, where weaker standards of one state could be understood as improper competition with the productive enterprises of other states which impose *stricter* standards.

Specifically, this implied jail time for placing a good manufactured by child labor in interstate commerce. This ruling reinforces Congressional authority to regulate anything that affects interstate commerce, be it wages or the ages of workers.[57] Ultimately, Congress decides what counts as rational or not. The Court will not second guess Congress regarding economic regulation. Congress can use criminal law to enforce its interstate commerce power by threatening jail time to violators. This power is pervasive.[58] In *West Coast Hotel Co. v. Parrish,*[59] the Supreme Court ruled in favor of a minimum wage for women.

What about production? It is also regulated with Supreme Court approval. In *Wickard v. Filburn,*[60] this Court analyzed the case of a farmer (Filburn) from Ohio who harvested an amount of wheat beyond that which was allowed to him by the Agricultural Adjustment Act (1938). The high court judges, despite the farmer's argument that this extra wheat was for his own private use, still ruled against him. The reason given was that since Congress may regulate commerce, it can influence prices. But Filburn's additional supply lowered the price of wheat compared to the level which would otherwise have obtained had he not done so. Therefore, intrastate production, *despite not being used for interstate commerce* (or any commerce at all), can be said to have an impact on it, and thus falls under Congress's regulations. The Court admitted that what Filburn did had only a marginal effect, but if many Filburns appear, then in the *aggregate* they will affect interstate commerce, so Congress *can* regulate them. If limits on farmers producing wheat for their own tables can be imposed, it is difficult to see what cannot be controlled by Congress.

---

[55] Although "irrational" is often understood as hatred, false statements, etc.

[56] *United States v. Darby*, 312 U.S. 100 (1941), *Justia*, https://supreme.justia.com/cases/federal/us/312/100/ (last visited Aug. 28, 2019).

[57] Joke: Luckily the court was not formed by praxeologists, because otherwise they would have ruled that even autistic exchange (Mises, 1949), is part of interstate commerce and therefore it could regulate all human action.

[58] As an example, see *Martino v. Michigan Window Cleaning Co.*, 327 U.S. 173 (1946).

[59] *West Coast Hotel Co. v. Parrish*, 300 U.S. 379 (1937), *Justia*, https://supreme.justia.com/cases/federal/us/300/379/ (last visited Aug. 28, 2019).

[60] *Wickard v. Filburn*, 317 U.S. 111 (1942), *Justia*, https://supreme.justia.com/cases/federal/us/317/111/ (last visited Aug. 28, 2019).

But surely the right to eat the food you grow on your own property[61] is a *fundamental* liberty. It should thus be out of the reach of government or Court.[62]

The slippery slope of legitimizing commercial regulation would eventually lead to cover work and production as well. This Constitutional interpretation is a recipe for interventionism on a massive scale.

True enough, the Supreme Court also ruled against regulating production in other cases, such as in *United States v. Butler.*[63] Here, the judges ruled against the application of a tax on commodities by Congress, under the Agricultural Adjustment Act (1933). The reasoning was that this tax was not imposed in order to collect revenue, but to control production so as to influence commodity prices. However, it was determined that this is a field outside the province of Congress. The power to tax and spend under the Constitution is conditioned by the legitimate powers of government.[64] Taxes were supposed to be imposed only to support those powers, but once the precedent of approving of the federal government's control of production and commerce was given, cases could go both ways, and were left to the *discretion* of the Supreme Court, instead of production and commerce being an absolute right protected by the Constitution.

What about private contracts? As *Home Building & Loan Ass'n. v. Blaisdell*[65] shows, the Supreme Court ruled in favor of the Minnesota Mortgage Moratorium Law (1933) that affected execution sales of property and mortgage foreclosures during the Great Depression. Thus, contracts were defaulted by *law* in favor of debtors, leaving a precedent for moral hazard and adverse selection. Although presented as a measure in favor of the public interest due to the systemic nature of the Depression and its impact on debtors, the fundamental premise is that the government can abrogate contracts freely agreed upon by private individuals. Specifically, Blaisdell could not pay the mortgage he owed. Hence, the state imposed a moratorium and banks could not implement foreclosures during the term of this moratorium. This, of course, negatively impacted banks, and violated the Contracts Clause. Equality before the law was set aside.

In *Home Building & Loan Ass'n v. Blaisdell*[66] we also read:

> I quite agree with the opinion of the court that whether the legislation under review is wise or unwise is a matter with which we have nothing to do. Whether it is likely to work well or

---

[61] See Block (1998, 2008c, 2014a) and Block and Block (1996). But see this for an alternative viewpoint. Tullock (1996).

[62] For other issues pertaining to property rights, see Barnett II and Block (2007, 2009), Block (1977, 1995, 1996, 2000, 2003c, 2006b, 2010b, c, d), Block et al. (2005), Cordato (1992a, b, 1997, 1998, 2000), Fox (2007), Krecke (1996), Krauss (1999), Rothbard (1982), Stringham and White (2004), and Terrell (1999).

[63] *United States v. Butler*, 297 U.S. 1 (1936), *Justia*, https://supreme.justia.com/cases/federal/us/297/1/ (last visited Aug. 28, 2019).

[64] See fn. 434, *supra*.

[65] *Home Building & Loan Ass'n. v. Blaisdell*, 290 U.S. 398 (1934), *Justia*, https://supreme.justia.com/cases/federal/us/290/398/ (last visited Aug. 28, 2019).

[66] P. 290, U.S. 483.

> work ill presents a question entirely irrelevant to the issue. The only legitimate inquiry we can make is whether it is constitutional. If it is not, its virtues, if it have any, cannot save it; if it is, its faults cannot be invoked to accomplish its destruction. If the provisions of the Constitution be not upheld when they pinch, as well as when they comfort, they may as well be abandoned. Being unable to reach any other conclusion than that the Minnesota statute infringes the constitutional restriction under review, I have no choice but to say so.

Taking the opposite track, the Supreme Court also ruled against state annulment of private contracts, in *Allied Structural Steel Co. v. Spannaus*.[67] Here it ruled against legislation passed in Minnesota, which penalized companies that were moving out of state or not continuing pension plans for their employees. As we can see, rulings can go both ways, according to which constitutional interpretation the Court is applying.[68] But the literal word of the Constitution is not taken as a given neither for private property rights nor free trade.

Another intervention of the federal government on state prerogatives was, for example, the withholding of Federal Highway Funds from those that did not mandate a minimum drinking age of 21. The Supreme Court, in *South Dakota v. Dole*,[69] supported this decision of Congress.

The right to own guns is also a burning issue. The Supreme Court has, at least so far, protected this 2nd Amendment right and prevented Congress from riding roughshod via through its usual tool, the Commerce Clause. A case in point is *United States v. Lopez*,[70] where a high school student was charged with violating the Gun-Free School Zones Act (1990). The Court ruled such Act unconstitutional. This case was important because it was, essentially, the first relevant challenge to the powers of the Commerce Clause. The court said that the Commerce Clause must be used only when dealing with a real commercial activity (despite Congress having used this clause several times during more than 150 years arguing the *opposite*), for the purpose of defending and regulating interstate commerce. If no commercial transaction exists, then the Commerce Clause, powerful though it be, cannot apply. In order to be defined as a commercial act, the *actors*, *conduct* and *purpose* involved must be commercial. None of these conditions applied here.

More recently, in *National Federation of Independent Business v. Sebelius*,[71] the Supreme Court did not prevent Congress from implementing the Patient Protection and Affordable Care Act (popularly known as Obamacare). In effect, it not only treated health care under the usual tool of the Commerce Clause, but also forced all

[67] *Allied Structural Steel Co. v. Spannaus*, 438 U.S. 234 (1978), *Justia*, https://supreme.justia.com/cases/federal/us/438/234/ (last visited Aug. 28, 2019).

[68] That is a polite way of referring to contradictory judicial findings.

[69] *South Dakota v. Dole*, 483 U.S. 203 (1987), *Justia*, https://supreme.justia.com/cases/federal/us/483/203/ (last visited Aug. 28, 2019).

[70] *United States v. Lopez*, 514 U.S. 549 (1995), *Justia*, https://supreme.justia.com/cases/federal/us/514/549/ (last visited Aug. 28, 2019).

[71] *National Federation of Independent Business v. Sebelius*, 567 U.S. 519 (2012), *Justia*, https://supreme.justia.com/cases/federal/us/567/519/ (last visited Aug. 28, 2019).

Americans to be insured. This is an entirely new step on the road to interventionism,[72] since this not only regulated commerce, consumption and production, but actually *compelled* business relations among citizens without their consent.

Medical insurance, here, is considered by some members of court as a tax, and following Art. 1, Sec. 8 of the Constitution, it could be interpreted as on behalf of the "general Welfare":

> The Congress shall have Power To *lay and collect Taxes*, Duties, Imposts and Excises, to pay the Debts and provide for the common Defence and general Welfare of the United States; but all Duties, Imposts and Excises shall be uniform throughout the United States (emphasis added).

Observe that the slippery slope extends a long way here. Previously, Congress may regulate interstate commerce but could not force an individual to buy insurance or engage in any *particular* type of interstate commerce. Now, the amount to be paid as medical insurance could be called a penalty (and not a tax because otherwise people would see that it is a tax increase). This, of course, is incompatible with the provision that health, safety, welfare and morality are a province of the states, not the federal government. Hence, there is no constitutional role for federal government in healthcare.

The long line of interventions legitimized by the Supreme Court ends with private property itself, through eminent domain.[73] For instance, as in *Kelo v. New London,*[74] the Supreme Court ruled in favor of this Connecticut city in its seizure of private property with the goal of selling it to other private developers. Here, the excuse was that seizure with the purpose of "public use" was to be understood as in the benefit of the *public*, since this action would promote development in the city. The "public" was an excuse in order to seize property from some of that "public", in favor of other members of it. Again, we find a performative contradiction: acting for the public, against the public.[75]

---

[72] Hayek (1944); was prescient.

[73] On the issue of eminent domain, see Block and Epstein (2004); Walter E. Block and Richard Epstein, *supra* note 422, *Debate on Eminent…*; Block (2006a). For zoning laws, see Goldberg et al. (1980), Siegan (1970, 1972), and Block (2014b).

[74] *Kelo v. New London*, 545 U.S. 469 (2005), *Justia*, https://supreme.justia.com/cases/federal/us/545/469/ (last visited Aug. 28, 2019).

[75] As in the fifth Amendment: "No person shall be held to answer for a capital, or otherwise infamous crime, unless on a presentment or indictment of a Grand Jury, except in cases arising in the land or naval forces, or in the Militia, when in actual service in time of War or public danger; nor shall any person be subject for the same offense to be twice put in jeopardy of life or limb; nor shall be compelled in any criminal case to be a witness against himself, nor be deprived of life, liberty, or property, without due process of law; *nor shall private property be taken for public use, without just compensation*" (emphasis added).

7.4 Conclusion

After this brief survey of interventionism sanctioned by the Supreme Court, we are now able to see more clearly the path taken by this institution, and how one intervention made the next one possible. First, we have the contradictions in the Constitution, allowing, for instance, eminent domain. The principle of Judicial Review meant that the Supreme Court had the last word on the legitimacy of the law legislated by Congress, in the light of this Constitution. In *Martin v. Hunter's Lessee*[76] we saw that private property rights controversies were not settled through *homesteading* considerations, but by strictly *legal interpretation*, such as treaties signed by the federal government. This was yet another step in the path for the federal government supremacy over the states.

Next, the possibility of government banks was sanctioned by *McCulloch v. Maryland*.[77] Later, the Commerce Clause appeared, at *Gibbons v. Ogden*.[78] The power of Congress to regulate interstate commerce, sanctioned by the court, meant that it would soon have the power to regulate everything *related* to commerce, not just interstate commerce itself, be it lottery tickets (*Lottery Case*[79]) or railroads (*Shreveport Rate Cases*[80]).

With that foundation, Congress garnered the power to intervene in production and its conditions within states, if produce was later traded through interstate lines (*Hammer v. Dagenhart*[81]). Also, this led to labor regulations (*National Labor Relations Board (NLRB) v. Jones & Laughlin Steel Corporation*[82]) and direct prohibition in some cases where the legislators did not find reasons for free trade *compelling* (*United States v. Carolene Products Co.*[83]). Further regulations on labor and wages were sanctioned (*United States v. Darby*;[84] *West Coast Hotel Co. v. Parrish*[85]). Since production (conditions), and prices (wages) were regulated, supply surely followed (*Wickard v. Filburn*[86]).

The breach of contracts, and the subsequent denial of equality before the law were next (*Home Building & Loan Assn. v. Blaisdell*[87]). Further regulations on employment were sustained (*Allied Structural Steel Co. v. Spannaus*[88]).

---

[76] 14 U.S. 1 Wheat. 304 304 (1816).

[77] 17 U.S. 4 Wheat. 316 316 (1819).

[78] 22 U.S. 9 Wheat. 1 1 (1824).

[79] 188 U.S. 321 (1903).

[80] 234 US 342 (1914).

[81] 247 U.S. 251 (1918).

[82] 83 F.2d 998 (5th Cir. 1936).

[83] 304 U.S. 144 (1938).

[84] 312 U.S. 100 (1941).

[85] 300 U.S. 379 (1937).

[86] 317 U.S. 111 (1942).

[87] 290 U.S. 398 (1934).

[88] 438 U.S. 234 (1978).

Virtually all of this was based on the power of Congress to regulate interstate commerce.

Moreover, decisions that are of the sole power of the states were affected (*South Dakota v. Dole*[89]). Finally, after intervention in production, trade, consumption, and private property, exchanges were compelled in the form of taxes or "penalties" (*National Federation of Independent Business v. Sebelius*[90]).

As we can see, the monopoly power to interpret law[91] and the undermining of private property rights subsequently lead to intervention in trade, production, consumption, and finally private actions.

The contradictions in the Constitution, and the subsequent rulings of the Supreme Court based on them (despite some of these being later abandoned), were the slippery slope on which the path to big government developed. This, of course, is far from an exhaustive analysis of the subject. But we believe it is accurate enough to indicate the steps that took place for interventionism to grow,[92] and for the US to persist in this road.

Bibliography

Alston, Wilton D., and Walter E. Block. 2007. Reparations, Once Again. *Human Rights Review* 9: 379.

Andersson, Anna-Karin. 2007. An Alleged Contradiction in Nozick's Entitlement Theory. *Journal of Libertarian Studies* 21: 42.

Baird, Charles. 1990. American Union Law: Sources of Conflict. *Journal of Labor Research* 11: 269.

———. 2000. Unions and Antitrust. *Journal of Labor Research* 21: 585.

———. 2013. American Unionism and Freedom of Association. *Journal of Private Enterprise* 28: 1.

Barnett II, William, and Walter E. Block. 2007. Coase and Van Zandt on Lighthouses. *Public Finance Review* 35: 710.

———. 2009. Coase and Bertrand on Lighthouses. *Public Choice* 140: 1.

Benson, Bruce L. 1990. *The Enterprise of Law: Justice Without The State*. San Francisco: Pacific Research Institute for Public Policy.

———. 2002. Justice without Government: The Merchant Courts of Medieval Europe and Their Modern Counterparts. In *The Voluntary City: Choice, Community and Civil Society*, ed. Beito, Gordon, and Tabarrok, 127–150. Oakland: The Independent Institute.

———. 2018. The Enterprise of Customary Law. *Mises Daily*. https://mises.org/library/enterprise-customary-law.

Berman, Harold J., and Felix J. Dasser. 1990. The 'New' Law Merchant and the 'Old': Sources, Content and Legitimacy. In *Lex Mercatoria and Arbitration: A Discussion of the Law Merchant*, ed. Thomas E. Carbonneau. Dobbs Ferry: Transnational Juris Publications.

[89] 483 U.S. 203 (1987).

[90] 567 U.S. 519 (2012).

[91] For private, alternative law systems, see Benson (1990, 2002, 2018), Berman and Dasser (1990), Friedman (1979, 1989), Osterfeld (1989), Peden (1977), Rothbard (1973b, 1991b), Stringham (1998–1999), Tannehill and Tannehill (1984, 2001), Thierer (1992), and Woolridge (1970).

[92] For more on this, see Napolitano (2004, 2006, 2014a, b).

Block, Walter E. 1969. Voluntary Slavery. *The Libertarian Connection* 1: 9.
———. 1977. Coase and Demsetz on Private Property Rights. *Journal of Libertarian Studies* 1: 111.
———. 1979. Book Review of Nancy C. Baker, Baby Selling: the Scandal of Black Market Adoptions, New York: The Vanguard Press, 1978. *Libertarian Review* 7: 44.
———. 1988. Rent-a-womb market. *Thunder Bay Ontario Daily*.
———. 1990. Earning Happiness Through Homesteading Unowned Land: a comment on 'Buying Misery with Federal Land' by Richard Stroup. *Journal of Social Political and Economic Studies* 15: 237.
———. 1993. Malcolm X. *Fraser Forum* 18.
———. 1995. Ethics, Efficiency, Coasean Property Rights and Psychic Income: A Reply to Demsetz. *The Review of Austrian Economics* 8: 61.
———. 1996. O.J.'s Defense: A Reductio Ad Absurdum of the Economics of Ronald Coase and Richard Posner. *European Journal of Law and Economics* 3 (265).
———. 1998. Roads, Bridges, Sunlight and Private Property: Reply to Gordon Tullock. *Journal des Economistes et des Etudes Humaines* 8: 315.
———. 1999. Market Inalienability Once Again: Reply to Radin. *Thomas Jefferson Law Review* 22: 37.
———. 2000. Private Property Rights, Erroneous Interpretations, Morality and Economics: Reply to Demsetz. *The Quarterly Journal of Austrian Economics* 3: 63.
———. 2001a. Alienability, Inalienability, Paternalism and the Law: Reply to Kronman. *The American Journal of Criminal Law* 28: 351.
———. 2001b. The Moral Dimensions of Poverty, Entitlements and Theft. *The Journal of Markets and Morality* 4: 83.
———. 2002a. A Libertarian Theory of Secession and Slavery. *Lew Rockwell*. http://www.lewrockwell.com/block/block15.html.
———. 2002b. Homesteading City Streets; An Exercise in Managerial Theory. *Planning and Markets* 5: 18.
———. 2002c. On Reparations to Blacks for Slavery. *Human Rights Review* 3: 53.
———. 2003a. National Defense and the Theory of Externalities, Public Goods and Clubs. In *The Myth of National Defense: Essays on The Theory and History of Security Production*, ed. Hans-Hermann Hoppe, 301–334. Mises Institute: Auburn.
———. 2003b. Toward a Libertarian Theory of Inalienability: A Critique of Rothbard, Barnett, Gordon, Smith, Kinsella and Epstein. *The Journal of Libertarian Studies* 17: 39.
———. 2003c. Private Property Rights, Economic Freedom, and Professor Coase: A Critique of Friedman, McCloskey, Medema and Zorn. *Harvard Journal of Law & Public Policy* 26: 923.
———. 2004. Are Alienability and the Apriori of Argument Logically Incompatible? *Dialogue* 1.
———. 2005. Ayn Rand and Austrian Economics: Two Peas in a Pod. *The Journal of Ayn Rand Studies* 6: 259.
———. 2006a. Epstein on Alienation: A Rejoinder. *International Journal of Social Economics* 33: 241.
———. 2006b. Coase and Kelo: Ominous Parallels and Reply to Lott on Rothbard on Coase. *Whittier Law Review* 27: 997.
———. 2007a. Secession. *Dialogue* 4: 1.
———. 2007b. Alienability: Reply to Kuflik. *Humanomics* 23: 117.
———. 2008a [1976]. *Defending the Undefendable*. Auburn: The Mises Institute.
———. 2008b. *Labor Economics from a Free Market Perspective: Employing the Unemployable*.
———. 2008c. Homesteading, Ad Coelum, Owning Views and forestalling. *The Social Sciences* 3: 96.
———. 2009a. Yes, Sell Rivers! And Make Legal Some Slave Contracts. *The Tyee*. http://thetyee.ca/Opinion/2009/07/24/SellRivers/.
———. 2009b. Privatizing Rivers and Voluntary Slave Contracts. *Lew Rockwell*. http://www.lewrockwell.com/block/block134.html.
———. 2010a. Are Unions Criminal Gangs? *Global Virtue Ethics Review* 6: –28.

———. 2010b. A Response to Brooks' Support of Demsetz on the Coase Theorem. *Dialogue* 2.

———. 2010c. Rejoinder to Brooks on Coase and Demsetz. *The Quarterly Journal of Austrian Economics* 13: 56.

———. 2010d. Rejoinder to Boettke on Coasean Economics and Communism. *Romanian Economic Business Review* 5: 9.

———. 2014a. A Collection of Essays on Libertarian Jurisprudence: Sunshine and Property Rights. *Saint Louis University Law Journal* 58: 541.

———. 2014b. Private Urban Planning and Free Enterprise. In *Cities and Private Planning: Property Rights, Entrepreneurship and Transaction Costs*, eds. David Emanuel Andersson and Stefano Moroni, 93, 96–97.

———. 2016a. So-called Privacy Rights Are Incompatible with our Libertarian Philosophy. *Lew Rockwell*. https://www.lewrockwell.com/lrc-blog/called-privacy-rights-incompatible-libertarian-philosophy/.

———. 2016b. Ex post facto law and slavery. *Lew Rockwell*. https://www.lewrockwell.com/lrc-blog/ex-post-facto-law/.

———. 2017. Privacy Rights? No. *Lew Rockwell*. https://www.lewrockwell.com/lrc-blog/privacy-rights-no/.

Block, Walter E., and Matthew A. Block. 1996. Roads, Bridges, Sunlight and Private Property Rights. *Journal des Economistes et des Etudes Humaines* 7: 351.

Block, Walter E., and Michael R. Edelstein. 2012. Popsicle Sticks and Homesteading Land for Nature Preserves. *Romanian Economic and Business Review* 7: 7.

Block, Walter E., and Richard Epstein. 2004. Block-Epstein Debate on Eminent Domain. *Mises.Org*. https://mises.org/library/block-epstein-debate-eminent-domain.

———. 2005. Debate on Eminent Domain. *NYU Journal of Law and Liberty* 1: 1144.

Block, Walter E., and Peter Lothian Nelson. 2015. *Water Capitalism: The Case for Privatizing Oceans, Rivers, Lakes, and Acquifers*. New York City: Lexington Books, Rowman and Littlefield.

Block, Walter E., and Guillermo Yeatts. 1999–2000. The Economics and Ethics of Land Reform: A Critique of the Pontifical Council for Justice and Peace's 'Toward a Better Distribution of Land: The Challenge of Agrarian Reform. *Journal of Natural Resources and Environmental Law* 15: 37.

Block, Walter E., William Barnett II, and Gene Callahan. 2005. The Paradox of Coase as a Defender of Free Markets. *NYU Journal of Law & Liberty* 1: 1075.

Block, Walter E., Stephan Kinsella, and Roy Whitehead. 2006. The Duty to Defend Advertising Injuries Caused by Junk Faxes: An Analysis of Privacy, Spam, Detection and Blackmail. *Whittier Law Review* 27: 925.

Boldrin, Michele, and David K. Levine. 2008. *Against Intellectual Monopoly*. Cambridge: Cambridge University Press.

Brilmayer, Lea. 1991. *Secession and Self-Determination: A Territorial Interpretation*, 16 YALE J. INT'L L. 177, 181.

Bylund, Per. 2005. *Man and Matter: A Philosophical Inquiry into the Justification of Ownership in Land from the Basis of Self-Ownership*. Master thesis, Lund University.

———. 2012. Man and Matter: How the Former Gains Ownership of the Latter. *Libertarian Papers* 4.

Cordato, Roy E. 1992a. Knowledge Problems and the Problem of Social Cost. *Journal of the History of Economic Thought* 14: 209.

———. 1992b. *Welfare Economics and Externalities in an Open-Ended Universe: A Modern Austrian Perspective*. Boston: Kluwer.

———. 1997. Market-Based Environmentalism and the Free Market: They're Not the Same. *The Independent Review* 1: 371.

———. 1998. Time Passage and the Economics of Coming to the Nuisance: Reassessing the Coasean Perspective. *Campbell Law Review* 20: 273.

———. 2000. Chasing Phantoms in a Hollow Defense of Coase. *The Review of Austrian Economics* 13: 193.
Cowen, Tyler, ed. 1988. *The Theory of Market Failure: A Critical Examination*. Fairfax: George Mason University Press.
Crepelle, Adam, and Walter E. Block. 2017. Property Rights and Freedom: The Keys to Improving Life in Indian Country. *Washington & Lee Journal of Civil Rights and Social Justice* 23: 314.
de Jasay, Anthony. 1989. *Social Contract, Free Ride: A Study of the Public Goods Problem*. Oxford: Oxford University Press.
DiLorenzo, Thomas J. 1996. The Myth of Natural Monopoly. *The Review of Austrian Economics* 9: 43.
———. 2004. The Union Myth. *The Free Market* 24.
DiLorenzo, Thomas. 2011. A Note on the Canard of 'Asymmetric Information' as a Source of Market Failure. *Quarterly Journal of Austrian Economics* 14: 249.
Evans, Jason, and Walter E. Block. 2002. Labor Union Policies: Gains or Pains. *Cross Cultural Management* 9: 71.
Fox, Glenn. 2007. The Real Coase Theorems. *The Cato Journal* 27: 373.
Frederick, Danny. 2014. Voluntary Slavery. *Las Torres de Luca* 4: 115.
Friedman, David. 1979. Private Creation and Enforcement of Law – A Historical Case. *The Journal of Legal Studies* 8: 399.
———. 1989. *The Machinery of Freedom: Guide to Radical Capitalism*. 2nd ed. La Salle: Open Court.
Futerman, Alan G. 2014. Hacia una Teoría de los Bienes Públicos como Bienes Políticos y el Rol Estatal. *Revista Procesos de Mercado* 11: 221.
Goldberg, Michael, et al. 1980. In *Zoning: Its Costs and Relevance for the 1980s*, ed. Walter Block, 40–41.
Gordon, David. 1986. *Hermeneutics vs. Austrian Economics*. Auburn: The Ludwig Von Mises Institute.
Grotius, Hugo. 1814. *Law of War and Peace* (De Jure Belli Ac Pacis). Trans. A.C. Campbell, London.
Habeas Corpus. 2017. Legal Information Institute, Cornell Law School. https://www.law.cornell.edu/wex/habeas_corpus. Last visited September 10, 2019.
Hayek, Friedrich. 1944. *The Road to Serfdom*. Chicago: The University of Chicago Press.
Heldman, Daniel C. 1977. *American Labor Unions: Political Values and Financial Structure*.
Heldman, Daniel C. et al. 1981. *Deregulating Labor Relations*.
Higgs, Robert. 2005. *How Many Divisions Does the Pope Have?* The Independent Institute. http://www.independent.org/news/article.asp?id=1492.
Hoppe, Hans-Hermann. 1989a. Fallacies of the Public Goods Theory and the Production of Security. *Journal of Libertarian Studies* 9: 27.
———. 1989b. In Defense of Extreme Rationalism: Thoughts on Donald McCloskey's The Rhetoric of Economics. *The Review of Austrian Economics* 3: 179.
———. 1993. *The Economics and Ethics of Private Property: Studies in Political Economy and Philosophy*. Boston: Kluwer.
———, ed. 2003. *The Myth of National Defense: Essays on the Theory and History of Security Production*. Auburn: The Ludwig von Mises Institute.
———. 2011. Of Private, Common, and Public Property and the Rationale for Total Privatization. *Libertarian Papers* 3: 1.
Hummel, Jeffrey. 1990. National Goods vs. Public Goods: Defense, Disarmament and Free Riders. *The Review of Austrian Economics* 4: 88.
Hutt, W.H. 1973. *The Strike Threat System: The Economic Consequences of Collective Bargaining*.
———. 1989. Trade Unions: The Private Use of Coercive Power. *The Review of Austrian Economics* 3: 109.
Jefferson, Thomas. 1958. *Thomas Jefferson to James Madison* 15: 392–398 (27 March 1789 to 30 November 1789). Princeton University Press. https://jeffersonpapers.princeton.edu/selected-documents/thomas-jefferson-james-madison#notes28b. Last visited September 8, 2019.

Jevons, William Stanley. 1871 [1965]. *The Theory of Political Economy*. 3d ed. London/New York: Macmillan and Co.

Kauffman, Bill. 1992. The Child Labor Amendment Debate of the 1920's; or, Catholics and Mugwumps and Farmers. *Journal of Libertarian Studies* 139.

Kershnar, Stephen. 2003. A Liberal Argument for Slavery. *Journal of Social Philosophy* 34: 510.

Kinsella, Stephan N. 2003. A Libertarian Theory of Contract: Title Transfer, Binding Promises, and Inalienability. *Journal of Libertarian Studies* 17: 11.

———. 2009a. What Libertarianism Is. In *Property, Freedom and Society: Essays in Honor of Hans-Hermann Hoppe*, ed. Jörg Guido Hülsmann and Stephan Kinsella. Auburn: Mises Institute.

———. 2009b. Homesteading, Abandonment, and Unowned Land in the Civil Law. *Mises Wire*. https://mises.org/wire/homesteading-abandonment-and-unowned-land-civil-law.

Krauss, Michael. 1999. Tort Law, Moral Accountability, and Efficiency: Reflections on the Current Crisis. *Markets and Morality* 2.

Krecke, Elisabeth. 1996. Law and the Market Order: An Austrian Critique of the Economic Analysis of Law. *Journal des Economistes et des Etudes Humaines* 7: 19.

Lester, Jan Clifford. 2000. *Escape from Leviathan*. St. Martin's Press.

Locke, John. 1948. An Essay Concerning the True Origin, Extent and End of Civil Government. In *Social Contract*, ed. E. Baker, 17–19. New York: Oxford University Press.

Long, Roderick T., and Tibor R. Machan, eds. 2008. *Anarchism/Minarchism: Is Government Part of a Free Country?* Burlington: Ashgate.

Machan, Tibor R. 2002. Anarchism and Minarchism: A Rapprochment. *Journal des Economistes et des Etudes Humaines* 12: 569.

Machan, Tibor R., Ayn Rand, and Murray Rothbard. 2012. Diverse Champions of Liberty. *The Daily Bell*. http://www.thedailybell.com/3435/Tibor-Machan-Ayn-Rand-Murray-Rothbard-Diverse-Champions-of-Liberty.

McChesney, Fred. 1991. Antitrust and Regulation: Chicago's Contradictory Views. *Cato Journal* 10: 775.

McElroy, Wendy. 2001. Legal Child Abuse. *The Free Market* 19.

Menger, Carl. 1950 [1871]. *Principles of Economics*, editors and translators, James Dingwall and Bert F. Hoselitz. Glencoe: Free Press.

Mill, John Stuart. 1870 [1909]. In *Principles of Political Economy with Some of Their Applications to Social Philosophy*, ed. William James Ashley. London: Longmans, Green and Co.

Mosquito, Bionic. 2015. Walter Block, Specific Performance Contracts, and Abortion. *Bionic Mosquito*. http://bionicmosquito.blogspot.com/2015/07/walter-block-specific-performance.html.

Napolitano, Andrew P. 2004. *Constitutional Chaos: What Happens When the Government Breaks Its Own Laws*. Nashville: Nelson Current.

———. 2006. *The Constitution in Exile: How the Federal Government Has Seized Power by Rewriting the Supreme Law of the Land*. Nashville: Thomas Nelson.

———. 2014a. *Suicide Pact: The Radical Expansion of Presidential Powers and The Lethal Threat To American Liberty*. Nashville: Thomas Nelson.

———. 2014b. A Legal History of National Security Law and Individual Rights in the United States. *New York University Journal of Law & Liberty* 8: 396.

Nardinelli, Clark. 1990. *Child Labor and the Industrial Revolution*. Bloomington: Indiana University Press.

Nozick, Robert. 1974. *Anarchy, state, and Utopia*, 162. Oxford: Blackwell Publishing.

O'Driscoll Jr., Gerald P. 1982 [1983]. Monopoly in Theory and Practice. In *Method, Process, and Austrian Economics, Essays in Honor of Ludwig Von Mises*, 189–213. Lexington Books.

Osterfeld, David. 1989. Anarchism and the Public Goods Issue: Law, Courts and the Police. *Journal of Libertarian Studies* 9: 47.

Pasour Jr., Ernest C. 1981. The Free Rider as a Basis for Government Intervention. *Journal of Libertarian Studies* 5: 453.

———. 1982 [1983]. Monopoly Theory and Practice – Some Subjectivist Implications: Comment on O'Driscoll. In *Method, Process, and Austrian Economics, Essays in Honor of Ludwig Von Mises*, 215–223. Lexington Books.

Paul, Ellen Frankel. 1987. *Property Rights and Eminent Domain*. Livingston: Transaction Publishers.

Peden, Joseph R. 1977. Property rights in Celtic Irish law. *Journal of Libertarian Studies* 1: 81.

Petro, Sylvester. 1957. *The Labor Policy of the Free Society*.

Pufendorf, Samuel. 1673. *Natural Law and the Law of Nations, de Officio Hominis et Civis Juxta Legem Naturalem Libri Duo*. Buffalo: Hein; reprint of New York, Oxford University Press, 1927.

Reynolds, Morgan O. 1984. *Power and Privilege: Labor Unions in America*.

———. 1987. *Making America Poorer: The Cost of Labor Law*.

———. 2009. *A History of Labor Unions from Colonial Times to 2009*. http://mises.org/daily/3553.

Rojas, Rod. 2010. The Fallacy of 'Child-Labor-Free'. *Mises Daily*. https://mises.org/library/fallacy-child-labor-free.

Rose, Jim. 1998. Child Labor, Family Income, and the Uruguay Round. *The Quarterly Journal of Austrian Economics* 1: 75.

Rothbard, Murray N. 1969. *Confiscation and the Homestead Principle*. *The Libertarian Forum* 1.

Murray N. Rothbard. 1973a. *For a New Liberty*. New York: Macmillan. http://mises.org/rothbard/newlibertywhole.asp.

Rothbard, Murray N. 1973b. Free Market, Police, Courts, and Law. *Reason*: 5–19.

———. 1982. Law, Property Rights, and Air Pollution. *Cato Journal* 2. In *Economics and the Environment: A Reconciliation*, ed. Walter E. Block, 233–279. Vancouver: The Fraser Institute, 1990.

———. 1985. Airport Congestion: A Case of Market Failure? *The Free Market*.

———. 1989. The Hermeneutical Invasion of Philosophy and Economics. *The Review of Austrian Economics* 3: 45.

———. 1991a. The Union Problem. *Free Market* 9: 1.

———. 1991b. On Denationalizing the Courts. In *Rothbard-Rockwell Report*, vol. 2. Burlingame: Center for Libertarian Studies.

———. 1996. Intimidation by Rhetoric. *The Review of Austrian Economics* 9: 173.

———. 1997. *The Logic of Action: Applications and Criticism from the Austrian School*. Vol. II. Cheltenham: Edward Elgar.

———. 1998 (1982). *The Ethics of Liberty*, 51–52. New York: New York University Press.

———. 2003. War, Peace, and the State. In *The Myth of National Defense: Essays on the Theory and History of Security Production*, ed. Hans-Hermann Hoppe, 65, 66. Auburn: Ludwig von Mises Institute.

Schmidt, Emerson P. 1973. *Union Power and the Public Interest*.

Schmidtz, David. 1991. *The Limits of Government: An Essay on the Public Goods Argument*. Boulder: Westview Press.

Sechrest, Larry. 2003. Privateering and National Defense: Naval Warfare for Private Profit. In *The Myth of National Defense: Essays on the Theory and History of Security Production*, ed. Hans-Hermann Hoppe, 239–274. Mises Institute: Auburn.

———. 2004a. Public Goods and Private Solutions in Maritime History. *Quarterly Journal of Austrian Economics* 7: 3.

———. 2004b. Private Provision of Public Goods: Theoretical Issues and Some Examples from Maritime History. *The ICFAI Journal of Public Finance* 2: 45.

———. 2007. Privately Funded and Built U.S. Warships in the Quasi-War of 1797–1801. *The Independent Review* 12: 101.

Shea, Brian. 2010. Solidarity Forever: The power invested in worker collectives under United States law. *Journal of Libertarian Studies* 22: 219.

Siegan, Bernard H. 1970. Non-Zoning in Houston. *The Journal of Law and Economics* 13: 71–120.

———. 1972. *Land Use Without Zoning*, 95–96.

Simpson, Brian. 2005. *Markets Don't Fail*. Lanham: Lexington Books.

Spooner, Lysander. 1966 (1870). *No Treason: the Constitution of no Authority and a Letter to Thomas F. Bayard*. Larkspur: Rampart College.

Steiner, Hillel. 1994. *An Essay on Rights*, 232. Oxford: Blackwell Publishers.

Stringham, Edward. 1998–1999. Justice Without Government. *Journal of Libertarian Studies* 14: 53.

Stringham, Edward Peter, and Mark White. 2004. Economic Analysis of Tort Law: Austrian and Kantian Perspectives. In *Law and Economics: Alternative Approaches to Legal and Regulatory Issues*, ed. Margaret Oppenheimer and Nicholas Mercuro, 374–392. New York: M.E. Sharpe.

Tannehill, Morris, and Linda Tannehill. 1984. *The Market for Liberty*. New York: Laissez Faire Books.

———. 2001. Arbitration of Disputes. *Mises Daily*. https://mises.org/library/arbitration-disputes.

Terrell, Timothy D. 1999. Property Rights and Externality: The Ethics of the Austrian School. *Journal of Markets and Morality* 2.

Thierer, Adam. 1992. *Judgement Day: The Case for Alternative Dispute Resolution*. London: Adam Smith Institute.

Thomson, Judith Jarvis. 1994. *The Realm of Rights*, 283–284. Cambridge, MA: Harvard University Press.

Tucker, Jeffrey. 2008. The Trouble with Child Labor Laws. *Mises Daily*. https://mises.org/library/trouble-child-labor-laws.

Tullock, Gordon. 1996. Comment on 'Roads, Bridges, Sunlight and Private Property', by Walter E. Block and Matthew A. Block. *Journal des Economistes et des Etudes Humaines* 7: 589.

Von Mises, Ludwig. 2002 (1927). *Liberalism: In the Classical Tradition*, 109. Auburn: The Ludwig Von Mises Institute.

——— 2011 (1976). *A Critique of Interventionism 13*. Auburn: The Ludwig Von Mises.

Walras, Leon. 1874. *Principe d'une 'Théorie Mathématique de L'Échange. Mémoire lu a l'Académie des Sciences Morales et Politiques* (Seances des 16 et 23 aout 1873). Paris: Guillaumin.

Watner, Carl. 1982. The Proprietary Theory of Justice in the Libertarian Tradition. *Journal of Libertarian Studies* 6: 289.

Woolridge, William C. 1970. *Uncle Sam the Monopoly Man*. New Rochelle: Arlington House.

Chapter 8
Public Policy

Vices are not Crimes

Lysander Spooner (2010)

Abstract This chapter is divided in two sections, both dealing with public policy from an Austro-libertarian perspective. Section 1 deals with the War on Drugs. Most modern societies prohibit the use of addictive drugs such as cocaine and heroin. We contend this is a mistake. They should all be legalized, forthwith, since their usage constitutes a victimless crime. Moreover, most of the evils associated with drug production, distribution and consumption are due to the War on Drugs itself, and not because of the drugs themselves. The War on Drugs is the modern-day Prohibition. And just as it occurred during that tragic era, including the Mafia, widespread murder, poisoned liquor, etc., the same is being repeated now with drugs. But if the same course of action is taken, the same results are to be expected. The only way to effectively fight Cartels and drug-related tragedies, is to decriminalize drug production, distribution, and consumption. In other words, to end this War.

Section 2 consists in a short essay attempting to show how a truly free society would deal with a pandemic such as COVID-19. Mainly through the functioning of the market as guided by the price system and the incentives promoted by capitalist institutions such as private property rights, free association, and non-aggression.

Keywords Legalization · Addiction · Victimless crimes · Drugs

---

This section of the present chapter is based on our paper Futerman, Alan G., and Block, Walter E. 2021. "The Harmful Addiction to the War on Drugs". *Touro Law Review*, Vol. 37: No. 1, Article 3.

A. G. Futerman, W. E. Block, *The Austro-Libertarian Point of View*,
https://doi.org/10.1007/978-981-16-4691-1_8

8.1 The Case Against the War on Drugs

8.1.1 *Introduction*

In the last years, we have seen the tragedy of at least 42,000 dead in Mexico (Carpenter 2011), more than 61,000 vanished (Villegas 2020), and the futility of hundreds of billions of taxpayer dollars spent by governments, with an economic loss of $88 billion per year to the USA,[1] because of the War on Drugs started by Richard Nixon in 1971 (although prohibition policies began many decades before).[2] Because of this, many world leaders have asked for the decriminalization of production, distribution, and consumption of drugs (Boyle 2014).

The important question is not only if this war is a monumental failure,[3] but why. How is it that a cause that is supposed to be moral and practical, and supported by billions of taxpayer dollars has failed so dramatically? The answer is simple: *it is neither moral nor practical.*

8.1.2 *Government Legislating Morality?*

The proper function of government[4] is to protect individual rights, which means to protect the freedom of the individual from force. This means that the state should not pass laws on morality, since not only is it not its function but also because morality is voluntary. Therefore, individuals should be free to act as they choose as long as they do not violate other people's rights. Since in this view, each individual has property over his own body, we should all be able to choose what to do with it. Whether an individual wants to eat unhealthy food or consume drugs, it must not be a concern of the government, which is entitled to act only if individual rights are

---

[1] Miron and Waldock (2010), at 12.

[2] According to the Drug Policy Alliance: "The first anti-opium laws in the 1870s were directed at Chinese immigrants. The first anti-cocaine laws in the early 1900s were directed at black men in the South. The first anti-marijuana laws, in the Midwest and the Southwest in the 1910s and 20s, were directed at Mexican migrants and Mexican Americans." *A Brief History of the Drug War*, Drug Pol'y All., https://www.drugpolicy.org/issues/brief-history-drug-war (last visited July 15, 2020).

[3] For the claim that this is indeed true, see Block (1993, 1996, 2016), Block et al. (2003), Cussen and Block (2000), Friedman (1992), Hanke and Walters (2016), Block and Obioha (2012); Szasz (1985); Szasz (1992) (hereinafter Our Right to Drugs); Thornton (1991b); Vance (2012); Whalin and Block (2017).

[4] If it has any function at all, to which classical liberalism and minarchism respond in the affirmative. For the view that it does not, see Anderson and Hill (1979), Benson (1989, 1990), Block (2011), Hasnas (1995), Hoppe (2008); Rothbard (1973); Rothbard (1982); Edward P. Stringham, Anarchy and the Law: The Political Economy of Choice (2007); Tannehill and Tannehill (1970), Tinsley (1999). See also Chap. 6.

violated. With regard to drugs, this has been the policy since consumption began near 2000 BCE until the twentieth century came.

An objection to the foregoing is that taking heroin, for example, is indeed a rights violation since the individual who does so will not be able to fulfill his obligations to others. For example, a father or mother to their small children. But, if this is a rights violation, so would be getting drunk, being lazy, not being a good parent, etc. What about running a marathon race and then being too tired to perform one's usual duties? How about reading into all hours of the night and then oversleeping? Here, too, dependents can suffer. If any of these flaws could land people in jail, it would be the rare person still free. Naturally, these simple examples would not be as remotely as harmful as drug addiction, but they are a *reductio ad absurdum* to prove our point. Crime, properly understood, requires a perpetrator and a direct victim, not an indirect one such as a family dependent. Murder, rape, kidnapping, carjacking are all real crimes. Possibly ruining your body with addictive drugs is something entirely different, whatever its painful consequences to you and those close to you may be. It is a categorical mistake to conflate them.

8.1.3 Same Story, Same Results

The same logic affected Prohibition, which took place from 1920 to 1933 (Thornton 1991a), and the same results appeared. Actually, the drug business was taken by the Mafia when they realized that since alcohol became a subject of entrepreneurs in the market, they had to find some new profitable trade.[5]

The economics of the matter is clear. The fact that drugs are being sold in black markets increases risks, and therefore prices, which makes other drugs profitable (such as synthetic ones, which are worse than natural and therefore create much more harm). The illegal commerce of drugs does not allow consumers to be protected by courts and doctors if they are victims of fraud and also makes consumers into criminals, even in cases where they are consuming for medical purposes[6] because they still have to engage in an illegal transaction.

The analogy between addictive drugs and addictive alcohol is a strong one. Both are harmful. When the latter was prohibited by law, there was the phenomenon of "bathtub gin:" poisoned liquor. When legalized, that rarely, if ever, occurs. Similarly, before the advent of laws prohibiting drugs, this too was a rare occurrence. We refer here to the lack of information of how illegal drugs are made and what ingredients they actually contain. For instance, in the case of synthetic drugs.

Also, under alcohol prohibition, people were shooting each other over turf. In the modern era, this industry is normalized; no violence is associated with its provision.

---

[5] For an attempt to explain why young Italian men, not blacks, were involved in the illegal trade of booze during Prohibition, and their positions are now to a great degree but not entirely reversed with regard to drugs, see Whalin & Block, *supra* note 497.

[6] *See* Our Right to Drugs, *supra* note 497.

In like manner, drug production and distribution are now a very violent enterprise; but not before, when it was legal.

Money laundering is closely linked to drugs, thus making part of the financial system a partner in the business. In order to avoid legal consequences, the economic and political system begins to be corrupted in every corner: politicians who maintain the prohibition and therefore safeguard the business of the cartels[7] (although many do it because they actually believe the war works), the police by looking aside (sometimes being themselves part of the business), and many others, such as the military, the courts, etc. (Coyne and Hall 2017). As the war increases, violence rises, the drug dealers expand their networks, and therefore drug production and consumption expand exponentially.

8.1.4 *Private Property Under Risk, Life Under Risk*

The intrusion by government into private property is a necessity under the war, since the entire market works in the shadows. Therefore, governments look into bank accounts and phone conversations, imprison innocents, and intrude much more into private lives and properties, thus using valuable taxpayer resources in order to persecute innocent individuals exercising the right to the property of their bodies and not to persecute true criminals.[8]

Criminals involved in the business do not participate because drugs are necessarily a criminals' market but *because drugs are illegal, and criminals work in illegal markets* (such as what happened during Prohibition). The same happens with consumption: *the relevant point is not how many criminals are drug addicts or users, but how many drug addicts or users are criminals*. And in any case, criminals under the influence of drugs should be penalized harder because they are willingly under drugs while knowing they will not be fully conscious and therefore become much more harmful than otherwise under the same circumstances (in a robbery or other crimes).

At the time of this writing, the Black Lives Matter movement is properly vitriolic about the needless and senseless death of Breonna Taylor.[9] How did she die? She was shot. Who killed her? The police. Why did they do so? They had a "no knock"

---

[7] South of the Rio Grande River, these organizations fight the military of many of those nations almost on an even basis, in terms of power. *See* Ioan Grillo, *How the Sinaloa Cartel Bested the Mexican Army*, Time (October 18, 2019, 7:39 PM), https://time.com/5705358/sinaloa-cartel-mexico-culiacan/

[8] Just like with any other tax, these are resources driven out of the economic system, and therefore, production, growth, and capital formation are decreased, thus generating a negative impact on incomes, wages, savings, and investments.

[9] *See* Alisha Haridasani Gupta, *Why Aren't We all Talking About Breonna Taylor?* N.Y. Times, https://www.nytimes.com/2020/06/04/us/breonna-taylor-black-lives-matter-women.html (Oct. 30, 2020); *see also* Black Lives Matter, *Happy Birthday, Breonna* (June 5, 2020), https://blacklivesmatter.com/happy-birthday-breonna/; *see also* Anna North & Fabiola Cineas, *The Police*

warrant; they broke into her house without announcing themselves as police. Her boyfriend shot at the police. Breonna, an entirely innocent young woman, was killed. Why did the police have a "no knock" warrant which they mistakenly used at her home? They were seeking drug law violators.[10] The point is, if drugs were legal, all of them without exception, this young woman would still be alive today. Strangely, given that all lives matter, most certainly including black ones, there is little or no call on the part of protestors to legalize drugs. Instead, they focus on defunding the police.[11]

8.1.5 Poverty Is not the Problem

Drug addiction must not be blamed on poverty; economic position is irrelevant to the consumption of these addictive substances. Yes, addicts tend to be poor (and their drug addiction indeed exacerbates their situation). But at least part of the reason is that what they consume is so expensive. And why, in turn, are these products so pricey? It is due to the fact that they are illegal. In addition to the ordinary costs of bringing them to market, the risks undertaken mainly on the supply side drive their prices through the roof. If they were legal, they would be far less expensive.[12] Even if some addicts keep spending all their money on these substances, at least they would be able to get higher quality drugs, which are ultimately less harmful. For instance, the use of "crack" became widespread because other drugs, such as cocaine, were more expensive. And the former is much more harmful than the latter.

Would the entire population become addicts if drugs were legalized? It all depends upon the elasticity of the demand curve. What empirical evidence we have strongly mitigates against any such possibility. Before drug prohibition, when drugs were relatively inexpensive, not everyone used them. Marijuana is now legal in Canada and in several U.S. states, not only for medicinal purposes but also for recreation, and we do not find massive numbers of people consuming them on a daily basis.

Shooting Death of Breonna Taylor, Explained, VOX, https://www.vox.com/2020/5/13/21257457/breonna-taylor-louisville-shooting-ahmaud-arbery-justiceforbreonna (July 13, 2020, 12:36 PM).

[10] Gupta, *supra* note 505; North & Cineas, *supra* note 505.

[11] Sam Levin, *Movement to Defund Police Gains 'Unprecedented' Support Across US*, GUARDIAN (June 4, 2020, 6:00 PM), https://www.theguardian.com/us-news/2020/jun/04/defund-the-police-us-george-floyd-budgets.

Limited government libertarians are ambivalent about this. On the one hand, the police are absolutely necessary to prevent mayhem, shootings, rapes, etc. On the other hand, they contribute to the mayhem they are supposedly created to reduce by pursuing victimless criminals such as drug dealers and users. Naturally, if the latter also engage in other crimes (such as Cartels, which are truly evil organizations), involving victims, that is another issue altogether. But that is not our point.

[12] Many of them grow like weeds, need little care, etc., and would be very cheap if legal.

8.1.6 The Moral Is the Practical

We must take into account that decriminalizing only *consumption* is not the solution since this would increase demand, but not supply, therefore increasing prices and profits for the cartels. The solution is to decriminalize *both production and consumption*, which would take criminals out of the market and turn drugs as any other ordinary good or service in the market (Ostrowski 1989): entrepreneurs competing for the favor of the consumer by developing much safer and cheaper drugs, thus potentially saving millions of lives (of the drug addicts themselves and of everyone affected by the war).

The entire society is corrupted by this drug prohibition. It not only increases the extent and profits of the suppliers but is also responsible for causing all the boomerang effects: the needless deaths. The destruction of Mafia networks, their link with terrorist organizations,[13] the reduction of drug abuse and more, are going to be achieved when drugs are legalized and considered as a good like shoes and t-shirts. The same thing would happen if shoes were banned to the public; criminals would take over the market and soon we would have a *War on Shoes*.

The known cases of decriminalization show mixed results, although many are successful beyond any doubt like the case of Portugal, which after 2001 decriminalized all drugs.[14] As a result, drug usage rates remained the same or slightly decreased compared to other European Union countries, but drug-related pathologies declined significantly.[15] Thus, we are able to see that negative results, where they appear, are due to wrong policies, such as those experienced in the Netherlands where syringes were being given out for free to drug addicts (Lynch 2021). Government should not interfere, neither *prohibiting nor subsidizing drug consumption or production*, in the same way as it should not interfere with or subsidize the consumption or production of tomatoes.

8.1.7 Conclusion

Although drugs are obviously bad for a person's organism[16] and psyche, it is not the morality of the consumption that is under debate in this War but the *morality of individual rights*, specifically, the morality of *the right of the individual to his own*

[13] Terrorist organizations are often involved in the drug business because of its big profits that help to finance their operations. See, for instance, John Fernandez, *The DEA's Targeting of Hezbollah's Global Criminal Support Network*, WASH. INST. (Jan. 10, 2020), https://www.washingtoninstitute.org/policy-analysis/deas-targeting-hezbollahs-global-criminal-support-network

[14] Although only consumption was legalized in Portugal. Glenn Greenwald, *Drug Decriminalization in Portugal: Lessons for Creating Fair and Successful Drug Policies*, CATO INST., April 2, 2009.

[15] *Id.*

[16] Eating too much chocolate and ice cream is also harmful; it leads to obesity. It is no longer possible to limit ourselves to theoretical *reductio ad absurdum*. When he was mayor of New York City,

body. Even taking into account the positive results of decriminalization, the main reason for decriminalization of production, distribution, and consumption of drugs remains the same: *vices are not crimes, and the government should fight crime, not vices.*

We will give credit to advocates of drug prohibition for one thing: they are good virtue-signalers. They come across as being filled with the milk of human kindness. Their main, no, practically their only goal they would have us believe, is to protect the rest of us from our weaknesses. But beneath this velvet glove there lies an uglier aspect, coercive racism. As Ann Fordham explains:

> Racism also played a key role in the push for prohibition, as substances like opium and cannabis were associated with Chinese and Mexican immigrants and African Americans, while cocaine was linked to Black men…[17]

There is also a phenomenon akin to a logical contradiction that accompanies the drug war. On the one hand, prohibitionists are paternalists. They think that the average citizen is too stupid, or too weak, to resist the siren song of drugs. On the other hand, they support our democratic institutions. But if people are unable to resist their primal urges to become drug-besotted, how can we trust them to exercise judgment in the voting booth. And, if they are allowed to cast a ballot, does that not imply that they have a modicum of common sense? Is the average adult member of society (paternalism is justified for children, not grown-ups) supposed to be too feeble-minded to resist the lure of drugs, but intelligent enough to vote for politicians who will rein him in in this regard? Strictly speaking, logical contradictions cannot exist in the real world, but our drug laws come mighty close to overturning this fact of nature.

Mike Bloomberg actually prohibited the sale of soft drinks greater than sixteen ounces. *See* Rachel Weiner, *The New York City Soda Ban Explained*, WASH. POST. (Mar. 11, 2013, 5:19 PM), https://www.washingtonpost.com/news/the-fix/wp/2013/03/11/the-new-york-city-soda-ban-explained/; *see also Here He Goes Again: Bloomberg Set To Ban All Sugary Drinks Over 16 Ounces*, CBS (May 30, 2012, 11:59 PM), https://newyork.cbslocal.com/2012/05/30/here-he-goes-again-bloomberg-set-to-ban-all-sugary-drinks-over-16-ounces/; *see also* Sondra Clark, *Michael Bloomberg's Ban on Soda: Where Will the Regulation Stop?*, MY HERITAGE, https://www.myheritage.org/news/michael-bloombergs-ban-on-soda-where-will-the-regulation-stop/ (last visited Jan. 27, 2021).

[17] Ann Fordham, *The war on drugs is built on racism. It's time to decolonise drug policies*, INTERNATIONAL DRUG POLICY CONSORTIUM (June 26, 2020), https://idpc.net/blog/2020/06/the-war-on-drugs-is-built-on-racism-it-s-time-to-decolonise-drug-policies. See also Desmond Manderson, *Symbolism and racism in drug history and policy*, 18 DRUG AND ALCOHOL REVIEW 179–186 (1999).

8.2 The Free Society in a Pandemic[18]

> There always remains an orbit that to the limited knowledge of man appears as an orbit of pure chance and marks life as a gamble. Man and his works are always exposed to the impact of unforeseen and uncontrollable events.
>
> Ludwig Von Mises (1962, 65–66)

How would a libertarian limited government deal with a pandemic, such as the one we are now living with COVID-19?[19] By promoting liberty, not by calling for the death of capitalism and the free market as we hear all too often. Economic freedom is most needed precisely when we have to deal with a serious crisis.

If no big government is expected to bail out businesses and private individuals during a disaster, people will engage, during good times, in precautionary activities. For example, they will act more like the proverbial ants, than grasshoppers. The cognoscenti sneer at people who prepare, the preppers, but the latter are far better prepared to protect themselves and their families. Tail hedging is not only advisable for trading, but for all aspects of life.

Bail outs and their effect, moral hazard, create the opposite incentive. If companies knew there would be no subsidies forthcoming, they would pay better attention to their bottom lines. Take, for instance, an airline. Would they operate normally and fill their planes to maximum capacity, or serve fewer customers on each plane with more distancing, while also requiring protective masks? They would do this for a simple reason: if a customer becomes infected during a flight, the airline could get sued.[20]

If streets were private, would the company that own them allow people to walk without masks? Not likely, and for the same reason. The same considerations would apply to every other business, particularly shops, malls, cinemas, natural or themed parks, or any other services that require physical presence, particularly under crowded circumstances. And customers, at the same time, would feel safer and therefore more intensively attend those places that take more precautions. Airports would not wait for political decrees to shut down flights from areas where the virus is hitting hard: its future cash-flows depend on it.

But the above could very well work the other way around. If there are people who are willing to take more risks, they could attend other businesses, or contract those very same services, but with lower security measures (or none), at a different price. The key to the analysis is that the market would give people freedom of choice, and not bound them to government decrees.

---

[18] This section of the present chapter is based on our article Futerman, Alan G., and Block, Walter E. 2020. "How Would A Libertarian Society Deal With A Pandemic?". *Zero Hedge*, May 20. Available at https://www.zerohedge.com/economics/how-would-libertarian-society-deal--pandemic (last visited May 8. 2021).

[19] We write in mid-2021.

[20] According to some libertarian authors, this may be controversial, given *caveat emptor*, but that would be the legal regime under which they would likely have to operate.

Medical insurance companies would also be guided by incentives. When there is a bank run not everyone can get their money. The same happens if we all want to access the hospital at the same time. An insurance company, then, can deal with a class of events that usually follows a normal distribution. But a pandemic, with a new virus, has an unknown distribution (which may be asymmetric to the left, fat tailed, etc.). In which direction do incentives lie in such unusual circumstances? Is it to prevent people from taking risks by not ensuring this type of event, or charging extra fees if the customer takes more risks of infection, or heavily investing in R + D to find a cure or treatment? Answer: All of the above. Moreover, insurance companies and private hospitals would likely take on the task of mass testing. Then, prevention (before and during pandemics) would be a key role of such companies, since their business depends on it.

Pharmaceutical companies could innovate faster to find new and better treatments and tests, or a cure, without having to comply with stultifying regulations of the sort promulgated by the Food and Drug Administration, while private certification companies would rush these to trial. The market, not difficult to remove bureaucrats, will judge if they fail to provide safety.

Think of a person who wants to leave his house. If medical insurance does not cover his infection, he will think twice. If he can infect someone else, and will be liable for it, he will more seriously consider the risk. If a restaurant is not insured in case someone becomes infected while eating dinner, then it will likely take measures to prevent it. It may close altogether, seat diners far away from one another, or offer only takeout meals. Some governments have already mandated such changes of course, but these orders might well have been superfluous. In the free society, responsibility is not only a moral ideal, but has concrete consequences insofar as one's pocket and health is concerned. It is the people themselves who have now taken precautions before governments mandated them.

The bottom line is that a libertarian society would not operate as a chaotic jungle where everyone does as he pleases on other people's property. It would rather function as a system where incentives are aligned with behavior so as to reduce costs as identified through the price mechanism.

In today's world, governments own public transportation, roads, public services, etc. How can they know what is the optimum amount of social distancing or how long businesses can be in quarantine until the economy completely collapses? They cannot, they lack the knowledge. Moreover, in the absence of tax postponements, companies are more focused in paying taxes instead of working as fast as possible to changing their business practices. With big bailout government, they are more focused in asking for subsidies than in innovating.

A free market would not be able to solve the crisis automatically, but it would have the mechanism to identify mistakes through losses and thus help to correct them as fast as possible. Moreover, a localist approach to society assures that different business models and prevention measures can compete and be compared. This would take us to better solutions, faster. A centralized response, on the other hand, renders us blind to alternatives, concentrating ignorance. And time, these days, costs lives.

What we need is not more government intervention, but more freedom. Liberty, by itself, will not cure COVID-19, but is surely the system that will allow us to get there, or to prevent a crisis such as this one from happening again when a new pandemic occurs.

Two more issues must be addressed for a more complete libertarian consideration of the COVID-19 pandemic.

First, we must inject a bit of modesty into our analysis. As economists, we support the notion of specialization and division of labor. It applies not only in the usual arenas of economics, such as production, the labor market, etc., but, also, insofar as intellectual issues are concerned. To wit, we must ask, do libertarians have any particular comparative advantage concerning the facts of the matter about COVID-19? About just how infectious it is? Regarding the safety of vaccines, the benefits of wearing a mask, isolating, etc. And the answer which comes readily to mind is, of course not. Therefore, everything libertarians, such as the present authors say about these issues must be taken not with a grain of sand, but with an entire bucketful. The facts are crucially important. Without them, we are in no position to say, definitively, that it would not be justified to compel people to take the vaccine, or to prohibit them from so doing. Either, or, conceivably, both, might constitute a physical threat against other. A modicum of agnosticism, thus, is entirely justified (Block 2020).

Second, if we know for sure that a pandemic virus can travel only 6 feet or less, and thus when people maintain this distance from one another or more they are safe, they are not infecting each other, they are not violating each others' rights, all is well. We can, in the verbiage of mainstream economists, "internalize the externality." Each property owner, of shopping malls, stadiums, airplanes, airports, train stations, can offer COVID-19 rules to his customers, and people can sort themselves out as they wish, based not only on the usual types of competition, but, now, also, on the basis of these rules.

However, suppose that exhaling out of doors allows the virus to travel 20 miles away, onto the property of entirely different owners. Then, this sort of rules competition cannot be a definitive answer to the challenges we face. Under these circumstances it would be justified to compel people to wear masks, even outdoors, for as long as the pandemic was a threat. And who, pray tell, is to determine the answer to that vital question? The typical response would be of course the government. However, we have said enough in this entire book to lead the reader into thinking that this would not be our public policy recommendation. Rather, we would rely upon private courts to make such determinations.

Bibliography

Anderson, Terry, and P.J. Hill. 1979. An American Experiment in Anarcho-Capitalism: The Not so Wild, Wild West. *Journal of Libertarian Studies* 3: 9. http://mises.org/journals/jls/3_1/3_1_2.pdf.

Benson, Bruce L. 1989. Enforcement of Private Property Rights in Primitive Societies: Law Without Government. *Journal of Libertarian Studies* 9: 1. http://mises.org/journals/jls/9_1/9_1_1.pdf.

———. 1990. Customary Law with Private Means of Resolving Disputes and Dispensing Justice: A Description of a Modern System of Law and Order without State Coercion. *Journal of Libertarian Studies* 9: 25. http://mises.org/journals/jls/9_2/9_2_2.pdf.

Block, Walter E. 1993. Drug Prohibition: A Legal and Economic Analysis. *Journal of Business Ethics* 12: 689.

———. 1996. Drug Prohibition and Individual Virtue. *Review of Political Economy* 8: 433. http://www.tandfonline.com/doi/abs/10.1080/09538259600000077.

———. 2011. Anarchism and Minarchism; No Rapprochement Possible: Reply to Tibor Machan. *Journal of Libertarian Studies* 22: 741. http://mises.org/journals/jls/22_1/22_1_37.pdf.

———. 2016. Is Ross Ulbricht of Silk Road a Libertarian Hero? *Journal of Economic Social Thought* 3: 327. http://www.kspjournals.org/index.php/JEST/article/view/909.

Block, Walter E., and Violet Obioha. 2012. War on Black Men: Arguments for the Legalization of Drugs. *Criminal Justice Ethics* 31: 106. http://www.tandfonline.com/doi/pdf/10.1080/0731129X.2012.719671.

Block, Walter E., et al. 2003. Re-evaluating America's Failing Drug Control Laws: A Legal, Philosophical, and Economic Proposal. *Oklahoma City Law Review* 28: 119.

Boyle, Catherine. 2014. World Leaders Slam War on Drugs as 'a Disaster'. *CNBC* (Jan. 23, 2014, 12:57 PM). https://www.cnbc.com/2014/01/23/why-world-leaders-think-drugs-should-be-decriminalized.html

Carpenter, Ted Galen. 2011. Undermining Mexico's Dangerous Drug Cartels. *Cato Institute* (Nov. 15, 2011). https://www.cato.org/publications/policy-analysis/undermining-mexicos-dangerous-drug-cartels

Coyne, Christopher J., and Abigail R. Hall. 2017. Four Decades and Counting: The Continued Failure of the War on Drugs. *Cato Institute* (April 12, 2017). https://www.cato.org/policy-analysis/four-decades-counting-continued-failure-war-drugs#_idTextAnchor012

Cussen, Meaghan, and Walter E. Block. 2000. Legalize Drugs Now! An Analysis of the Benefits of Legalized Drugs. *American Journal of Economics and Sociology* 59: 525.

Friedman, Milton. 1992. The Drug War as a Socialist Enterprise. In Milton Friedman & Thomas S. Szasz, *On Liberty and Drugs,* ed. Arnold S. Trebach & Kevin B. Zeese. http://www.druglibrary.org/special/friedman/socialist.htm

Hanke, Steve H., and Stephan J. K. Walters. 2016. One Year After: Freddie Gray and 'Structural Statism'. *Cato Institute* (April 22, 2016). http://www.cato.org/publications/commentary/one-year-after-freddie-gray-structural-statism

Hasnas, John. 1995. The Myth of the Rule of Law. *Wisconsin Law Review* 199.

Hoppe, Hans-Hermann. 2008. Reflections on the Origin and the Stability of the State. *Lew Rockwell* (June 23, 2008). http://www.lewrockwell.com/hoppe/hoppe18.html

Lynch, Alberto Benegas. 2021. Thirty-two Reflections to Free the Drugs. *Libertad Digital.* https://www.clublibertaddigital.com/ilustracion-liberal/43/treinta-y-dos-reflexiones-para-liberar-las-drogas-alberto-benegas-lynch-h.html (Last visited Feb. 9, 2021).

Miron, Jeffrey, and Katherine Waldock. 2010. *The Budgetary Impact of Ending Drug Prohibition.* Washington, DC: Cato Institute.

Ostrowski, James. 1989. Thinking About Drug Legalization. *Cato Institute* (May 25, 1989).

Rothbard, Murray N. 1973. *For a New Liberty: The Libertarian Manifesto*. New York: Macmillan.

Rothbard, Murray N. 1982. *The Ethics of Liberty*, 2nd ed., 1998. New York: New York University Press.

Spooner, Lysander. 2010. *Vices are Not Crimes: A Vindication of Moral Liberty.* In 5 The Collected Works of Lysander Spooner (1834–1886), in 5 Vols. 1.

Szasz, Thomas. 1985. *Ceremonial Chemistry: The Ritual Persecution of Drugs, Addicts, and Pushers*. Bradenton Beach: Learning Publications.

Szasz, Thomas. 1992. *Our Right to Drugs: The Case for a Free Market.* Syracuse: Syracuse University Press.

Tannehill, Linda, and Morris Tannehill. 1970. *The Market for Liberty.* Laissez Faire Books, 1984.

Thornton, Mark. 1991a. Alcohol Prohibition was a Failure. *Cato Institute* (July 17, 1991). https://www.cato.org/policy-analysis/alcohol-prohibition-was-failure

Thornton, Mark. 1991b. *The Economics of Prohibition.* Salt Lake City: University of Utah Press.

Tinsley, Patrick. 1999. With Liberty and Justice for All: A Case for Private Police. *Journal of Libertarian Studies* 14: 95. http://www.mises.org/journals/jls/14_1/14_1_5.pdf.

Vance, Laurence M. 2012. *The War on Drugs is a War on Freedom.* Orlando, FL: Vance Publications.

Villegas, Paulina. 2020. A New Toll in Mexico's Drug War: More Than 61,000 Vanished. *N.Y. Times* (Jan. 6, 2020). https://www.nytimes.com/2020/01/06/world/americas/mexico-drug-war-death-toll.html

von Mises, Ludwig. 1962. *The Ultimate Foundation of Economic Science.* New York: D. Van Nostrand.

Whalin, Luke L., and Walter E. Block. 2017. Racial Discrepancies in the Participation Between Alcohol Prohibition and the Drug War. *Acta Economica Et Turistica* 3: 119. https://content.sciendo.com/view/journals/aet/3/2/article-p119.xml.

Block, Walter E. 2020. A Libertarian Analysis of the Covid-19 Pandemic. *Journal of Libertarian Studies* 24(1): 206–237. Available at https://mises.org/library/libertarian-analysis-covid-19-pandemic (Last visited May 23, 2021).

Chapter 9
Final Thoughts

This book is called *The Austro-Libertarian Point of View*.

What kind of a title is this? The "Austro" stands for Austrian economics. As is well known amongst the cognoscenti, this has nothing whatsoever to do with the economic situation of that particular European country. Rather, this school of thought is so-named since its founders – Carl Menger, Eugen von Böhm-Bawerk, Ludwig von Mises and Friedrich A. Hayek (among others) – all started their careers there. (In similar manner, the Chicago School of Economics rarely even discusses, let alone is predicated upon, the business situation in that midwestern city; its leaders, too, Milton Friedman, George Stigler, Gary Becker, were all associated at one time or another, with the University of Chicago). As such Austrian economics, as in the case of all other schools in the dismal science, is a purely positive enterprise: it deals in questions such as what causes unemployment, the genesis of business cycles, which is the most efficacious way of wrestling inflation to the ground.

Libertarianism, in very sharp contrast, is a normative discipline. It focuses entirely on just law. Should drugs be legalized? Should the minimum wage law be enacted? Is it just that prostitutes who limit themselves to consenting adults be imprisoned?

That being the case, how can there be any such thing as Austro (Austrian) libertarianism? The two are in effect polar opposites. The normative, and the positive. The is, and the ought. They go together as well as oil and water, that is, not at all. Seemingly, never the twain shall meet. If the two are incompatible with one another, how can there be any such thing as a book, for example, this very one, dedicated to both? We might as well have book titles such as Mozart and shoelaces, or fish and bicycles, or the Moon and green cheese.

Not so fast. Things are not quite that bad. There is at least some method in our seeming madness.

First of all, it just so happens that virtually all economists who have ever characterized themselves as Austrians have also adhered to the libertarian philosophy. There are exceptions of course. The birth of this school of thought was in 1870. Its

A. G. Futerman, W. E. Block, *The Austro-Libertarian Point of View*,
https://doi.org/10.1007/978-981-16-4691-1_9

earliest supporters were in Austria. What was true of this nation in the late 1920s to the mid 1940s? Why, Naziism reared its ugly head. Thus, there were indeed Austrian economists who were also National Socialists, the very polar opposite of libertarianism. They may have been good economists, but they were of course evil. But such people were exceedingly few and far between even during that epoch. In the modern era, it would be the rare follower of Austrianism who is not also a devotee of the libertarian philosophy.

Of course, the obverse does not hold. That is, it is by no means true that virtually all libertarians are Austrians. For in order to be counted in the latter category, you must first be an economist, and only a small portion of libertarians fit that bill.

Secondly, it is by no means an accident that with but very few exceptions, all Austrians are also devotees of libertarianism. Consider the Austrian Business Cycle theory. It is predicated on the claim that an artificial lowering of interest rates is responsible for the boom bust cycle.[1] And which institution is responsible for that? Well, it is not the free enterprise system. Or consider the fact that Austrianism objures interpersonal comparisons of utility.[2] That pretty much eliminates the economic justification on grounds of efficiency for antitrust legislation and egalitarian welfare laws. Then there is the issue of the minimum wage enactments and labor unions.[3] The Austrian insight concerning discounted marginal revenue productivity puts paid to notions that laws, institutions, of this sort can promote economic development. Perhaps the most powerful inclination of Austrians in the direction of economic liberty emanates from the views of this school of thought on socialism and central planning, in the absence of market prices indicating consumer desires and subjective costs.

So, while at first glance there would seem to be an incompatibility between the two foundational aspects of this book, liberty and Austrian economics, upon a deeper analysis, the gap is not so wide at all. At the same time, there is a great deal of work to be done in expanding both disciplines, and this is not at all incompatible with building more bridges among the two.

As such, this brief conclusion works as well as a summary. There is no necessary connection between Austrian economics and the philosophy of libertarianism, but as we have tried to show throughout this book, there is a sufficient one. In a deeper sense, both support each other. Perhaps making the reader put on a smile, we cannot say this is an *a priori* proposition, but we can defend it anyway. The reader will judge if we did so satisfactorily or not.

---

[1] See Chap. 4.

[2] See Chap. 2.

[3] See Chap. 3.